The Constitution of the City

Allen J. Scott

The Constitution of the City

Economy, Society, and Urbanization in the Capitalist Era

palgrave macmillan

Allen J. Scott
Geography and Public Policy
University of California
Los Angeles, California, USA

ISBN 978-3-319-61227-0   ISBN 978-3-319-61228-7 (eBook)
DOI 10.1007/978-3-319-61228-7

Library of Congress Control Number: 2017946742

© The Editor(s) (if applicable) and The Author(s) 2017
This work is subject to copyright. All rights are solely and exclusively licensed by the Publisher, whether the whole or part of the material is concerned, specifically the rights of translation, reprinting, reuse of illustrations, recitation, broadcasting, reproduction on microfilms or in any other physical way, and transmission or information storage and retrieval, electronic adaptation, computer software, or by similar or dissimilar methodology now known or hereafter developed.
The use of general descriptive names, registered names, trademarks, service marks, etc. in this publication does not imply, even in the absence of a specific statement, that such names are exempt from the relevant protective laws and regulations and therefore free for general use.
The publisher, the authors and the editors are safe to assume that the advice and information in this book are believed to be true and accurate at the date of publication. Neither the publisher nor the authors or the editors give a warranty, express or implied, with respect to the material contained herein or for any errors or omissions that may have been made. The publisher remains neutral with regard to jurisdictional claims in published maps and institutional affiliations.

Cover illustration: © Rudy Malmquist / GettyImages

Printed on acid-free paper

This Palgrave Macmillan imprint is published by Springer Nature
The registered company is Springer International Publishing AG
The registered company address is: Gewerbestrasse 11, 6330 Cham, Switzerland

Preface

I seek in this book to reconsider the foundations of urban theory and to propose a robust concept of the city. These aims revolve around two interrelated tasks. The first is to explain the persistent tendency for durable but diverse clusters of human activity to form on the landscape. The second is to show how this primary urge sets in motion powerful space-sorting crosscurrents that shape and reshape the city as a nexus of interrelated social and economic undertakings. This general argument is filled out in empirical terms by reference to the historical and geographical character of urbanization in the era of capitalism.

There is an abundance of books devoted to explaining how cities come into being, how they function, and how their diverse problems can be addressed. The conscientious reader may well therefore question the wisdom of putting forth yet another effort that plows very similar furrows. I fully recognize the appropriateness and force of this challenge, but I am also firmly persuaded that urban studies today is facing a crisis whose origins reside at least in part in a pervasive eclecticism that tends to lose sight of what is essential and central to the city as such, and that by default transforms it into an all-purpose receptacle of virtually anything and everything connected to life in organized society. In recent years, some theorists have gone even further by more or less dispensing with any notion of the urban as a geographically finite phenomenon and submerging it into an all-encompassing amalgam of social and economic entities at the planetary scale.

Of course, cities are indeed marked by high levels of substantive heterogeneity and interconnection. There is no reason whatever why we should not celebrate the complex personality and idiosyncrasy of particular places that we take to be interesting or unusual. Nor can we overlook the increasing functional integration of cities into global capitalism generally. My aim in this book is not to dispute the evident diversity of cities or their openness to the outside world but to attempt to recalibrate the conceptual apparatus that we bring to bear on them so that the basic features that they all share in common as dense clusters of ordered human existence come more sharply into view. An alternative way of saying the same thing is that I am intent here on an effort to identify what it is that enables us to distinguish the city as a concrete social and spatial entity from the rest of reality in general.

To begin with, I develop a broad conceptual account of urbanization that I contend makes systematic sense of the enormous variety of cities over geographic space and historical time. This is an audacious declaration, I know, and it will be taken amiss by the many urban analysts today who have put their faith in a "new particularism" that insists on the distinctiveness and irreducible complexity of every individual city, and hence—by inadvertence more than by explicit acknowledgment—that in essence sees every city as a special case requiring its own special kind of explanatory apparatus. The robust alternative to this analytical impasse is the admittedly risky but potentially highly rewarding strategy of insisting on the search for conceptual generality. Besides, in any given intellectual enterprise, there is no reason, in principle, why we cannot retain an appreciation of empirical diversity alongside a determined effort of theoretical abstraction. I should point out immediately that while such a strategy motivates the writing of the present book, the theoretical proposals that I advance are not a bid to compress all the minutiae of city life into a single comprehensive formula, but rather to show how a common underlying *urban process* brings these minutiae into generalizable mutual relations that occur in differing combinations and intensities in different cities.

We must also acknowledge that the logic and dynamics of the city are always embedded in and in turn act back upon much more extensive systems of social relationships and forces. Accordingly, the argument to be developed pays considerable attention to the reflexive interactions that are invariably in play between the city and society in the context of a wide geographical frame of reference. This phase of the analysis focuses above all on cities of the last century or two and more specifically on the varieties of urban development that have come and gone in relationship to the historical unfolding and global expansion of capitalism. Above all, I put great emphasis on an attempt to reveal the deeply rooted mutations of capitalism in the twenty-first century and the resulting major shifts that are currently proceeding in the form and functions of cities today. To be sure, these trends operate with widely contrasting intensities in different social milieus and in different parts of the world. I recognize and pay attention to these modulations as they work themselves out in diverse historical and geographical contexts, and I recognize that we can speak of varieties of cities just as we can speak of varieties of capitalism. However, as will appear in the later discussion, I take issue with the argument that circulates in some quarters today to the effect that the cities of different geographic provinces are fundamentally incommensurable with one another.

The field of urban studies has been much agitated throughout its relatively short history by many different theoretical proclamations and political advocacies. I pay some explicit attention to the diverse debates and theoretical claims that have come and gone in the field over the years, and I draw on an extensive body of already published literature for diverse factual and analytical material, but by and large I refrain from engagement in a systematic critique of that literature. The exceptions to this statement consist of certain mainly current ideas that collide head-on with my own and that cannot simply be passed over without some due diagnostic assessment. As it happens, the conceptual analysis that I present is perfectly amenable to hybridization with many other approaches to urban investigation, and it is arguable that the theoretical interpretations I offer may allow at least some controversies about cities to find more common ground than they otherwise might. This is a contentious proposition, but part of my justification for it is that the theoretical thrust of the book is directed not just to a synchronic concept of the city, but also, and crucially, to an account of the genetics of urbanization as a general process. Moreover, much of the argument is translatable into testable propositions that I believe can stand up to rigorous efforts of disconfirmation. This, at any rate, is an open invitation to the reader to make the attempt.

I should also say a few words here about the broad discursive strategy that I adopt. It is the height of fashion in urban studies today to proceed in a very self-conscious way by invoking the writings of various philosophers, and above all Continental intellectuals of a post-structuralist or phenomenological bent. These thinkers undeniably provide crucial insights about basic ontological and epistemological issues in social research. Many of the philosophers invoked in this manner have indisputably important things to say about the human predicament. Some of them, for example Michel

Foucault and especially Henri Lefebvre, also have important and directly relevant thoughts to offer about the urban condition, but most of them provide commentaries that at the outset have a rather oblique relationship to the city in any significant sense of the term. I am definitely not of the opinion that we can dispense with this material as a general guide to intellectual work, though I would certainly argue that it is broached by urban theorists more often in the hope that it will shed light on practical urban predicaments than in the actual accomplishment of this feat. In parts of the following text, I cite a select few of these philosophers, but I have preferred to adopt a *sotto voce* attitude to philosophy generally in the present argument, not out of philistinism or a naïve empiricism, but on the grounds that an unobtrusive realist epistemology provides us with most of what we need (such as the apparently surprising idea in some quarters that there is a fundamental distinction between necessary relationships and mere association) to make sense of the kinds of questions examined here. The most pressing task ahead, in short, is to bring the substantively *urban* content of urban analysis into the limelight.

I owe a debt of gratitude to many colleagues, students, and friends, who have helped me over the years to refine my own thought and to deepen my knowledge of cities. It would be invidious to attempt to sort out just what I owe specifically to each of them. I do, however, want to make acknowledgment to two individuals who have played a uniquely important role in the development of my own academic work. Shoukry Roweis stimulated me some time ago to embark on a major reassessment in my thinking about cities, if not the world in general. The concept of the "urban land nexus," which runs through the whole of the following text, is originally his. Michael Storper has been a constant companion and intellectual collaborator over the years and has been a discerning critic of my work. In many different ways, the influence of both of these friends, colleagues, and coauthors is detectable in all that follows. I alone am responsible for the errors of fact, emphasis, and interpretation that will doubtless be detected by the attentive reader.

Contents

1 City and Society   1

2 In Search of the City   11

3 Industrialization and Urbanization in Early Capitalism   39

4 Triumph and Tribulations of the Mass-Production Metropolis   61

5 Cities in a Globalizing World   83

6 The Third Wave   105

7 Mainsprings of Resurgence   131

8 Social Differentiation and Forms of Life   155

9	Through the Kaleidoscope	187
10	The Urban Commonwealth	215
Index		237

List of Figures

Fig. 4.1	The city as conceived by E. W. Burgess	68
Fig. 4.2	Schematic representations of the city in terms of concentric zones, sectors, and multiple nuclei	69
Fig. 5.1	The 50 largest metropolitan areas in the United States arrayed by rank	85
Fig. 5.2	Percentage of total population living in cities in 190 different countries as a function of GDP per capita, 2014	88
Fig. 5.3	Number of cities worldwide with populations of one million or more, 1950–2015	92
Fig. 5.4	World geographical distribution of cities with populations of one million or more	93
Fig. 5.5	The global multiplex of city-regions within the world system: a schematic representation	96
Fig. 6.1	US labor force characteristics, routine and non-routine task content, 1960–1998	116
Fig. 6.2	Workers in the labor force in selected occupational groupings as a percentage of the total labor force in the United States, 1980 and 2010	118
Fig. 8.1	Wage and salary income in constant 2010 dollars for the labor force in US metropolitan areas, 1950 and 2010	156
Fig. 8.2	Percent of the labor force with a bachelor's degree or equivalent versus the logarithm of population in US metropolitan areas, 1950 and 2010	163
Fig. 8.3	Human capital and work indexes by metropolitan size class in the United States	165
Fig. 10.1	Hierarchical classification of the urban commons	220

LIST OF TABLES

Table 5.1	Percentage of total population living in urban areas by major world region, 1955–2015	89
Table 5.2	Total world population living in urban areas by different size categories, 1955–2015	90
Table 5.3	Number of cities worldwide in different size categories, 1950–2015	91
Table 7.1	Selected transnational producer service firms, showing the top 15 cities ranked from top to bottom in order of the number of facilities belonging to each firm	142
Table 8.1	Wage and salary income of employed workers in US metropolitan areas by percentile, 1950–2010	157
Table 8.2	Employment levels by occupational category in US metropolitan areas, 1950–2010	159
Table 8.3	Percentage of labor force with a bachelor's degree or equivalent in different occupational categories in US metropolitan areas, 1950–2010	164
Table 8.4	Percentage of the labor force composed of African Americans, Asians, Hispanics, and European-born in US metropolitan areas, 1950, 1980, 2010	168
Table 8.5	Percentage occurrence of selected population groups in selected occupational categories in US metropolitan areas, 1950 and 2010	169
Table 8.6	Percentage occurrence of female workers in selected occupational categories in US metropolitan areas, 1950 and 2010	172

CHAPTER 1

City and Society

PROLOGUE

Toward the end of the eighteenth century, Dr. Samuel Johnson is reported by Boswell to have observed that "when a man is tired of London, he is tired of life; for there is in London all that life can afford."[1] Only a few decades later, William Cobbett referred to London as the "great wen," a tumor seething with thieves and prostitutes, a monstrosity shackling "the affairs of the nation" and impeding its accession "to a happy state."[2] Like so many others who have come before and after him, Johnson saw the city as the very condition of civilized existence and a monument to human accomplishment. Cobbett, also like many others, thought of it as an inferno undermining the order and welfare of society. In the two centuries and more that separate Johnson and Cobbett from our own era, a virtually endless sequence of variations on these contrasting judgments on the city have come and gone. The substance and tone of these judgments have varied greatly at different times and in different places, but they remain as enduring elements of both popular and academic opinion about cities. To borrow a turn of phrase from Balzac, the splendors and miseries of urban life always exist cheek by jowl though they are never democratically allocated in equal measure across the citizenry at large. To the contrary, as Balzac's novels tell us so cogently, these features are invariably spread about in lopsided proportions following the vagaries of class, race, gender, education, and sometimes, simply, luck. In a recent book, Edward Glaeser has uncompromisingly celebrated the *triumph* of the city,³ and while he is right to point to the benefits that urbanization brings in its wake, a more insightful analysis would surely have also stressed the numerous *tribulations* that are intrinsic to urban life and the political strife that continually rises to the surface as they take on tangible social form.

Cities have grown persistently in size and number since the time of Johnson and Cobbett, and they have diffused steadily over an ever-expanding geographical range. Their successes and failures have evolved through many different permutations, and these shifting phases have come and gone with increasing rapidity as capitalism, with its accelerated dynamic of social and economic change, has deepened its hold on the urban process. To be sure, cities have existed in various parts of the world beginning in the Neolithic Age some 10,000 years ago, and they have proliferated through countless mutations ever since.⁴ But it was capitalist industrialization with its peculiar social and property relationships that set in motion the epochal, and so far irreversible, rise of large-scale urbanization after the eighteenth century, and that has been the principal force underlying the concentration of more and more of the world's population and productive capacity in cities. The same dynamic has pushed aggressive forms of urbanization out to even the most secluded fringes of the inhabited world. Traditional non-industrial and non-capitalist cases of urban development can still be observed in many parts of the world today, but these are now virtually everywhere articulated in diverse ways with the global economy, and are in many instances undergoing rapid transformation by intercalations and erasures that for better or worse reflect the imperatives of modern capitalism. This is not to say that cities have everywhere become—or are becoming—homogeneous replicas of one another. To the contrary, casual observation alone reveals that cities differ enormously from country to country and even from region to region within any given country just as the evolutionary trajectories of individual cities over the modern era typically display wide variations. Every city, in other words, represents a unique combination of built structures, people, economic activities, social problems, cultural resources, and political institutions, to mention only a few of the common attributes of the urbanization process. This point takes on special resonance at a time when some commentators are proposing to submerge the notion of the city into a theory of "planetary urbanism," which proposes that the urban in the contemporary era simply dissolves away into the singularity of global capitalism.[5] Cities do certainly exist at the core of wider articulations of social and economic relations within world-encircling networks. However, the city is far from dissolving away within these networks, for as the following chapters will demonstrate in detail, the city is always a forceful presence with an assertive identity by reason of its collective internal structure and dynamics reflecting not just the simple aggregation of its individual components but in addition, and more importantly, the distinctive synergistic logic of their interplay.

This logic, as I shall argue at length in the succeeding discussion, can be represented in terms of a general theoretical archetype even as it is simultaneously expressed in specific historical and geographical urban forms rooted in often sharply contrasting social conditions. For the purposes of the present book, attention is focused above all on issues of urbanization in the capitalist era, though a number of critical distinctions still need to be dealt with under this general rubric. It is useful here to think of cities in capitalism as evolving through space and time within broad waves (or regimes of accumulation[6]), each reflecting a specific social formation in regard to technology, the organization of production and markets, basic class and political alignments, and an associated set of urban outcomes. It is important to note that when I speak of "waves" I am not referring to a teleological dynamic of advancement but to particular conjunctures of capitalism within which these outcomes share certain generic characteristics. In brief, we should think of each wave as relating to a unique period of historical time and a finite expanse of geographic space and as being subject to often wayward evolutionary tendencies. Three main waves, in particular, can be identified in the capitalist epoch. These assuredly do not exhaust the complete spatio-temporal record of capitalist development, but they do represent critical conjunctures that reveal in striking ways the shifting character and contours of capitalism itself, and, as a consequence, patterns of urbanization on the ground. They also provide significant clues about the political alignments and collisions that constantly come and go as the work and life of cities proceed. In any case, the main point here is to present a preliminary empirical sketch of the intimate connections between prevailing forms of capitalism and the broad character of the urban milieu as a way of entering into the basic theoretical discussion that follows in Chap. 2.

Waves of Capitalist Urbanization

The First Wave

The origins of the first main wave of capitalist development and urban growth can be detected in the seventeenth and eighteenth centuries when early forms of industrialization began to make their appearance in Britain and subsequently in parts of North America and continental Europe. The formation of this urban economic order with its principal foundations reposing on an emerging workshop and factory system together with rapidly expanding trade relationships, stimulated the growth of existing cities and encouraged the proliferation of new urban centers at locations where advantages such as access to energy sources like coal and water power were obtainable and where strategic transport routes intersected to form nodal centers. The main foci of production also became specialized in particular lines of business, as illustrated in Britain in the late eighteenth and nineteenth centuries by cotton production in the towns of Lancashire, woolens in Yorkshire and fabricated metal goods in the Midlands. At the same time, and even at this early stage, a geographical separation between manufacturing and finance had started to come about as nationally dominant cities like London, New York, and Paris emerged as important commercial and financial centers serving both national and international markets.

Most of the industrial towns that developed during this early version of capitalism were subject to very limited regulatory controls so that their physical expansion proceeded in rather haphazard ways, with notably deleterious effects on workers' housing and health. Social relations were marked by a sharp division between an impoverished working class, most of whom resided in cheap terrace housing close to factory locations in inner parts of the city, and a bourgeoisie made up of factory owners, merchants, and various professional castes who for the most part occupied large houses in the urban fringe. Working-class political agitation was endemic in these towns, not only in regard to matters of wages and working conditions but also housing, transport, education, and other social issues. Beyond Western Europe and North America, diverse colonial outposts of the major capitalist powers were also emerging at this time in response to ever-rising demands in the core countries for industrial raw materials and foodstuffs. These outposts functioned as administrative, commercial and entrepôt centers, often grafted onto preexisting indigenous settlements.

The Second Wave

As the nineteenth century came to a close, this first wave of capitalism gave way to a second wave that was attended by the intensified mechanization of production, the rise of large industrial corporations, increasing workers' wages (partly in response to growing union power), and the greatly accelerated expansion of cities. These trends gathered momentum in the first couple of decades of the twentieth century, driven especially by the large-scale, capital-intensive manufacturing systems that were then becoming technically and organizationally feasible, as exemplified above all by Henry Ford's introduction of the moving assembly line in his Highland Park car plant in Detroit in 1913. So strong is the symbolism of this event that the period from the turn of the twentieth century down to the 1970s and 1980s is nowadays often referred to, in terms first coined by Antonio Gramsci in the 1930s, as an era of "fordism" or "fordist capitalism."[7] Industry-driven urbanization at this time flourished above all in the so-called Manufacturing Belt in the northeast of the United States stretching from Boston and Baltimore in the east through Pittsburgh, Buffalo, Cincinnati, Cleveland, Detroit, and Chicago to St Louis in the west, and complemented by a Canadian segment extending from Halifax through Montreal to Toronto. A parallel, though smaller and more geographically fragmented Manufacturing Belt also came into being in Europe, anchored by burgeoning cities like Glasgow, Manchester, Birmingham, Lille, Charleroi, Rotterdam, Essen, and Dortmund, (with offshoots into southeast Germany and Silesia, which, after World War II, were absorbed into communist Eastern Europe).

North America and Western Europe represented the heartland of fordist capitalism over much of the twentieth century, with the United States emerging after World War II as the undisputed hegemon of the international system. This system itself rapidly came to be seen as a tripartite world order comprising a First World (initially North America and Western Europe and later incorporating Japan), a Second World (the Soviet Union and its satellites) and a Third World (comprising diverse colonial and ex-colonial territories and protectorates). The post-War period in North America and Western Europe was also marked by a major boom driven by the continued dynamism of the mass production system with its multiple tiers of direct and indirect input suppliers feeding into the voracious demands of major lead plants producing cars, machinery, chemicals, and so on, at the pinnacle of the system. This so-called Long Post-War Boom stretching from the early 1950s to the early 1970s promoted rapid growth of the main industrial cities of the First World transforming them into large-scale metropolitan regions with ever-extending outer boundaries. Residential neighborhoods in the core areas of these metropolitan regions remained for the most part the preserve of the blue-collar working class while white-collar families dominated in the suburbs, though even in the 1950s a degree of reversal of these patterns was already under way, along with the increasing suburbanization of industry. By the 1960s, the early symptoms of industrial decentralization started to give way to a more aggressive form of dispersal, first of all to various peripheral regions (such as the American South and the Italian *Mezzogiorno*) in the main capitalist countries and subsequently to selected parts of the Third World where import substitution and growth-pole policies were being widely promoted and where, as a result, industrial-urban expansion was proceeding rapidly. Japan also participated in many aspects of the core capitalist developmental model in the post-War years, at first hesitantly and essentially on the basis of expanding home markets, but then as the 1960s wore on, with increasing success on the international front.

For complex reasons that need not detain us at this stage, fordist capitalism in Western Europe and North America entered a period of serious crisis in the 1970s that left many of the major metropolitan regions that had flourished under the mass-production system in a state of near devastation. Japan initially managed to stave off crisis conditions by means of assertive export policies and innovative reorganization of its major factories on the basis of a highly productive and relatively flexible "neofordism," though eventually Japan too started to face serious problems. By the late 1970s and 1980s it seemed evident that the main industrial centers of North America and Western Europe were entering into a new developmental phase that soon came to be known as "post-fordism."[8] This was a period when digital technologies were starting to replace more purely mechanical forms of production, when labor relations were shedding much of the rigidity that they had acquired over the fordist period, and when a more open global economy was beginning to override earlier versions of the international order.

The Third Wave

With the wisdom of hindsight, it now appears that post-fordism was in reality a transitional phase leading from fordism, as such, to a more clearly identifiable "cognitive-cultural" capitalism with its key features residing not just in digital technologies but also in the formation of a new class of knowledge workers and a general restratification of urban society.[9] These social changes, in turn, have fostered a number of important shifts in intraurban residential space, partly reflected in the intensifying phenomenon of gentrification. By the end of the twentieth century, then, the main outlines of a third wave of capitalism, and, as a corollary, dramatic shifts in patterns of urbanization were becoming increasingly clear. For our purposes, the most obvious factor underlying this trend has been the rise of a series of new industries at the leading edges of capitalist expansion, as represented by sectors producing the technologies of the new economy together with finance, business and professional services, the media and cultural products, but also including more traditional branches of production undergoing extensive technological retooling. These trends have been occurring, moreover, not only in more economically advanced countries but in many parts of the former Third World too, and nowhere more so than in China and other rapidly developing nations of East and South Asia. Concomitantly, the cities that are most intensely implicated in these developments are rapidly coming to form a global mosaic bound together by extensive networks of competition and collaboration.

At the same time, this emerging third wave of capitalism is exacerbating many long-standing social predicaments of cities. Urban poverty, in particular, is an age-old problem but has taken on fresh and aggravated dimensions in North America and Western Europe as the former welfare arrangements of fordism have fallen by the wayside before the much less forgiving social policies of the current neoliberal order. In parts of Asia, Latin America and Africa, too, insistent pauperization has resulted in a situation where enormous masses of individuals live from hand to mouth in extended urban slums. Indeed, the deepening income and social inequalities in cities throughout the world today suggest that this third wave has inherently explosive tendencies that will require deeply rooted policy corrections if it is to survive over the long run.

SPECIFICITIES AND GENERALITIES OF URBANIZATION

The wider implications of these three brief sketches will be elaborated in subsequent chapters, where despite widely held opinion to the effect that "there can be no uniform approach to the city,"[10] I will make an attempt to develop a broad but parsimonious concept of urbanization. I seek to achieve this goal, not by an attempt to compress all of the minutiae of urban life into a single formula, but rather to provide guidelines that indicate how the genetics of dense agglomerations of human activity can be understood as a general social process and how this then leads on to the specific kinds of space-sorting dynamics that are always operative in the extensive development of the city. As the argument of the book proceeds, I advance the claim that the elaboration of these insights permits us to identify a specifically *urban* social logic and to distinguish the city as a material phenomenon embedded in and structured by society as a whole.

This is no easy challenge, for even at this early stage in the discussion it is evident that the substantive character of cities and their modes of work and life have changed time and time again over the course of history as a function of the complex interplay between the internal and external pressures that act upon them. These broad structuring processes have varying effects in different times and places depending on prevailing levels of technological development, resource availability, human capital, class relations, political power, and other important drivers of urban development. In capitalist society, as the subsequent argument will show, these drivers are actually bound up in powerful reflexive relationships with urbanization, for not only do they mold the physical and social character of urban centers but they are also themselves partly shaped by city-forming processes. Cities, in other words, provide essential foundations for the continued social reproduction of capitalism itself, and there is, indeed, no version of capitalism anywhere at any time that is not intimately associated with some form of urban development. Of course, not all that goes on in cities is immediately reducible to the logic of capitalism, and many aspects of urban life call for supplementary forms of explanation, as in the case of, say, spatial segregation or political contestation over land-use conflicts. Equally, many cities in different parts of the world today, perhaps most especially smaller cities in low- and middle-income countries, still remain in significant ways outside the principal orbit of capitalist production, trade, and social exchange, though this situation is clearly shifting rapidly as globalization proceeds.

In the ensuing chapters, we will pursue these and related themes through a series of analytical and descriptive maneuvers in which I seek to lay out the foundations of a generalized concept of the city and to show how this can be operationalized in substantive terms. The discussion will culminate in the second half of the book in a detailed examination of the complex forms of social and economic development and urbanization in the third historical wave that is now opening up before us.

NOTES

1. James Boswell, *Life of Johnson*, Oxford: Oxford University Press, 2008 (originally published in 1787).
2. William Cobbett, *Rural Rides*, London: Penguin, 2005 (originally published in 1830).
3. E. Glaeser, *Triumph of the City: How Our Greatest Invention Makes Us Richer, Smarter, Greener, Healthier, and Happier*, London: Penguin, 2011.
4. J. Robinson, A. J. Scott and P. Taylor, *Working, Housing: Urbanizing*, Berlin: Springer, 2016.
5. N. Brenner and C. Schmid, "The urban age in question," *International Journal of Urban and Regional Research*, 38, 2014, 731–755.
6. For an exposition of the notion of a regime of accumulation, see R. Boyer, *La Théorie de la Régulation: Une Analyse Critique*, Paris: Algalma, 1986; and A. Lipietz, "New tendencies in the international division of labor: regimes of accumulation and modes of social regulation," pp. 16–40 in A. J. Scott and M. Storper, *Production, Work, Territory: The Geographical Anatomy of Industrial Capitalism*, Boston: Allen and Unwin, 1986.
7. A. Gramsci, "Americanism and fordism," pp. 275–299 in D. Forgacs (ed.) The Gramsci Reader: Selected Writings, 1916–1935, New York: New York University Press, 2000.
8. A. Amin (ed.) *Post-Fordism: A Reader*, Oxford: Blackwell, 1994.
9. A. J. Scott, "Capitalism and urbanization in a new key? The cognitive-cultural dimension," *Social Forces*, 85, 2007, 1465–1482.
10. P. Perulli, *The Urban Contract: Community, Governance and Capitalism*, London: Routledge, 2017, p. 22.

CHAPTER 2

In Search of the City

What Is the City?

Definitional Dilemmas

In his short novel, *Species of Spaces,* Georges Perec warns us not to be too hasty in any attempt to define the city: "it is much too big and there is every likelihood that you will get it wrong."[1] Perec's warning is not to be taken lightly, for the history of thinking about cities is littered with an abundance of different and often-conflicting identifications of their supposed essential features. Here are few sample opinions (each taken out of a much larger body of work) about the nature of the city as offered by various luminaries in the field over the last century:

> [A city is] a continuous area having everywhere 10,000 or more people to the square mile. Mark Jefferson (1909)[2]

> The city is a collection of one or more separate dwellings in a closed settlement. Max Weber (1921)[3]

> A city may be defined as a relatively large, dense and permanent settlement of socially heterogeneous individuals. Louis Wirth (1938)[4]

> The city … is a geographic plexus, an economic organization, an institutional process, a theater of social action, and an aesthetic symbol of collective unity. Lewis Mumford (1938)[5]

> By its nature, the metropolis provides what otherwise could be given only by traveling; namely, the strange. Jane Jacobs (1961)[6]
>
> The city is a social product resulting from conflicting social interests and values. Manuel Castells (1983)[7]
>
> The city is everywhere and in everything ... What is not the urban? Ash Amin and Nigel Thrift (2002)[8]
>
> Cities are ... fundamentally about the display of wealth and power. Richard A. Walker (2016)[9]

My objective in listing these opinions is neither to disparage nor to endorse them, but simply, for the moment, to illustrate something of the plethora of different perspectives on the city that have been expressed at various points in time. In addition to these kinds of pronouncements, the literature contains a multitude of vignettes that seek to capture the essential qualities of urban structure and life in terms like captive cities, manipulated cities, postmodern cities, insurgent cities, consumer cities, cities as entertainment machines, the carceral city, the neoliberal city, the fragmented city, the dual city, the digital city, the global city, the post-fordist city, the creative city, the informational city, and scores if not hundreds more of other characterizations.[10] Many of these statements pick up on genuinely important aspects of cities, but even taken jointly, they still leave us very much in the dark about how and why cities come into being and what processes sustain them over time. Are we condemned, then, simply to reiterating the widely accepted judgment that cities are intrinsically resistant to any generalized assessment other than that they are "complex" and "diverse" foci of human settlement?

Theoretical Entanglements

At least one such generalized assessment had a considerable influence over an extended period of time on the intellectual development of urban studies and is still present in the background of much research today. I am referring here to the theoretical ideas propounded by the so-called Chicago School of Urban Sociology in the 1920s and 1930s. The main protagonists of this school of thought claimed to have identified the basic logic of urbanization as a function of the differential power of selected social groups, defined in terms of income, ethnicity, and race, to carve out ecological niches for themselves in the residential space of the city. This point of departure then led Park, Burgess, and McKenzie in their class work, *The City*, published in 1925, to posit a conception of intraurban space as a system of concentric zones, with blue-collar families and various ethnic and racial minorities distributed in neighborhoods around the urban core, while more affluent white-collar families occupied residential zones lying in the periphery.[11] Louis Wirth, another member of the Chicago School, provided a yet more encompassing theory of the city, deriving in part from Simmel's idea to the effect that modern urban life fosters individualism and the substitution of secondary for primary social bonds.[12] Wirth identified three major variables as forming the mainsprings of social existence in cities, namely, density, heterogeneity, and size, leading, respectively, to a spirit of competition, social fluidity, and the decay of tradition. The fact that Chicago School theory as a whole resided both explicitly and implicitly on an intellectual scaffolding derived from Social Darwinism brought it under increasing attack, especially after the 1950s and 1960s, when biologistic metaphors postulating a view of urban society as an "organism" came to be seen by social scientists as deeply suspect from both an analytical and a political perspective. Many of the ideas of the Chicago School lived on over the post-War decades in the guise of social area analysis, a mode of description that relentlessly catalogued the different varieties of socio-spatial balkanization observable in cities in terms of class, race, and ethnicity, but that largely abandoned any overt theoretical propositions about the underlying drivers of urban social geography.[13]

Chicago School theory and social area analysis finally gave way over the 1960s and 1970s to a powerful resurgence of Marxian and *marxisant* ideas in the domain of urban analysis. This intellectual thrust involved a set of approaches rooted in political economy and the analysis of capitalist class relations and focused in particular on the agonistic political divisions that permeate much of intraurban space. Henri Lefebvre's work, dating from the late 1960s, was an early, and still today influential, attempt to posit a Marxian interpretation of the city as an arena of class struggle and the site of a specifically normative project focused on the democratization of urban space and the "right to the city."[14] The sociologist Manuel Castells and the geographer David Harvey were much influenced by the work of Lefebvre and were also in the forefront of the intellectual shift away from the ideas of the Chicago School.[15] Castells' and Harvey's research efforts differ from one another in significant respects, but both were deeply concerned with the politics of public investments in items of collective consumption in the city and the class-*cum*-ethnic dimensions of conflict around their spatial allocation. Feminist scholars added an important dimension to these lines of radical analysis in urban research by pointing to the deeply rooted gender imbalances that run throughout the city, from discrimination in the workplace, through biases in urban service provision, to inequalities in the structure of family life.[16]

A further set of theoretical approaches deriving partly out of these earlier efforts, addressed the intensifying process of globalization that was becoming steadily more evident in the 1980s and after. These advocacies directed attention to the increasing integration of cities in different countries into worldwide networks of trade, reciprocity, and migration flows. A pioneering paper by Friedmann and Wolff pointed to the incipient formation of a network of "world cities" and the role of these cities in anchoring the emerging system of global capitalism.[17] Saskia Sassen then carried the discussion forward in a proposed synthesis of urban outcomes and globalization processes by stressing the important part that major metropolitan areas like New York, London, and Tokyo were playing as centers of corporate decision-making and high finance, and hence as centers of command and control in the world economy.[18] In the two or three decades since these founding ideas were published, a vast literature has accumulated around issues of global cities and global city-regions and how they have come insistently to the fore not only in North America and Western Europe but in many former Third World countries as well.[19]

More recently, various other analysts have advocated that urban theory now needs to veer toward post-structuralist visions of the city. In this vein, some urban scholars have claimed that we should approach investigation of the city as an intricate system of finely grained or rhizomatic networks binding together the social and the material elements of urban existence into "assemblages" of non-hierarchical relationships. This view places special emphasis on issues of agency or effectivity as residing in *both* human and non-human actors so that the citizenry at large and the artifacts that are part of the materiality of the city are seen as equally active participants in shaping urban outcomes.[20] Other analysts, drawing on post-colonial theory, suggest that we must start to correct or rethink our notions of urbanization by giving due weight to the experiences of cities in the Global South in our investigations. This is certainly a most welcome recommendation given the relative neglect of these cities in the published corpus of urban studies, though it often comes with the more controversial claim that theoretical ideas developed in the Global North are by definition Eurocentric and therefore irrelevant to the analysis of cities elsewhere in the world.[21] Yet other recent theoretical proposals revolve around declarations that the city as we usually think of it is a purely ideological construction. In this latter school of thought, with its central focus on the idea of "planetary urbanism," the twenty-first-century city is seen as having essentially been absorbed into a sort of overarching capitalist protoplasm spanning the entire globe.[22] Brenner expresses this idea in the remark that "it is the uneven extension of [the] process of capitalist creative destruction onto the scale of the entire planet … that underpins the contemporary problematic of planetary urbanization."[23] I shall have more to say about these issues later.

Toward a Reconsideration

These all-too-brief allusions to some of the leading ideas that have circulated in the urban studies literature over the years represent a sampling of the multiplicity of theoretical approaches that have been advocated by different schools of thought. Many of these approaches provide extremely useful insights into urban processes; others offer more dubious counsel. The questions that now evidently pose themselves are these: What common denominators, if any, can be adduced as minimal points of reference in debates about urban analysis? Are there foundational issues of urbanism that can help us in this task? If so, how do we use them to move further forward? And, more immediately, is it possible to establish a criterion of judgment that allows us to discriminate between the different ideas alluded to above and to sort out those that seem likely to offer the most promise for continued research and policy guidance from those that lead us away from these goals?

Almost everyone is likely to concur with the proposition that more or less all cities can be represented as dense clusters of people, but beyond this meager first step, points of agreement about the nature of cities are few and far between. Even if we accept this point of departure, there are likely to be immediate disagreements as to what size a settlement must be and what functions it performs before it can be considered to be a city. Some scholars have argued that there is in fact no single theoretical statement that can be usefully applied to all cities and that urban theory must be "provincialized" or compartmentalized in order to accommodate the allegedly incommensurable features of urbanization in different times and different places.[24] Given the oft-repeated description of cities—typified by the quotation from Perec above—as impenetrably complex and multifaceted entities, there is certainly on the surface something persuasive about this point of view. Alternatively, as Saunders wrote almost four decades ago, perhaps there is nothing especially distinctive about the city at all beyond its status as an arbitrary arena of social life whose dynamics are shaped by relationships that can only be understood by reference to society as a whole.[25] From this standpoint, the city is just modern society, *tout court*.

Part of my objective in this book is to cut through these contending views and to identify a durable theoretical construct that reveals certain intrinsic and generalizable features of cities and that can help us to distinguish specifically urban phenomena from the rest of society. This construct will be deployed at a later stage to show that however much individual cities may differ from one another empirically across time and space, they are all marked by a common underlying logic of socio-spatial integration that enables us to recognize what it is that constitutes their inherently *urban* character. In other words, and in order to ensure that the following chapters remain tethered to a disciplined treatment of the theme of the city, we must distinguish those phenomena that function intrinsically as elements of an urban process from those that may also be found in cities but have no necessary relationship to urbanization as such. Rest assured, I am not aiming to propose the impossible in the guise of a grand theoretical synthesis that will finally lay to rest all future debate about the city. My objective here, rather, is to offer an essentially simple concept of some core components of urban development processes and to clear away at least some of the incoherence that has accrued over a long period of time around the idea of the city. As I will demonstrate, the conceptual apparatus that I offer can then be hybridized in combination with other social variables, while simultaneously—and this is crucial—maintaining a disciplined distinction between those phenomena that are innately urban from those that are just happenstance occurrences in cities. To make the same point in another way, I propose to construct an argument that shows why a phrase like, say, "sex and the city," is, in the absence of further elaboration, empty of meaning. Our entry point into this exercise is a brief interlude on the historical origins of cities.

The Origins of Urbanization

Let us begin with a deceptively obvious truism: Every city coincides in the first instance with a place or locale where people congregate together over more or less extended periods of time. This truism provides us with an important point of focus, for it instantly brings us face-to-face with a central puzzle, namely, *why* is it that people congregate together in geographic space, and when does any resulting cluster constitute a city? Any meaningful answer to this question should ideally satisfy three main criteria, namely, it should provide a reasoned theoretical statement about the ontogenesis of cities as relatively dense and clustered aggregations of human activity, it should demonstrate that cities have significance as concrete social phenomena distinct from but contained within society as a whole, and it should be open to the full complexity of cities as substantively realized entities.

The Earliest Cities

A common starting point for thinking about the historical origins of cities is the observation that there must be a surplus of food production that allows for a social division between those who produce the food on the one side and other members of society on the other, no matter what the social condition of these other members may be (e.g. legislators, priests, soldiers, craftsmen, merchants, or a leisured aristocracy).[26] The generally accepted opinion in most studies of the origins of ancient cities is that the food surplus was produced by agriculturalists, but in her book, *The Economy of Cities*, published in 1969, Jane Jacobs argued strongly for an alternative view. She proposed that the first cities were sustained by hunting and gathering activities and that agriculture followed on from this initial stage.[27] The first chapter of her book is entitled "Cities First—Rural Development Later," where she makes the case that it was knowledge and technology developed in cities that made agriculture possible at the outset. Her argument relies heavily on the case of the oldest town yet known, Çatal Hüyük (located in southeastern Anatolia and dating from 7000 B.C.), where it appears that a population of hunters and gatherers was responsible for an overall food supply that supported many different craftsworkers engaged in activities such as obsidian carving, metal working, and the production of textiles.²⁸ The degree to which Jacobs' hypothesis is generalizable to the historical origins of cities as a whole remains open to debate, though it strains credulity to suppose that urbanization was without exception a precursor to agricultural development in the cases of other early city-based civilizations in places such as Egypt, Mesopotamia, the Indus Valley, the North China Plain, Middle America, the Central Andes, and Yorubaland in West Africa. The hypothesis seems all the more limited in its applicability given that hunting and gathering would require an exceptionally dense distribution of game and edible plants within feasible geographic range of the city in order to feed a permanent population beyond a few hundred or at most a few thousand souls. Certainly many authorities in the fields of urban archaeology and history, such as Childe and Bairoch, are in favor of an argument that insists on the primary importance of agriculture as a prelude to urbanization.²⁹ In any case, this question need not detain us further in the present context since we are only concerned here to affirm the importance of a food surplus, no matter what its source, before urbanization can occur.³⁰

The availability of a food surplus may constitute a necessary condition for cities to form, but it is actually not a sufficient condition. Specifically, it does not offer any particular insight as to why the spatial clustering or agglomeration of consumers of the agricultural surplus should occur. Indeed, we can readily envisage scenarios where consumers are spread out geographically in dispersed formations, whether stable or nomadic. One response to the puzzle is to invoke factors such as the foundation of ceremonial-*cum*-religious centers, the consolidation of administrative or military power, or the search for self-glorification on the part of the dominant class by means of monumental buildings.³¹ There is, indeed, no reason why spatial aggregations of these sorts should not have ignited the initial spark behind the formation of early cities, though even in the ancient world, cities were almost always much more complex than the signs and residues left by putatively initiating circumstances like these.³² Moreover, there are many cases, such as many of the Iron Age *oppida* of Northern Europe, that appear to have lacked monumental structures, and to have been purely economic centers with well-developed artisanal production activities.³³ If we are to formulate a general concept of urbanization, we must assuredly be able to go beyond the idiosyncrasies and limited occurrence of monumental gestures and identify at a minimum some basic conditions of existence that all cities share in common.

A well-trodden pathway around this challenge—like the call for the provincialization of urban theory—is to claim that no such general concept is possible, and that cities are continually being reinvented so that they represent irretrievably dissimilar species of phenomena in different times and places. In opposition to this claim, I propose that a general theoretical construct can in fact be successfully adduced, and that it can be identified in terms of an approach that builds upon—but then goes beyond—spatial and temporal dynamics rooted in economies of proximity, scale, and specialization.

The Division of Labor and the Growth of Cities

Our analytical departure point is once again focused on the early historical origins of cities. Let us suppose that a sufficient food surplus is available, and that a given fraction of the population can now survive by pursuing activities other than hunting and gathering or agriculture. Some or all members of this fraction may gather together in one place where they engage in non-economic avocations or employments of different sorts, but under what circumstances and with what consequences will this occur? So long as the place in question remains no more than an internally undifferentiated aggregation composed of a dominant social cohort (e.g. a political or religious elite) and its retainers, I propose that it should be referred to as a *proto-city* or a *proto-urban* form. I suggest, in addition, that we reserve the term *urban* for types of human settlements that are marked by the specialization and functional interdependence of their component social units accompanied by an internal dynamic of nucleation and land-use differentiation. In point of fact, such a process may very well already have been present in early proto-urban centers, for even in these cases, divisions of labor were likely to have occurred as individuals and groups sought to carry out their functions more effectively. A more important point is that with an adequate food surplus, production and trade can also come into being thus emphatically opening the way to detailed divisions of labor, thereby enhancing efficiency and productivity. Metallurgical workers, for example, might begin severally to specialize in individual tasks like smelting, molding, hammering, and polishing, and textile workers might divide into distinct trades like spinning, weaving, and dyeing. At the outset, these production activities were often dependent on serving a local elite, but they were also increasingly likely to form the basis of exchange relationships that occurred over a much wider social and geographical range. Specialized artisans were already strongly in evidence in ancient Çatal Hüyük, a place where public buildings were notably absent, and where evidence of extensive trade connections has been found.

The division of labor is the basis of what Durkheim called "organic solidarity," that is, the organization of society on the basis of multiple and specialized conjoint activities.[34] Organic solidarity in this sense represents a basic and recurrent condition for the agglomeration of human activities in geographic space and provides the crucial organizational underpinning of the city. Those members of society who are caught up in the division of labor in non-agricultural sectors will by the same token be bound together in webs of interlinkages involving interpersonal cooperation and transfers of materials, messages, and people across space. These interlinkages inevitably incur costs as a function of distance. There will therefore be strong incentives for selected individuals in non-agricultural sectors to agglomerate together in geographic space in order to achieve some degree of organizational and productive efficiency. Equally, increasing levels of agglomeration and hence rising opportunities for individual specialization will tend to encourage yet further deepening of the division of labor. The economy is undoubtedly the main sphere of society where trends such as these are likely to be most insistent, but even priestly, administrative, and military functions as noted earlier will tend to be subject to similar processes of differentiation and locational agglomeration, with or without symbolic elaboration.[35]

In general, we can say that the availability of a food surplus has a double relevance to any attempt to understand the origins of cities. In the first place, it enables a fraction of the population to undertake activities other than food production, though this factor by itself cannot account for significant spatial clustering effects. In the second place, the same fraction of the population may be subject to internal functional specialization leading to the formation of networks of specialized but complementary activities. At least some parts of these networks will agglomerate together around their own center of gravity, and because this enhances overall productivity, there will be some tendency for the resulting cluster to grow. These processes are likely to be particularly vigorous in the case of economic activities when wider markets provide an outlet for exports, allowing production levels to expand and thus facilitating advances in the division of labor.[36] Rising numbers of producers will help to boost the local population, as will incursions of ancillary workers and their families, and these trends will induce further local increases in production and trading. In this manner, and so long as a food supply remains available, intensifying centripetal and virtuous circles of growth can be expected to occur.

Cities hence appear and constantly reappear throughout history and over geographic space as dense congeries of differentiated human activities with an endemic but never automatic propensity to grow as their functional foundations expand and the division of labor proliferates. As Paul Bairoch, Peter Taylor, and others have pointed out, moreover, the growth of cities, right from the beginning, has always depended on long-distance interactions.[37] Even the earliest cities, including Çatal Hüyük, Jericho, Babylon, Mohenjodaro, and others, were tied into long-distance trade networks. In many different social formations, and in many different concrete forms, processes like these have always played a prominent role in the rise and growth of cities and their transformation through cycles of technological and organizational change. In particular, the forces of capital accumulation and economic innovation set in motion by the Industrial Revolution unleashed the unprecedented and constantly widening rounds of urbanization that have become one of the hallmarks capitalism.

Analytical Reprise

The highly stylized account of urban development that I have given thus far is expressed in a way that reproduces certain echoes of the actual historical order of things, but it can also be recast into an analytical order that is more self-consciously abstract. The argument thus far has proposed that cities are an outcome of organizational and spatial forces promoting the agglomeration of diverse socio-economic phenomena and above all productive activities embedded in detailed divisions of labor. What specific sorts of activities are at issue here is immaterial relative to the fundamental point that they constitute networks of specialized and interdependent units of human effort whose interactions or linkages with one another make it advantageous for them to cluster together in geographic space. Even today, when transport and communication costs have fallen to unprecedentedly low levels, it has been shown by economic geographers and urban economists that intraurban linkages typically involve high costs per unit of distance.[38] These costs are especially burdensome where the linkages are small in scale, variable over time, constantly shifting in regard to origins and destinations, and entail the need for face-to-face contact, and these are precisely the kinds of linkages that predominate in urban areas.[39]

The phenomenon of agglomeration induced by the division of labor and the spatial costs of interaction is reinforced by a set of complementary processes generated by the burgeoning mass of the city. These processes reside primarily in the many-sided increasing-returns effects (or economies of scale) that typically intensify as any city grows in size leading to increased efficiency and productivity of its internal operations. To be more accurate, it should be said that as the city grows, both increasing and decreasing returns come into being, though as and when the latter begin to threaten the viability of critical urban operations, at least some attempts at corrective intervention can usually be expected to ensue. The varying substance of these relationships can be expressed in terms of three broad processes identified by Duranton and Puga as *matching, sharing*, and *learning*.[40] First, increasing urban size simplifies the recurrent problem of matching in cities as epitomized by situations where there are numerous buyers and sellers of goods and services (including labor services). The matching process is facilitated not only in the sense that buyers and sellers can identify one another with relative ease in dense agglomerations but can also engage in comparative assessments of different possibilities before actually engaging in an exchange. Second, as cities grow, increased opportunities for sharing make possible the more efficient provision and utilization of public goods. Sharing means that large fixed capital investments in artifacts, such as roads and sewage systems, can be supplied at diminishing per capita cost as a function of urban size. Third, learning is typically at a high level in large cities as a consequence of the frequent, many-faceted interpersonal contacts that are one of the major features of urban life. Learning helps to sustain the creative and innovative potentialities of the city and is one of the cornerstones of the evolving habits of thought and imaginative flair that have always been primarily associated with large urban centers.

The net result of these different symbiotic forces in combination with the heightened levels of interindividual accessibility offered by agglomeration is that many cities are endowed with significant competitive advantages. In the case of modern cities, these advantages enable local producers to lower their costs, to intensify their innovative capacities, and to contest wider global markets, thus promoting possibilities for the formation of forceful virtuous circles of growth.

The Urban Land Nexus

These remarks about the genesis and growth of cities take us part of the way toward a disciplined minimal concept of the urban, but still by no means the whole way. We have examined in a preliminary manner how the persistent agglomeration of multiple and disparate human activities comes about, but we have not yet considered the consequences in terms of the organization of the internal spaces of the city. Obviously, these activities cannot all occupy the single, dimensionless point that constitutes the gravitational center of the agglomeration. Rather, they must necessarily arrange themselves at different locations around this center subject to their different economic and political resources and functional interdependencies with one another. The properties of this particular space-sorting process and its end result in terms of the spatial and physical form of the city are an organic complement to agglomeration, and as such, a description of them is required to round out our basic concept of the city. We may refer to this end result as the *urban land nexus*, that is, a set of interrelated locations forming a composite integument and anchored geographically by the forces of agglomeration.[41] As such, the urban land nexus can also be provisionally identified as a spatially ordered kaleidoscope of use values and exchange values forming the internal space of the city.

The Spatial Organization of the City

When we examine a map of any actual city, we are virtually always struck by the regularities that usually run through intraurban space as expressed in wide swaths of different types of land use. Equally striking, however, is the heterogeneity of the detailed social, economic, and physical elements into which these swaths of land use themselves decompose. In modern cities, and probably most cities in the past as well, these patterns can generally be broken down in a first round of description into three different categories reflecting fundamental attributes of urban existence, namely, spaces of production where economic activities and employment sites are concentrated, spaces of residential and social activity given over to areas dominated by housing and family life, and spaces of circulation comprising the physical networks that allow for movement through the urban land nexus. In some instances, these spaces interpenetrate and overlie one another; in other instances, they are geographically separate but functionally integrated, as exemplified by modern cities where physical separation between employment places and home places is the general rule. In certain situations, we may need to add a fourth category representing the symbolic (ceremonial or political) spaces of the city, as in the case of the monumental structures of the Aztec cities recorded by Michael Smith[42] or the palaces of the ancient Aegean world described by Hammond.[43] These broad types of spaces represent different aspects of the forces of agglomeration and their expression in the urban land nexus. In more specific terms, the city, and its materialization in the urban land nexus, can be represented as *a mode of spatial integration* of many disparate social and economic phenomena whose urbanity flows from the fact that they are drawn together by the imperative of mutual proximity. Jane Jacobs in her *Death and Life of Great American Cities* has captured the same idea with her "uniquitous principle" of urbanization, namely, "the need of cities for a most intricate and close-grained diversity of uses that give each other constant mutual support both economically and socially."[44] It is this basic concept of urbanization that allows us to distinguish between phenomena that exist *in* the city (but are not part of its quintessential urban character) from phenomena that are *of* the city (and that constitute the city as such). In line with these remarks, a school or a hospital is intrinsically a component of the urban process when it has spatial relations to and impacts on other components of the city but neither the teaching methods of the school nor the internal administrative arrangements of the hospital are likely to have any particular relationship to the city as such, or, rather, *they are relevant only to the degree that they intersect in some functionally meaningful way with the forces of agglomeration and the spatial logic of the urban land nexus*. For example, curriculum arrangements in schools are usually not especially relevant to the urban land nexus, but when they underpin training that matches demands by local employers, they are certainly of relevance because they are directly implicated in the functions of the city as an agglomerated mass of interdependent phenomena. Similarly, the architectural landscape of the city constitutes an organic aspect of the urban land nexus not only because of the ways in which it embodies and expresses particular kinds of land use but also by reason of the compositional effects created by the spatial juxtaposition of many individual buildings. As Ruskin writes, "… architecture differs from painting peculiarly in being an art of *accumulation*" leading to the "concerted music of the streets of the city"[45] though he might just as easily have mentioned how often the music is disconcertingly discordant.

Notwithstanding this highly generalized definition of the urban land nexus, each individual case always represents a unique combination of social and economic phenomena arranged in unique spatial patterns so that every individual city is immediately distinguishable from every other. At the same time, cities are always embedded in a wider social formation that leaves certain traces on their physiognomy, and we can thus frequently recognize distinctive families or classes of cities that share certain basic features characteristic of a particular historical period or geographical territory. Some of the important overarching variables that exert important effects on urban form and function can be catalogued as follows (cf. Storper and Scott[46]):

- the organization and level of economic activity, which in turn determine basic configurations of production and material culture;
- prevailing resource allocation rules, especially in regard to the ownership, use, and exchange of land;
- structures of social stratification and differentiation, which play an important role in marking out lines of residential separation in the city and in the provision of shelter;
- cultural norms and traditions, with their multidimensional effects on the form and visual appearance of the city as well as on modalities of interaction among the citizenry; and
- relations of political authority and power, which have direct impacts on the character of urban governance and collective decision-making in regard to remedial and strategic action in the urban land nexus.

The observable qualities of cities, then, are always expressed in ways that reflect both the character of the society out of which they emerge and the special dynamics that spring from the operation of agglomeration and the urban land nexus as an integrated socio-spatial system. This double determination of the urban is equivalent to what Henri Lefebvre refers to as the "far order" (society at large) in relation to the near order (the city in all its specificity).[47] Moreover, cities are not just passive receptacles of this far order, for while they always reflect an overarching social logic, so also are they way-stations that play a decisive role in the reproduction of society as a whole. This reflexive relationship is emphatically present in capitalist societies.

Rent and Land Use

In capitalism, the primary mechanism shaping the division of labor and the agglomerative forces that lie at the root of urbanization is the production of goods and services in the context of the profit-seeking urges of firms in competitive markets. Equally, the city (i.e. the urban land nexus) plays a decisive role in securing many of the social and spatial conditions that facilitate profit-seeking and competition in capitalism. Agglomeration is critical in this regard because of its virtues as a source of cost reduction, efficiency, and innovation.

A supplementary constitutive condition of the capitalist city is the institution of private property, and most notably private property in land so that the competitive space-sorting mechanisms of the urban land nexus are structured above all by the phenomenon of land rent or value.[48] For any given configuration of intraurban space, each unit of land will have a rent reflecting the externalities that encroach upon it, where these externalities reflect the advantages and disadvantages of that unit *relative to* every other. In practice, access to the city as a whole is one of the most potent externalities of this sort, and hence locations close to the center of gravity of the urban land nexus are typically valued at higher levels than those in other parts of the city (and will also be occupied at notably higher densities). As we move outward from the center toward the urban fringe, both rent and density tend to decline steadily, though submaxima commonly occur at non-central sites where accessibility is relatively high or where special kinds of locational advantages are available, as in the case, for example, of local retail nodes. This process of location and land rent in the city is modulated by complementary mechanisms related to many additional kinds of externalities. Thus, all else being equal, firms will select locations in ways that seek appropriate trade-offs between land rents and the specific sorts of agglomeration economies at those locations. Likewise, families seeking residential accommodation will be likely to favor sites with compatible neighbors and will tend to be averse to sites where neighbors are perceived to be antipathetic or where properties are falling into disrepair. But each individual family's actual choice will also be shaped by a budget constraint, and if, as is likely, the contrasting qualities of the available sites are reflected in rent differentials, the family's final decision will in part be governed by the size of its budget in comparison with the rent of the land.

The interplay between rent formation and these complex mechanisms of site selection in the context of profitability criteria and budget constraints not only brings about the division of the urban land nexus into production, social, and circulation spaces but also encourages further detailed internal differentiation within each of these spaces. Thus, the production space of the city in contemporary capitalism includes factories, offices, warehouses, retail establishments, and other kinds of land uses, in some cases located in specialized quarters such as an industrial district or a downtown shopping area, in other cases dispersed over more extensive spatial niches such as the suburbs.[49] Social space is the privileged domain of housing activity and is invariably fragmented into different neighborhoods partly reflecting the affinities and aversions that exist between different groups depending on demographic and cultural factors such as class, race, ethnicity, religion, national origins, and so on. Circulation space comprises the arterial pathways that connect the varied land uses in the city into a functioning system of interdependencies and that also have major impacts on land rent and hence (again) land use. The net result of all these different crosscurrents is the complex but systematically organized patchwork of spaces and relationships that constitute the urban land nexus.

THE PUBLIC CITY

Externalities, the Commons and Collective Consumption

Externalities represent benefits or costs that spill over from land users or activities at one set of locations to land users or activities at another set of locations independently of any prior agreement between the parties concerned. Externalities thus circulate spontaneously through urban space irrespective of their desirable or undesirable qualities. As such, they are special cases of a wider set of phenomena that are of increasing importance in the urban milieu and that can be identified under the general rubric of the *commons*. Public goods or items of collective consumption are also instances of these phenomena, as are common-pool resources (which, like gated communities, are accessible to only designated groups of people), and the gifts of nature. The urban commons, in brief, are composites of all those features of the urban land nexus that lie beyond the claims of private property and market discipline and that constitute public and quasi-public assets of both positive value (e.g. parks, museums, transport networks, agglomeration economies, and the like) and negative value (e.g. air pollution and public health hazards). The city is an important fountainhead of the commons because the density, variety, relational interconnections, and frequent indivisibilities of its different elements create a milieu that is charged with extra-market effects and public assets.

Above all, from the very beginnings of capitalism, the *social and economic atmosphere* of the city has functioned as a multidimensional assemblage of common resources with profound impacts on urban development.[50] The importance of atmosphere to the urban economy was identified at the end of the nineteenth century by Alfred Marshall who described the city as a locus of critical informational assets and increasing-returns effects.[51] More recently, the role of atmosphere as a factor in molding the social reproduction and consciousness of the labor force has been underlined by Hardt and Negri in their discussion of the replacement of the traditional factory by the modern city as an instrument of habituation of the labor force into the rhythms and requirements of life in capitalism.[52] I shall have much more to say on these matters in subsequent chapters, and especially in Chap. 10 where I deal with the urban commonwealth. For the moment, we should note, in addition, that a convergence of the urban commons and the global commons is rapidly occurring as reflected above all in the extraordinary explosion of information storage and exchange capabilities based on digital technologies and the Internet. The rise of the vast and variegated commons that has accompanied the emergence global capitalism raises many new questions, as we shall see, about the constitution of the city.

The commons have many different and contradictory impacts on urban life, and even when their impacts are positive, they may be susceptible to degradation due to overexploitation. Collective intervention is hence often needed in order to harmonize their relationships to the rest of the urban system. In some instances, the resources of the commons are immune from overuse (as for example in the case of knowledge), but there still may be gains to be made from intervention in order to boost available benefits and to redirect them into designated channels. Three brief concrete examples demonstrate something of diversity and urgency of urban quandaries like these. First, there is a persistent tendency for roadways through the core of the city to become heavily congested in response to insistent commercial development in the central business district. Congestion will not only make commuting less efficient but also lead on to other functional inefficiencies such as rising labor costs at downtown locations. In situations like these, social costs and benefits can only be brought back into effective balance by effective regulation through mechanisms such as rationing or road pricing. Second, serious problems often ensue when incompatible or mutually disruptive types of land use come into close proximity with one another. Thus, encroachment by a factory or other noxious facility on a residential neighborhood is apt to engender significant dissonances due to factors such as increased traffic, noise, and blight, leading in turn to falling house prices, and in some cases, perhaps, to deterioration of the local social fabric. Third, continued outward expansion of the city by speculative building of low-density suburban housing puts rising fiscal burdens on local governments, which then have to provide for necessary infrastructure out of public funds. These and many other types of ingrained dilemmas that haunt the urban land nexus mean that agencies of collective order must be able to exercise powers of remedial intervention in order to bring a semblance of workability to the city.

Most of these dilemmas represent what neoclassical economists refer to as "market failures," but this terminology grants far too much, by implication, to the market as a normative ideal of social organization, and far too little to the collectivity as a source in its own right of socially rational decisions. Certainly, technical market failures such as externalities and free-rider problems abound in the urban land nexus, and while these are in some instances relatively limited in their impacts, they often call for massive strategic choices to be made, as, for example, in those not infrequent cases where a large employer decides to relocate to another part of the world leaving behind a devastated community, or where air pollution problems require major regulatory guidelines. The efficiency and social order of the urban land nexus are further dependent on the provision of items of collective consumption such as utilities, street lighting, and fire protection that would not otherwise appear spontaneously in the appropriate quantities and qualitative forms under market rules of supply and demand. Additionally, there is always the clear danger that lock-in problems may occur as the city evolves through time so that some degree of collective steering needs to be undertaken to help it select pathways leading to more desirable social and economic outcomes. It is clear that in a capitalist society, cities are unlikely to come even within striking distance of what Richard M. Hurd referred to as the "highest and best use of the land,"[53] unless markets are complemented by appropriate institutional controls.

Institutions of Governance

The discussion thus far underlines the point that market coordination can never secure the continued sustainability of the urban land nexus in contemporary capitalism. This remark applies to cities of all sizes but is most unambiguously illustrated by the case of large metropolitan areas where complex combinations of emergent effects produce a chronically shifting terrain of functional failures that constantly put the social and economic life of the city at risk. Institutions of collective decision-making and action, with command of the instruments of social coercion, eminent domain, and fiscal appropriation, and with a mandate to ensure smooth reproduction of the social order, are therefore indispensable as guarantors of the continued robust operation of the urban land nexus. Concomitantly, local government organizations in modern cities can be understood in significant ways as a response to the endemic breakdowns of the urban land nexus under capitalism. By and large, the work of these organizations entails fairly routine management operations though they also must deal with major strategic initiatives as well as with the political upheavals that break out from time to time as a consequence of both real and perceived inequities in intensities and directions of urban development. Other types of organizations (e.g. chambers of commerce, neighborhood groups, philanthropic associations) also play subsidiary roles in the planning process by addressing issues specific to their range of legitimate concerns.

The panoply of individual agencies and institutions that almost always make up the totality of municipal governance express the many-sided nature of the challenges that must be faced up to in cities, from dealing with infrastructural deficits, through development controls, to the social pacification of fractious neighborhoods. Enabling legislation by higher levels of government typically provides city governments with the broad tools that enable them to address these challenges and to engage in corrective action, but the tools are almost always deployed with very high levels of local discretion. To be sure, city governments also typically pay attention to matters that often go far beyond the specifics of the urban land nexus, and that include an enormous diversity of issues like health counseling, legal services, or certification programs extending into spheres of life that often are only indirectly, if at all, connected to urbanization processes in the strict sense. These issues reflect two interrelated circumstances: first, the fact that local authorities frequently act as relay stations for directives issued by higher-level political agencies, and second, the subsidiarity principle meaning that the locality is often simply the most efficient geographic unit for carrying out certain kinds of public service directives that in and of themselves have no special or necessary relationship to the urban land nexus. City governments, then, are almost always hybrid in nature; they act simultaneously both as constituent elements of the urbanization process (i.e. when they are engaged in the affairs of the urban land nexus) and as agents of a broader political apparatus that is accountable for much more extensive social responsibilities. There is unquestionably a very fine line between these two different sets of functions, but the advantage of making the distinction is that it helps us maintain a disciplined viewpoint about the nature of the city and its essential functions as opposed to the incoherent tangle of contingencies that are more usually thought of as ingredients of the urban crucible. It is possible that at least some of the perplexity concerning the aims and purposes of local political institutions (as expressed, for example, by Cochrane[54]) may be due to a failure to recognize this complex interpenetration of scales and functions in the management of cities and society at large.

The City in Focus

We are now in a position give a provisional definition of the city in relation to its fundamental genetic and organizational traits. If we gather together the individual strands of the argument thus far, we can formulate this definition by reference to the urban land nexus as a specifically local scale of economic and social interaction that is (a) generated by agglomeration processes deriving in the first instance from the division of labor; (b) reinforced by diverse economies of scale; (c) structured by prevailing modalities of decision-making and behavior in relationship to overall social and property relationships; and (d) almost always endowed with governance arrangements that attempt to deal with collective issues of coordination and management.[55] These comments can be seen as outlining the basic constitutive conditions of the urban land nexus in general and as guidelines for the analysis of urban outcomes in specific social formations. I should add a further proviso to these conditions, namely that throughout history, cities have always been linked over both short and long distances to locations beyond their own confines so that they invariably function as nodal hubs of far-flung external connections. Indeed these connections are critical to the survival of cities if only in the minimal sense that essential food supplies invariably need to be imported into the city from elsewhere.

Brenner and Schmid[56] have argued recently that the multiple external relationships of the city have become so integral to the urban condition that we have now entered an era of "planetary urbanism" in which the city, as such, has essentially receded before a continuous membrane of interacting social and economic activities circling the entire globe. To the degree that global space today is indeed virtually everywhere suffused by modern capitalism and that cities are inextricably embedded in this same space, Brenner and Schmid have a point of sorts. They err, however, in their radical depreciation of the city as a distinctive unit of social reality as well as in their unwarranted misappropriation of the term "urban" to refer to the totality of global space.[57] "The urban," they write, "cannot be plausibly be understood as a bounded, enclosed site of social relations that is to be contrasted with non-urban zones or conditions."[58] To the contrary, as I have repeatedly argued here, the city exists as a concrete social phenomenon that can be coherently conceptualized on the basis of the social and political dynamics that are unique to it. It is unquestionably true that the urban land nexus with its tapering outward spread is not spatially delimitable in any precise way, but, then, if boundedness and enclosure were a necessary condition of ontological integrity we would never, by analogy, be able to talk in a meaningful manner about any complex unit of space or time with blurred outer boundary zones such as a mountain versus a plain, a river versus the ocean, the stratosphere versus the troposphere, the spring versus the summer, or a white neighborhood versus an African-American neighborhood. What makes these phenomena ontologically distinguishable (and epistemologically knowable in realist terms) is that they possess coherence over some significant set of criteria that identify a meaningful constitutive inside. The existence or non-existence of a linear boundary is irrelevant to the presence or absence of this coherence. Similarly, it is the self-reinforcing process of agglomeration and the unique emergent effects of the urban land nexus that distinguish the city from the rest of geographic space even in the absence of any clear-cut spatial delimitation.

I have attempted in this chapter to preserve and sharpen the concept of the city by offering a theoretical synthesis that captures the essential logic and substantive character of urbanization by means of a focus on agglomeration and the urban land nexus. I say "essential" here because my objective is not to build a theory that accounts for all the detailed minutiae of human decision-making and behavior in the city, but rather to identify the skeletal groundwork that springs into being as these minutiae come into systematic spatial relationships with one another and take on the shape of an agglomerated urban land nexus. The net result in empirical reality is a multiplicity of urban forms that are all outwardly different from one another but that in aggregate share an inward genetic and generic resemblance. Actually, the stories we tell about cities are almost always implicitly or explicitly hybrid constructions, for the city in its diverse concrete realizations is a synthesis of constantly shifting empirical circumstances rooted in an enveloping social formation and concentrated within nucleated masses that give rise to complex emergent effects. From this perspective, virtually anything can *potentially* be urban, even though not everything that is found in the city is *actually* urban, for the urban, to repeat, is defined not by the things it contains but by their mode of spatial integration. This manner of conceptualizing the city, moreover, provides a disciplined means of grounding the *urban question*, where I mean by the latter term a scientifically and politically driven problematic of enquiry into the workings of the city and into the possibilities of progressive reform in any given conjuncture.

In the light of these arguments, we can dispense altogether with the rather barren debate about the lower bounds on the size of a settlement before it can be considered to be a city, and the equally futile attempt to distinguish towns from cities as distinctive scalar or functional entities. An urban process cannot be identified in terms of size or substantive functions, but only in terms of an agglomerated spatial logic relative to a congruent external environment. In those cases where cities have been founded *ex nihilo* as a conscious political gesture, these generalizations still apply, for even a city of this type comprises at a minimum an aggregation of specialized (e.g. administrative or ceremonial) functions together with an associated land nexus containing various social and economic appendages to these functions. Eventually, as illustrated by contemporary cases like Brasilia, Canberra, and Naypyidaw, more people will gravitate to the city and employment opportunities will tend to expand, filling out and widening the urban frame and creating a more extended terrain of interrelated land uses.

Notes

1. G. Perec, *Espèces d'Espaces*, Paris: Galilée, 1974, p. 119.
2. M. Jefferson, "The anthropography of some great cities: a study in distribution of population," *Bulletin of the American Geographical Society*, 41, 1909, p. 544.
3. M. Weber, *The City*, Glencoe: Free Press, 1966, p. 65 (translated from the German edition of 1921).

4. L. Wirth, "Urbanism as a way of life," *American Journal of Sociology*, 44, 1938, p. 3.
5. L. Mumford, *The Culture of Cities*, New York: Harcourt Brace Jovanovich, 1938, p. 480.
6. J. Jacobs, *The Death and Life of Great American Cities*, New York: Random House, 1961, p. 238.
7. M. Castells, *The City and the Grassroots: A Cross-Cultural Theory of Urban Social Movements*, Berkeley: University of California Press, 1983, p. 291.
8. A. Amin and N. Thrift, *Cities: Reimagining the Urban*, Cambridge: Polity, 2002, p. 1.
9. R. A. Walker, "Why cities?—A response," *International Journal of Urban and Regional Research*, 2016, DOI:10.1111/1468-2427.12335.
10. Taylor and Lang write that "this invention of concept after concept is hardly conducive to credible understanding of what is going on in and between our cities." See: P. J. Taylor and R. E. Lang "The shock of the new: 100 concepts describing recent urban change," *Environment and Planning A*, 36, 2004, 951–958.
11. R. E. Park, E. W. Burgess ad R. D. McKenzie, *The City*, Chicago: University of Chicago Press, 1925.
12. L. Wirth, *op. cit.*, 1938. G. Simmel, "The metropolis and mental life," pp. 409–424 in K. H. Wolff (ed.) *The Sociology of Georg Simmel*, New York: Free Press, 1950 (first published in German in 1903).
13. Early statements on the subject of social area analysis include: E. Shevky and W. Bell, *Social Area Analysis*, Stanford: Stanford University Press, 1955, and A. H. Hawley and O. D. Duncan, "Social Area Analysis: A Critical Appraisal," *Land Economics*, 33, 1957, 337–345.
14. H. Lefebvre, *Le Droit à la Ville*, Paris: Editions Anthropos, 1968.
15. M. Castells, *La Question Urbaine*, Paris: Maspéro, 1972; D. Harvey, *Social Justice and the City*. London: Edward Arnold, 1973.
16. Cf. D. B. Massey, *Space, Place, and Gender*, Minneapolis: University of Minnesota Press, 1994; L. McDowell, *Working Bodies: Interactive Service Employment and Workplace Identities*, Chichester: Wiley-Blackwell; 2009; K. England, "From social justice and the city to women-friendly cities? Feminist theory and politics," *Urban Geography*, 15, 1994, 628–643.
17. J. Friedmann and G. Wolff, "World city formation: an agenda for research and action," *International Journal of Urban Regional Research*, 6, 1982, 309–344.
18. S. Sassen, *The Global City: New York, London, Tokyo*. Princeton: Princeton University Press, 1991.
19. See, for example: A. J. Scott, *Global City-Regions: Trends, Theory, Policy*, Oxford: Oxford University Press, 2001.
20. C. McFarlane, "Assemblage and critical urban theory," *City*, 15, 2011, 204–224.

21. A. Roy, "Slumdog cities: rethinking subaltern urbanism." *International Journal of Urban and Regional Research*, 35, 2011, 223–238; see also J. Robinson, *The Ordinary City: Between Modernity and Development*. London: Routledge, 2006.
22. N. Brenner and C Schmid, "The urban age in question," *International Journal of Urban and Regional Research*, 38, 2014, 731–755; H. Angelo and D Wachsmuth, "Urbanizing urban political economy: a critique of methodological cityism," *International Journal of Urban and Regional Research*, 39, 2015, 16–27.
23. N. Brenner, "Theses on urbanization," *Public Culture*, 25, 2013, p. 109.
24. See, for example: H. Leitner and E. Sheppard, "Provincializing critical urban theory: extending the ecosystem of possibilities," *International Journal of Urban and Regional Research*, DOI 10.1111/1468-2427.12277, 2015.
25. P. Saunders, *Social Theory and the Urban Question*, London: Hutchinson, 1981.
26. V. G. Childe, "The urban revolution," *Town Planning Review*, 21, 1950, 3–17.
27. J. Jacobs, *The Economy of Cities*, New York: Random House, 1969.
28. Cf. J. Mellaart, *Çatal Hüyük: A Neolithic Town in Anatolia*, London: Thames and Hudson, 1967.
29. V. G. Childe, *op. cit.*, 1950; P. Bairoch, *De Jéricho à Mexico: Villes et Economie dans L'Histoire*, Paris, Gallimard, 1985.
30. An unspoken assumption here is that an overgrown village composed entirely of agriculturalists (or hunters and gatherers) does not constitute a city. The subsequent discussion provides a reasoned basis for this assumption.
31. R. A. Walker, *op cit.*, 2016.
32. Cf. B. G. Trigger, "Early cities: craft workers, kings, and controlling the supernatural," pp. 53–66 in J. Marcus and J. A. Sabloff (eds.) *The Ancient City: New Perspectives on Urbanism in the Old and New World*, Santa Fe: School for Advanced Research Press, 2008; A. T. Creekmore, "The social production of space in third-millennium cities of Upper Mesopotamia," pp. 32–73 in A. T. Creekmore and K. D. Fisher (eds.) *Making Ancient Cities: Space and Place in Early Urban Societies*, Cambridge: Cambridge University Press, 2014.
33. S. Fichtl, *La Ville Celtique: Les Oppida de 150 avant J.-C. à 15 après J.-C.*, Paris: Errance, 2005.
34. E. Durkheim, *De la Division du Travail Social*, Paris, Félix Alcan, 1893.
35. See, for example, C. Isendahl and M. E. Smith, "Sustainable agrarian urbanism: the low-density cities of the Mayas and Aztecs," *Cities*, 31, 2013, 132–143.

36. Cf. Adam Smith's celebrated dictum "the division of labor is limited by the extent of the market," A. Smith, *The Wealth of Nations*, Oxford: Oxford University Press, 2008 (originally published in 1776).
37. P. Bairoch, *op. cit., 1985;* P. J. Taylor, "Extraordinary cities: early city-ness and the origins of agriculture and states," *International Journal of Urban and Regional Research*, 36, 2012, 415–447.
38. See the review article by A. J. Scott, "Location and linkage systems: a survey and re-assessment," *Annals of Regional Science*, 17, 1983, 1–39.
39. See, for example, A. J. Scott, *Metropolis: From the Division of Labor to Urban Form*, Berkeley: University of California Press, 1988; M. Storper, *The Regional World: Territorial Development in a Global* Economy. New York: Guilford Press, 1997; J. E. Anderson and E. van Wincoop, "Trade costs," *Journal of Economic Literature*, 42, 2004, 691–751.
40. G. Duranton and D. Puga, "Micro foundations of urban agglomeration economies," pp. 2065–2118 in J. V. Henderson and J. F. Thisse (eds.) *Handbook of Regional and Urban Economics*, Vol. 4, Amsterdam: Elsevier, 2004.
41. A. J. Scott and S. T. Roweis, "The urban land question," pp. 38–73 in K. Cox (ed.) *Urbanization and Conflict in Market Societies*, Chicago: Maaroufa, 1978; A. J. Scott, *The Urban Land Nexus and the State*, London: Pion, 1980; A. J. Scott and M. Storper, "The nature of cities: the scope and limits of urban theory," *International Journal of Urban and Regional Research*, 39, 2015, 1–15.
42. M. E. Smith, "Aztec urbanism: cities and towns," in W. J. Bryant, D. L. Nichols and E Rodriguez-Alegria (eds.) *The Oxford Handbook of the Aztecs*, Oxford: Oxford University Press.
43. M. Hammond, *The City in the Ancient World*, Cambridge: Harvard University Press, 1972.
44. J. Jacobs, *The Death and Life of Great American Cities*, New York: Random House, 1961.
45. J. Ruskin, *The Seven Lamps of Architecture*, New York: John Wiley and Sons, 1889, p. 77. Italics in the original, as they should be.
46. Storper and Scott, *op. cit.,* 2016.
47. H. Lefebvre, *op. cit.,* 1968.
48. If R is the annual rent of a unit of land then the monetary value or price of that same unit is $V = R/r$, where r is the rate of interest. It is rent that determines the price of the land and not the other way around.
49. A. J. Scott, *op. cit.,* 1988.
50. M. Kornberger and C. Borch, "Introduction: urban commons," pp. 1–21 in C. Borch and M. Kornberger (eds.) *Urban Commons: Rethinking the City*, Abingdon: Routledge, 2015.

51. A. Marshall, *Principles of Economics*, London: Macmillan, 1890.
52. M. Hardt an A. Negri, *Commonwealth*, Cambridge, MA: Harvard University Press, 2009.
53. R. M. Hurd, *Principles of City Land Values*, New York: Record and Guide, 1903.
54. A. Cochrane, *Understanding Urban Policy: A Critical Introduction*, Oxford: Blackwell, 2006.
55. Based on the definition given in Storper and Scott, *op. cit.*, 2016.
56. N. Brenner and C. Schmid, "Towards a new epistemology of the urban," *City*, 19, 2015, 151–182.
57. All the more so as there are perfectly adequate and more serviceable terms for what they seem to be pointing to, for example, "planetary capitalism," the "global space-economy," or the "geographical anatomy of global society."
58. N. Brenner and C. Schmid, *op. cit.* 2014, p. 750.

CHAPTER 3

Industrialization and Urbanization in Early Capitalism

Preliminary Observations

Cities have been present in human society for the better part of nine or ten millennia. Over most of this period, cities were for the most part small, and, compared with today's world, few in number.[1] Until relatively recent times, individual cities rarely attained populations of more than a few thousand, though in some instances much larger sizes have been recorded, especially in cases where cities functioned as imperial capitals.[2] The population of Ancient Rome is said to have been over one million, and Hangzhou and Constantinople in the medieval period are estimated to have had close to the same number. However, it is only with the great growth of trade and industry after the seventeenth and eighteenth centuries that urbanization made its way into human society on a massively pervasive and ever-increasing scale.

The origins of this trend coincide with the rise of mercantilism and the increasing integration of major cities in Western Europe and North America into trans-Atlantic networks of trade including the notorious triangular trading system involving the shipment of manufactured goods, slaves, and sugar in a circuit encompassing Europe, West Africa, and the Caribbean and in a corresponding circuit based on the Northeastern United States. Mercantilism stimulated the growth of major seaports and commercial centers in Europe and North America and helped to establish the economic groundwork of the Industrial Revolution. As such, it also foreshadowed the emergence of capitalist society and its colonial extensions, which in turn further promoted urban growth in Europe and North America together with a special kind of urbanization based on entrepôt activities in various dependent territories. Much of this growth was sustained over the nineteenth century by the so-called old international division of labor in which manufactured goods were exported from industrial countries to the colonies, with a return flow of foodstuffs and raw materials feeding both the labor force and the factories of the main capitalist cities.

Mercantilism and capitalism arose at an early stage in Britain, and they not only stimulated exceptionally high levels of city growth but also new and hitherto unprecedented configurations of the urban land nexus. Bairoch and Goertz estimate that in England, the population living in cities of more than 5000 inhabitants increased from 15 percent to as much as 34 percent between 1700 and 1830.[3] By 1851, over 50 percent of the country was urbanized, with the major industrial centers of Birmingham, Bradford, Leeds, Manchester, and Sheffield and the ports of Liverpool and Bristol attaining over 100,000 inhabitants each. London alone reached a population of 2.7 million in the same year. Urbanization in the rest of Western Europe and in North America followed parallel patterns of growth and spread as capitalism and industrial development took deeper and deeper root in these parts of the world.[4] Why and how, we may ask, did capitalist industrialization lead to such rapid urbanization over wide areas in Western Europe and North America? How was this process expressed in the geometry of the urban land nexus? And what specifically was the role of the urban land nexus in accommodating and fostering this overall system of production and social life?

INDUSTRIALIZATION AND URBANIZATION

The Driving Force of Capitalism

The capitalist economy revolves centrally around the activities of private firms in which labor and materials are combined to produce final outputs in quantities and with qualitative attributes that reflect the pressures of market pricing and profitability criteria. Efficiency and competitive advantage are therefore critical to firms, and the quest to achieve these forms of leverage has important effects on the space and time dimensions of production. The urban land nexus—in the context of the external relations of the city—plays a critically important part in helping to underpin this quest through its copious agglomeration economies. Capitalist society is also marked by deep class divisions as represented on the one side by owners, managers, professionals, and other social fractions that benefit disproportionately from the status quo, and on the other side by wage-earning workers subject to economic and social subordination at the workplace and in the society at large. The precise social composition of these classes and the boundary line between them differ from place to place and from time to time, but they have remained as enduring elements of work and life throughout the history of capitalism. What is important above all for the present investigation is that the physical imprint and operational logic of these basic features of capitalism—that is, competitive profit-seeking units of production and the class relationships associated with them—are deeply engraved on the spatial organization of the urban land nexus.

At the same time, the urban land nexus is subject to constant structural and substantive change reflecting the evolutionary dynamic of capitalist society. This dynamic itself is generated out of a logic of accumulation based on the need for firms continually to reinvest their profits in improvements to product and process configurations or to risk the possibility of eventually being forced out of business by more entrepreneurial competitors. Accumulation in its turn is manifest in long-run propensities within capitalism to persistent growth and to constant qualitative change (i.e. development). These propensities sometimes proceed in the context of a more or less stable configuration of the social relations of production, and sometimes they bring about radical transformation of these matters. When accumulation moves forward in a relatively stable manner over some fairly durable lapse of time, we often identify the corresponding system of social and economic relationships as a *regime of accumulation*,[5] or, in an alternative phrase that I use throughout this book, a wave of capitalist development. I also argue that three very definite regimes, each associated with an unmistakably distinctive variety of urbanization, can be recognized, namely as already indicated in Chap. 1, early capitalism, fordist capitalism, and the knowledge- and culture-intensive capitalism of the twenty-first century.

Industrial Organization and Location

The competitive pressures and profitability imperatives of capitalism in any given regime of accumulation exert conspicuously strong effects on the organization and location of production and *a fortiori* on patterns of urbanization. In order to remain competitive, individual firms need to select appropriate configurations of available technologies and to identify productive combinations of inputs and outputs relative to the possibilities and constraints imposed by external markets. As they seek to construct an operational structure out of these variables, firms must also identify an optimal level of production (scale) and an optimal level of scope (a given range of outputs, e.g. iron and steel, or printing, bookbinding and publishing). Scale effects are notably visible in the so-called *horizontal* division of labor, as illustrated at one extreme by horizontally integrated sectors, where production of a given kind of final output is performed by a very small number of large firms and at the other extreme by horizontally disintegrated sectors where production is secured by many small firms. Scope effects, by contrast, are manifest in the *vertical* division of labor. Vertically integrated sectors are characterized by firms whose operational span covers a relatively large number of functionally interrelated products, whereas vertically disintegrated firms are specialized in only a few stages—or even just one stage—in a chain of input-output relationships.[6]

In principle, any and all combinations of scale and scope are possible in any given economic system, but one particular archetype is of special importance in regard to urbanization. This concerns firms that are relatively highly disintegrated in both the horizontal and vertical dimensions so that there is a preponderance (but not necessarily an exclusive set) of many small, specialized, and interrelated units of production. In these circumstances, given sets of individual firms will amalgamate into functional complexes held together by networks of input-output linkages. As we learned in the previous chapter, activities embedded in conjoint networks like this will have a definite tendency to converge in locational terms toward their common center of gravity, and this will be notably so where the linkages are small in scale and subject to fluctuation in their spatial and temporal arrangement so that they incur high costs per unit of flow per unit of distance. This logic of spatial gravitation will be accompanied by the formation of localized increasing-returns effects or agglomeration economies (related to processes of matching, sharing, and learning) thereby intensifying the tendency of firms to cluster together in geographic space. A subvariant of this archetype is represented by the case where many small firms exist, each producing a different kind of output, but where functional interlinkages are absent. In perhaps the majority of cases, there will be little incentive for these firms to locate in close proximity to one another. In some cases, however, the latent presence of localized increasing-returns effects alone will often induce them to cluster. A typical example is offered by groups of specialized traders whose joint presence at a given location attracts more buyers than would be the case if each trader occupied an isolated location. Both the archetype and the subvariant model are potentially capable of generating developmental seeds around which urban agglomerations come into being, but the former is more likely to promote successive rounds of growth because it is based on a logic of industrialization that is itself driven forward by powerful processes of technological development, accumulation, division of labor, and scale economies.

The clustering of producers of goods and services, obviously cannot occur in the absence of a labor force in the immediate vicinity. Accordingly, as any cluster starts to appear on the landscape, its viability will depend on the concomitant provision of workers' housing in surrounding areas, and as the cluster grows, more and more resident workers will be required to fill the expanding employment needs of the cluster. In this way, a primitive or proto-urban form will start to emerge comprising a small agglomeration of workplaces with employees' residences in immediately adjacent areas thereby reducing the distance and time costs of the journey to work as much as possible. The development of this agglomeration is likely to follow a path-dependent evolutionary trend, with firms attracting workers and workers attracting firms, but always with the agglomeration and growth of production activities as the primary motive force. Furthermore, the cost-reducing strategy underlying the formation of residential locations relative to workplaces will further accentuate overall clustering, as will the additional agglomeration economies that come into being in relation to the materialization of intraurban labor markets and the intensification of local socialization processes. For example, the circulation of relevant labor market information about employment possibilities and prospects will be enhanced as clusters develop, just as opportunities for worker training in locally relevant skills will in all likelihood expand.

The mutual agglomeration of firms and workers will also generate an embryonic urban land nexus reflecting the search by different land users for locations that offer selected forms of proximity and that ensure selected forms of avoidance. The term "embryonic" must be emphasized in this context, for at this stage of the analysis, the configuration of the urban land nexus is still far from being established in any viable form. In its final incarnation, the urban land nexus comprises much more than places of production and workers' residences, for its full functional integrity is intimately dependent on numerous emergent effects and contingent phenomena ranging from large-scale infrastructures, through diverse neighborhoods, to institutions of governance and collective order.

Urban Outcomes

The geography of early capitalism is replete with clear-cut cases of industrial and urban development that illustrate the substantive realization of these preliminary analytical principles. The textile towns of England that sprang up at the time of the Industrial Revolution offer notable empirical examples of industrialization and urbanization processes as intermediated through agglomeration and the urban land nexus. In the nineteenth century, cotton and woolen goods were manufactured in Lancashire and Yorkshire, respectively, in vertically disintegrated mills and workshops forming the core axes of employment in mushrooming industrial towns.[7] By way of contrast to this geographic pattern, large, standardized and vertically integrated cotton and woolen manufactories were spatially distributed in a much more dispersed way over the rest of the country.[8] Similarly, Birmingham in the Midlands of England was a hotbed of specialized industrial districts containing masses of small vertically disintegrated workshops involved in metal-working trades like nail-making, edge tools, screws, nuts and bolts, metal chains, springs, guns, locks, and jewelry.[9] The same kind of development is well illustrated in the United States by small-scale, labor-intensive boot and shoe producers bound together in tightly organized networks forming one of the major foci of employment in Boston and surrounding towns in the mid-nineteenth century.[10] Similar kinds of outcomes were observable wherever industrialization and urbanization were occurring in early capitalism. Small to medium-sized factories and workshops constituted the majority of producers in any given cluster. Large factories also participated in these local economic systems while others were often to be found at relatively isolated locations, usually in association with workers' villages or small towns. Familiar examples of the latter relationship are provided by Robert Owen's cotton mill at New Lanark in Scotland, the Schneider Iron Works in Le Creusot, France, and a number of big vertically integrated textile factories in specialized mill towns in New England. In the absence of complementary economic activities generating agglomeration effects, places of this sort typically remained small in size and were susceptible to prolonged crisis when the dominant employer encountered outside competitive threats.

With advancing accumulation, urbanization accelerated greatly over the nineteenth century, as expressed in the rapid growth of individual cities and continual increases in their number. This same trend has persisted, in fact, as a durable feature of capitalism since the Industrial Revolution. Already by 1802, London was the first city in the modern era to attain a million inhabitants, followed by Paris in 1850, New York in 1870, Vienna in 1878, and Berlin in 1880. In 1909, Mark Jefferson pointed to what was then often taken to be the astonishing emergence of "million cities" in different parts of Western Europe and North America.[11] Today, the million city is a commonplace phenomenon not only in Western Europe and North America but in the rest of the world as well. In 2014, according to the United Nations there were 662 cities with over one million inhabitants around the globe, and as many as 104 with over five million,[12] and all the signs point to a continuation of this trend. In short, while capitalism, economic growth, and urbanization constitute relatively distinctive spheres of social reality, they are also marked by deeply interpenetrating and mutually restructuring relationships that lead on perennially to an ever-changing social and economic landscape that now is global in extent.

Industrial Agglomerations in the Nineteenth Century

The Location of Cities

The Industrial Revolution ushered in the factory system and with it an enormous expansion of production capabilities and the growth of manufacturing towns. Processes of agglomeration operated with considerable force at this time as networks of specialized and complementary producers multiplied at various locations thus forming clusters that also drew growing numbers of workers into their spatial orbit. In Western Europe, and in Britain especially, the expansion of population at these locations was fed in large degree by the migration of displaced agricultural workers from the countryside. In North America, the insatiable demand for labor in the burgeoning port cities of the Atlantic coast and the newly emerging industrial towns of the northeastern states attracted droves of immigrants from Europe. Pred has shown that the rise and spread of towns in nineteenth-century America was enhanced by the extension of communications and transport networks, thereby boosting the interurban exchange of products and stimulating further developmental impulses at major industrial agglomerations.[13] In Britain in the nineteenth century, important coal resources were directly available in virtually all of the important manufacturing regions (each of them containing multiple urban centers) so that producers had ready access to a relatively cheap source of power for driving the industrial machinery. In the United States, early industrial and urban growth was associated with natural harbors along the east coast and with more inland locations where the abundant water power provided by streams and rivers descending from the New England uplands and the Appalachians to the Atlantic Ocean could be harnessed. As the frontier of development moved westward into Pennsylvania, Ohio, and beyond, new urban centers sprang up at resource sites (e.g. where coal and iron ore were available) as well as at transport nodes, especially where communications by land and water intersected with one another.[14]

These remarks indicate, among other things, that there was often a strong connection between the presence of specific site advantages and the growth of towns in early industrial capitalism as indeed there frequently is in other social contexts too. However, it is emphatically not the case that advantages of this sort must always exist before successful urban centers can appear. Both in theory and in empirical reality, vibrant urban development is a possibility even at essentially arbitrary locations. No matter how fortuitous an initial locational event may be, a thriving urban center can always come into being if there is subsequently a sequence of expansionary thrusts growing out of the division of labor and the formation of localized increasing-returns effects. When this occurs, even a perfectly random initiating incident is liable to evolve into a self-confirming agglomeration with endogenous growth potentials, irrespective of the presence or absence of local resources. Detroit is a clear example of how an unremarkable small settlement can turn into a flourishing metropolis on the basis of the organizational and locational dynamics underlying agglomeration processes and the formation of the urban land nexus, just as it also exemplifies how, when those same dynamics weaken as a result of changing external circumstances, the metropolis can retreat into stagnation and decline. The car capital of twentieth-century America was assuredly destined to materialize somewhere in the Manufacturing Belt, but its precise location at Detroit was a historical and geographical accident that could easily have occurred at countless other sites in this extended region.

Intraurban Patterns

Industrialization has complex effects on spatial structures within the urban land nexus, depending on the particular regime of accumulation that is under consideration. In nineteenth-century towns in Britain and the United States, industry tended to locate for the most part in the inner city where it also anchored workers' housing in nearby residential districts. Certain detailed variations on this theme are noteworthy, however, particularly in regard to two main categories of sectors, namely, on the one hand, large-scale materials-intensive processing activities such as many kinds of food production or heavy metallurgical industries, and, on the other hand, small-scale labor-intensive industries such as clothing, furniture, jewelry, and printing. The locations of the former sectors typically coincided with sites adjacent to major canal and rail transport routes, and they often followed these routes out toward the edges of the city. The locations of the latter sectors were more usually confined to clusters forming specialized industrial quarters lying close to the core of the city, as in the cases of the diverse metal-working trades of Birmingham and the more fashion-oriented clothing, furniture, footwear, and watchmaking industries of London analyzed by Hall.[15] A similar profusion of small-scale industries was to be found in core areas of nineteenth-century Paris, New York, and other large primate cities of Western Europe and North America.[16] Commercial and financial service firms, too, clustered tightly together in centralized clusters in these cities, where they acted as nerve centers of early capitalism in matters of investment, production, and trade.

These developments within the urban land nexus were accompanied by a number of other trends in the intraurban location of economic activity. In particular, even in the nineteenth century, a degree of decentralization of manufacturing to the urban periphery was already becoming evident. This trend involved not only the outward diffusion of industrial land use along urban canal and rail routes, but also followed on from the insistent capital intensification that was occurring in many sectors and that was encouraging significant increases in plant size, hence stimulating demand for locations where land was relatively cheap.[17] Capital intensification also fostered the routinization of production processes leading in turn to lower average costs via increased scale and standardization of input-output linkages, a factor that further enhanced producers' ability to adopt cheaper suburban locations. This point is dramatically illustrated by the case of the gun industry of Birmingham. Until the middle of the nineteenth century, the local gun industry comprised a large number of small, vertically disintegrated workshops concentrated in a tight cluster close to the center of the city. In 1861, a significant restructuring of a part of this industry occurred when the Birmingham Small Arms Company was established to supply mass-produced military guns to the British government during the Crimean War. As a corollary, the new company moved into a large, standardized, vertically integrated factory located in Small Heath in what was then the far suburban edge of the city. A further illustration of the same point is offered by the Singer Sewing Machine Company, which in 1867 set up operations in Britain in a relatively modest plant located in central Glasgow. With growing demand for the company's products, the plant moved to a more suburban location in Bridgeton; and with yet more expansion of demand, a new large state-of-the-art plant was set up in Kilbowie on the far western edge of Glasgow in 1882. An additional instance of the suburbanization of industry in nineteenth-century capitalism is offered by the case of Paris. The densely developed historic city *intra muros* harbored many specialized industrial districts comprising labor-intensive workshops and factories, but it was not especially receptive to large-scale industrial enterprise. As a result, suburbanization of industries like chemicals and textiles occurred on a major scale and at an unusually early stage in Paris.[18] The northern and eastern periphery of Paris, in particular, industrialized rapidly in the second half of the nineteenth century, partly as a result of spontaneous suburbanization and partly as a result of Haussmann's land clearances in central Paris. These events helped to initiate the early emergence in Paris of predominantly working-class suburban areas.

Urban Social Conditions and the Imperative of Planning

The growth of cities in early capitalism was accompanied by a great expansion of the proletarian population serving as cannon fodder for the burgeoning factory system as well as by striking changes in occupational structure and social class composition.[19] For the mass of working-class individuals, living standards were close to the subsistence level, though as the century wore on, wages slowly rose in response to worker demands and governmental legislation that increasingly extended the rights of labor.

The widespread poverty and the unremitting blight and pollution in industrial cities over much of the nineteenth century were manifest in extensive tracts of crowded, insalubrious housing, especially in core areas of the city where the working classes lived for the most part. In Britain and the United States, members of the business and professional classes tended to favor more spacious housing toward the city limits, though residential enclaves of business and professional people were also to be found in selected central areas, notably in the larger towns. In the working-class residential districts of the inner city, cheap housing, constructed by speculative builders, was typically arranged in narrow, serried rows. Physical conditions in these districts were often decrepit and almost always involved much crowding, and at their most degraded level, they faded into the slums and stews of the city, where, in Britain, much of the Irish immigrant population was concentrated.[20] In a celebrated passage from the *Condition of the Working Class in England*, Friedrich Engels paints a lugubrious picture of proletarian housing in Manchester in the 1840s:

> Right and left a multitude of covered passages lead from the main street into numerous courts, and he who turns in thither gets into a filth and disgusting grime, the equal of which is not to be found—especially in the courts which lead down to the Irk, and which contain unqualifiedly the most horrible dwellings which I have yet beheld. In one of these courts there stands directly at the entrance, at the end of the covered passage, a privy without a door, so dirty that the inhabitants can pass into and out of the court only by passing through foul pools of stagnant urine and excrement. This is the first court on the Irk above Ducie Bridge—in case anyone should care to look into it. Below it on the river there are several tanneries, which fill the whole neighborhood with the stench of animal putrefaction. Below Ducie Bridge the only entrance to most of the houses is by means of narrow, dirty stairs and over heaps of refuse and filth.[21]

Engels goes on to describe the spatial layout of Manchester, with its working-class quarters arranged in a ring about a mile and a half wide around the central commercial district, while beyond lay the regularly laid out neighborhoods of the middle and upper bourgeoisie succeeded by an outer zone of comfortable villas set in gardens. Analogous descriptions of deteriorated working-class areas and class segregation in cities in industrializing regions in Western Europe and North America proliferate in the writings of commentators on nineteenth-century urban conditions.[22] Small wonder that in his novel *Our Mutual Friend*, written in 1864–65,

Dickens sees fit to coin a metaphor for the city and its exploitative social relations in terms of "dust heaps" or garbage dumps (containing among other things fecal waste) combed by hordes of impoverished wretches for whatever they could dig up.

The two passages on Glasgow and Manchester quoted above point not only to the physical decay and deteriorated living conditions of a mostly brutalized and illiterate proletariat but also to the collapse of "respectability and morality" with all that this implies for the corrosion of urban order.[23] The calamitous conditions of the urban land nexus in nineteenth-century industrial cities threatened the physical, social, and psychological well-being of urban dwellers, and for the same reason had deeply negative consequences for the efficacy and discipline of the labor force in the workplace, and hence for accumulation at large. Marx had proposed in the *Economic Manuscripts of 1861–63* that workers' discipline was in part secured by what he called "formal subsumption," meaning the subjection of the labor force to the routines and pressures of work through regimentation and the exercise of managerial authority on the factory floor.[24] The blunt rituals of formal subsumption no doubt had much effect, but as capitalist economic development moved ahead, increasing demands for more amenable and self-motivated workers came steadily into collision with the circumstance that social conditions in the manufacturing cities were hostile to the emergence of more thoroughgoing forms of adaptation of the human animal into industrial-urban society.

Benevolo has shown that among early efforts to make progress in this regard were a number of town planning initiatives focused above all on public health legislation and physical environmental programs such as periodic street sweeping and the provision of clean drinking water.[25] These initiatives were especially important given the prevalence of cholera epidemics in the industrial towns of the period. As the century progressed, other critical interventions directed to the improvement of urban conditions and the social reproduction of the working class were put into effect. In 1843, Edwin Chadwick's *Report on the Sanitary Condition of the Labouring Population* drew widespread attention to the severe failures of British towns and was followed in subsequent years by a series of parliamentary acts providing for slum clearances, the repair of substandard housing, and the improvement of urban public health.[26] Critical issues of intraurban transport were also addressed. Thus, after 1860, the British government established a series of statutory measures facilitating the day-to-day functioning of local labor markets by making it possible for workers to avail themselves of early-morning and late-afternoon train transport. These measures allowed for the transport of workers from more outlying communities into the center of the city,[27] but, by the same token, fostered increasing separation between home and work.[28] In London, for example, the combination of rising land prices at the center of the city and cheap suburban transport facilities was already inducing workers to move out to places on the periphery like Edmonton, Finchley, and Walthamstow. These initiatives were complemented by a continually expanding body of social legislation in regard to health, education, and the conditions of factory work. In Paris, the urban crisis loomed especially large, partly by reason of the rebellious character of the popular classes crammed into dense housing in a maze of narrow streets, and partly because of the pressing need for modernization of the city's infrastructure. As already noted, Baron Haussmann dealt with these issues in an extended program of urban transformation in the two decades after 1851 by clearing away extensive slums, reorganizing the city's transport grid, and installing new sewage and water-supply systems.[29] Much of the growing proletarian population of the northern and eastern suburbs of Paris comprised workers who were displaced from more central locations by Haussmann's renovation projects. Other European cities like Barcelona and Brussels also reorganized their internal spatial structures by implementing versions of Haussmannization.

In many sundry ways, then, piecemeal but cumulatively powerful collective responses to the endemic problems of the urban land nexus in the nineteenth century were worked out and implemented in the interests of efficiency, social order, and continued economic growth. As such, they undoubtedly played a part in securing the real as opposed to the merely formal subsumption of the worker into capitalist reality, and eased the willing integration of the labor force into the coils of life and work in capitalism.[30]

Prophets of Doom and Redemption

From the very beginnings of capitalism, a growing chorus of voices was raised in protest against the irrationalities and human costs of industrial-urban society. In the nineteenth century, in particular, political radicals, philanthropists, social reformers, utopian thinkers, and gadflies produced a stream of critical diagnoses and suggested resolutions of urban social problems, not least of which was the program of revolutionary change advocated by Marx and Engels.

Among these critics was a group of individuals designated pejoratively by Marx and Engels in the *Communist Manifesto* of 1848 as "utopian socialists" on the grounds that they conceived of programmatic pathways to socialism via reformist gestures rather than by sweeping away the debris of capitalism altogether. These were individuals like Henri de Saint-Simon, Charles Fourier, Étienne Cabet, and Robert Owen who were much concerned with the improvement of society by means of egalitarian and communitarian principles that they thought would put humanity on a new and higher plane of existence. Some of them also carried out practical experiments by setting up small-scale model urban settlements, but they failed in almost all cases to produce anything that lasted for more than a brief interlude. Owen, for example, founded a utopian community in New Harmony, Indiana, in 1825, but this came to an end only two years after its establishment.

Another line of attack came from more aesthetically minded critics, most prominently Ruskin, who fulminated against the "rattling, growling, smoking, stinking" cities of the time and their morbid effects on the human spirit.[31] Ruskin's comment is all of a piece with his distaste for capitalism generally and the utilitarian doctrines that were advanced to justify it, though the romantic tenor of his approach with its allusions to a lost world of honest craftsmen laboring in a mist of traditional artisanal ideals rather blunted its practical force. An equally severe critic of the ugliness and injustices of capitalism and urban life was Ruskin's disciple, William Morris, the leader of the Arts and Crafts Movement, and, late in life, a committed socialist.[32] Morris' utopian novel, *News from Nowhere*, published in 1890, describes an idyllic future world in which work has finally recovered its non-alienated character as a craft activity and in which, crucially, there are no big cities. The novel (along with Bellamy's *Looking Backward*) is said to have influenced Ebenezer Howard's conception of the garden city as an answer to the evils of the large manufacturing towns.[33] Howard sought to implement this conception through the Garden City Movement with its practical agenda focused on the establishment of small, low-density urban centers with intermixed housing and green space and with sufficient employment for all residents. In the first two decades of the twentieth century, two such centers, Letchworth and Welwyn Garden City, were built under the auspices of the Garden City Movement.

Many of the views alluded to above formed part of the torrent of ideas criticizing large-scale urbanization formulated over the nineteenth and early twentieth centuries by what Marchand calls the "enemies of the city."[34] More importantly for our purposes is the case of a long line of paternalistic and philanthropic capitalists who experimented with building model factory villages and towns located in relative isolation from the anarchical social conditions in the large industrial centers and yet who were also concerned with the decidedly non-utopian goal of maintaining profitable business operations. Among the earliest practical experiments of this kind was the one undertaken by Robert Owen who assumed the management of a large cotton mill at New Lanark in Scotland in 1799 (well before he became the messianic prophet of New Harmony). Owen undertook not only to transform the operations of the mill itself but also to oversee the daily lives of the 2500 workers who inhabited the adjacent village. He accordingly established diverse welfare programs for his workers, including the founding of an Institute for the Formation of Character. He also inaugurated a nursery and a day school for the children of New Lanark and set up a village shop where workers could buy food at reduced prices. Owen showed in practice that higher productivity and profits in enterprise could actually be obtained by improving workers' living conditions and education, at least in the special circumstances of New Lanark.

Partly as a result of the widespread influence of Owen, analogous experiments were undertaken in different parts of Europe and North America in the nineteenth century. Perhaps none of these was as successful as Sir Titus Salt's project at Saltaire near Bradford, where he established a large woolen mill and a dependent workers' settlement. Saltaire was remarkable in its day for its well-constructed workers' houses set in wide streets and its many facilities for education, leisure pursuits, and religious uplift. These facilities included a large public park, a Mechanics' Institute and library, and a central Congregational Church, all of them provided by Salt himself. In addition, strict rules were applied with respect to standards of behavior, and these included a stringent prohibition on drinking.[35] Salt died in 1876, but the mill itself closed down only in 1986. Among the many workers' settlements that were established along similarly paternalistic lines in the late nineteenth and early twentieth centuries were Ackroyden, Bournville, and Port Sunlight in Britain, and Pullman and Hershey in the United States, to mention only some of the most prominent cases.

These diverse initiatives undoubtedly owe much to the laudable philanthropic motives of their instigators, but they can also be partially understood in terms of a wider social meaning and logic. Above all, they need to be set in the context of the pervasive nineteenth-century problems with respect to labor control and the socialization of the working class within the framework of the urban land nexus. They point, in particular, to the limits of management-labor interactions based on crude formal subsumption, and to the search by individual capitalists for possible solutions involving the reconstruction of labor relations on a more humane but also on a much more efficient basis. However, any attempt to achieve this goal in factories embedded within competitive labor markets in large industrial towns would almost certainly have encountered serious difficulties. For one thing, investments by individual factory owners in their own workers would in all likelihood have been partly dissipated by the counterinfluences of life in the disordered social spaces of the city. For another, effective action was also impeded by the logic of the free-rider problem in that any investments employers might make in upgrading their own workers were always liable to be tapped as positive externalities by other employers through labor market adjustments. Faced as they were with these problems, it is no surprise that many employers sought a logical (but ultimately non-generalizable) solution involving both physical exit from the city and the reorganization of the labor force into relatively sequestered communities, dependent on a single monopsonistic employer. As such, these experiments shared certain common features with the spirit of Bentham's Panopticon. Even in the twenty-first century, echoes of these efforts can still be observed, as, for example, at the three-square-kilometer industrial park of Longhua operated by Foxconn near Shenzen in China where the needs of 250,000 workers (many of them migrants from the countryside) are provided for by dormitories, canteens, and diverse social programs, though in something less than the all-intrusive bundle of housing and welfare arrangements instituted by Sir Titus Salt.

All that being said, and in spite of the success of some of these individual experiments in cultivating a captive and compliant labor force, they could never become models for a wholesale spatial reorganization of capitalism. A brief reconsideration of the logic and dynamics of the urbanization tells us why. As we have seen, the forces of agglomeration are of great potency. Indeed, despite the existence of certain kinds of negative externalities in the urban land nexus, a highly significant proportion of all capitalist producers persistently gravitate to spatial clusters where they can achieve superior efficiency levels, greater innovativeness, and more robust competitive advantages than they could at more dispersed locations. Moreover, the shared labor markets of large industrial towns offer definite advantages that a monopsonistic employer is denied. In a shared labor market, firms can all the more easily recruit new employees with skills that closely match job descriptions; and in times of economic downturn, they can lay off significant fractions of the labor force while facing a relatively low risk of not being able to rehire replacements when their economic fortunes revive. These different considerations mean that capitalist firms, especially in the nineteenth century, were tied in significant ways to industrial clusters and shared pools of labor in urban centers. To be sure, some types of firms can readily escape from this constraint, but these are above all large, standardized producers facing relatively steady markets so that they can maintain a stable labor force while their need for proximity to complementary producers and markets is correspondingly reduced.

As a consequence, capital continued to concentrate in urban areas so that correction of the very tangible social defects of the city as a reservoir of labor in the nineteenth century could only be achieved, if at all, on the basis of social reforms under the aegis of some institution of collective order. In another vocabulary, any shift from formal subsumption toward a broader system of real subsumption was at least in some major degree necessarily in the hands of governmental agencies (thus extending the range of the urban commons). As capitalism continued to develop, moreover, it called for an increasingly educated and effectively socialized work force, so that reform of this sort became steadily more urgent. After the mid-nineteenth century, extensive legislation in virtually all of the capitalist countries brought about social changes that pointed at least partly in this direction, and palliative collective action in the city played a vital role in this regard. Planning measures and public investments were undertaken with increasing intensity in cities in the second half of the nineteenth century in a broad political agenda devoted to bringing social reproduction processes in the urban land nexus into more effective alignment with the requirements of an increasingly demanding production system.

A Synoptic View

The economies of early capitalism expanded at a rapid pace on the basis on insistent industrialization, the expansion of trade, and the incorporation of colonial territories into their spheres of control. Urbanization had a critically important but exceptionally problematical role to play in this expansionary thrust.

As the economic and property relationships of capitalism took hold in the eighteenth and nineteenth centuries, industry and social life came into an uneasy symbiosis in the burgeoning cities of Europe and North America. The expression of this symbiosis in the urban land nexus created tensions that at times seemed to threaten the very existence of capitalism as a going concern. The social and economic viability of the city was constantly imperiled by a dearth of adequate urban infrastructure and services; effective social reproduction of the working class was curtailed by inferior housing conditions and the general degradation of residential areas; and the life and health of the labor force were endangered by a host of negative externalities brought on by industrialization combined with high rates of poverty and population density. These disruptive conditions not only had major urban repercussions, but also had negative impacts on the productivity and competitiveness of capitalist enterprise as whole.

In spite of many difficulties, including the often-bitter political struggles between the bourgeoisie and the working class in regard to the directions of reform, various collective efforts to deal with the manifold problems of the city were implemented over the nineteenth century in a spasmodic but cumulatively ameliorative progression. These efforts differed in their detailed practical expression from country to country, but all of them led in the direction of a rationalized urban land nexus in terms of transport, waste removal, public health, housing, the harmonization of land uses, the provision of open space, and related matters. Concomitantly, durable urban planning institutions were gradually pieced together as operating units within state apparatuses throughout Europe and North America, where they served as the main social frameworks for dealing with the wayward consequences of spontaneous urbanization in capitalism. In this manner, the first major wave of capitalist development and urbanization made its erratic evolutionary pathway forward over the nineteenth century, to be followed by a second wave marked by yet more assertive patterns of urbanization together with new but equally perplexing social and economic dilemmas.

Notes

1. G. Sjoberg, *The Preindustrial City, Past and Present*, Glencoe, IL: The Free Press, 1960.
2. J. Robinson, A. J. Scott, and P. J. Taylor, *Working, Housing: Urbanizing*, Berlin: Springer, 2016.

3. P. Bairoch and G. Goertz, "Factors of urbanisation in the nineteenth century developed countries: a descriptive and econometric analysis," *Urban Studies*, 23, 1986, 285–305. See also: C. M. Law, "The growth of urban population in England and Wales, 1801–1911," *Transactions of the Institute of British Geographers*, 41, 1967, 125–143.
4. For more statistical information on population growth in the nineteenth-century cities see: A. Weber, *The Growth of Cities in the Nineteenth Century*, New York: Macmillan, 1899.
5. See R. Boyer, *La Théorie de la Régulation: Une Analyse Critique*, Paris: La Découverte, 1986.
6. A. J. Scott, *Metropolis: From the Division of Labor to Urban Form*, Berkeley, CA: University of California Press, 1988; M. Storper, *The Regional World: Territorial Development in a Global Economy*, New York: Guilford, 1997.
7. S. J. Chapman and T. S. Ashton, "The sizes of businesses, mainly in the textile industries," *Journal of the Royal Statistical Society*, 77, 1914, 469–555.
8. This more dispersed geographic distribution can be attributed to the relative standardization and self-sufficiency of large vertically integrated textile mills. For one thing, they faced relatively low transport cost schedules; for another thing, they were not dependent on supporting (and unstable) networks of specialized upstream suppliers and downstream customers within an overall detailed division of labor.
9. G. C. Allen, *The Industrial Development of Birmingham and the Black Country, 1860–1927*, London: George Allen and Unwin, 1929. See also M. J. Wise, "On the evolution of the jewellery and gun quarters in Birmingham," *Transactions and Papers of the Institute of British Geographers*, 15, 1951, 57–72.
10. E. M. Hoover, *Location Theory and the Shoes and Leather Industries*, Cambridge: Harvard University Press, 1937.
11. M. Jefferson, "The anthropography of some great cities: a study in distribution of population," *Bulletin of the American Geographical Society*, 41, 1909, 537–566.
12. United Nations, *World Economic Prospects*, New York, 2014.
13. A. Pred, *Urban Growth and City-Systems in the United States, 1840–1860*, Cambridge, MA: Harvard University Press, 1980.
14. S. Kim, "Division of labor and the rise of cities: evidence from US industrialization, 1850–1880," *Journal of Economic Geography*, 6, 2006, 469–491.
15. P. G. Hall, *The Industries of London Since 1861*, London: Hutchinson, 1962.
16. J. Gaillard, *Paris, la Ville, 1852–1870*, Paris: Honoré Champion, 1977; R. M. Haig, *Major Economic Factors in Metropolitan Growth and Arrangement*, New York: Regional Plan of New York and its Environs, 1927.

17. A. J. Scott, "Locational patterns and dynamics of industrial activity in the modern metropolis: a review essay," *Urban Studies*, 19, 1982, 111–142.
18. J. Bastié, *La Croissance de la Banlieue Parisienne*, Paris: Presses Universitaires de France, 1964.
19. J. A. Banks, "The social structure of nineteenth century England as seen through the census," pp. 179–223 in R. Lawton (ed.) *The Census and Social Structure: An Interpretative Guide to Nineteenth Century Censuses for England and Wales*, London: Frank Cass, 1978.
20. A. Briggs, *Victorian Cities*, London: Odhams Press, 1963.
21. F. Engels, *Condition of the Working Class in England*, London: Panther Books, 1969, pp. 82–83.
22. For the case of France see M. Villermé, *Tableau de l'Etat Physique et Moral des Ouvriers Employés dans les Manufactures de Coton, de Laine et de Soie*, Paris: J. Renouard, 1840.
23. S. Pollard, *The Genesis of Modern Management*, London: Edward Arnold, 1965.
24. K. Marx, *Collected Works of Karl Marx and Friedrich Engels*, Vol. 33, New York: International Publishers, 1992.
25. L. Benevolo, *The Origins of Modern Town Planning*, Cambridge, MA: MIT Press, 1967.
26. E. Chadwick, *Report on the Sanitary Condition of the Labouring Population of Great Britain*, London: Her Majesty's Stationery Office, 1843.
27. S. T. Abernethy, "Opening up the suburbs: workmen's trains in London 1860-1914," *Urban History*, 42, 2015, 70–88; H. J. Dyos, "Workmen's fares in south London, 1860–1914," pp. 87–100 in D. Cannadine and D. Reeder, eds., *Exploring the Urban Past: Essays in Urban History*, Cambridge: Cambridge University Press, 1982.
28. H. Carter and C. R. Lewis, *An Urban Geography of England and Wales in the Nineteenth Century*, London: Edward Arnoll, 1990.
29. J. Gaillard, *Paris, la Ville, 1852–1870*, Paris: Honoré Champion, 1977.
30. Cf. M. Hardt and A. Negri, *Commonwealth*. Cambridge, MA: Belknap Press, 2009.
31. J. Ruskin, *The Crown of Wild Olive*, Orpington: George Allen, 1882.
32. E. P. Thompson, *William Morris: Romantic to Revolutionary*, New York: Pantheon Books, 1977.
33. F. S. Boos, "News from Nowhere and Garden Cities: Morris's Utopia and Nineteenth-Century Town Design," *Journal of Pre-Raphaelite Studies*, 7, 1998, 5–27.
34. B. Marchand, *Les Ennemis de Paris: la Haine de la Grande Ville des Lumières à nos Jours*, Rennes: Presses Universitaires de Rennes, 2009; see also M. White and L. White, *Intellectual Versus the City, from Thomas Jefferson to Frank Lloyd Wright*, Cambridge, MA: Harvard University Press, 1962.

35. N. Jackson, J. Lintonbon, and B. Staples, *Saltaire: The Making of a Model Town*, Reading: Spire Books, 2010; C. Stewart, *A Prospect of Cities*, New York: Longmans, Green, 1952; J. Minnery, "Model industrial settlements and their continuing governance," *Planning Perspectives*, 27, 2012, 309–321.

CHAPTER 4

Triumph and Tribulations of the Mass-Production Metropolis

EMERGENCE OF MASS PRODUCTION AND THE TWENTIETH-CENTURY METROPOLIS

The Mass-Production System

The assembly line has always been a feature of manufacturing activity in capitalism. Even in Adam Smith's eighteenth-century pin factory, work was organized in an internal (intrafirm or *technical*) division of labor along a line that extended through some 17 or 18 different stages ranging from cutting pieces of wire to affixing finished pins on strips of paper.[1] As technologies of production progressed in the main capitalist countries toward the end of the nineteenth century, it became possible in some sectors to operate sequential procedures like this on an enlarged scale, and eventually to automate the assembly line so that management could directly control the pace of work. Automation also encouraged a degree of vertical integration in production, though far from a wholesale abolition of the external (interfirm or *social*) division of labor. Production processes marked by these features usually entailed significant investments of capital so that manufacturing plants tended to be large in order to take advantage of internal economies of scale. Moreover, as the technical division of labor was pushed forward, work tasks were increasingly fragmented, thus promoting the deskilling of the individual worker and reducing much of the labor force to a pool of anonymous mutually substitutable units of employment. Not all sectors were prone to this kind of transformation but those that were became the core of the mass-production system that dominated the economies of North America and Western Europe over much of the twentieth century.

This system was focused above all on the production of standardized outputs in large batches in assembly industries such as cars, domestic appliances, and machinery. It also included a number of process or continuous flow-through industries such as petroleum refining, chemicals, and steel. The classic illustration of the large vertically integrated, capital-intensive, mass-production assembly plant in the early twentieth century was Henry Ford's River Rouge plant in Detroit. At its peak in the 1930s, this particular venture employed as many as 100,000 workers, though it was an extreme case and its size was rarely if ever matched in other mass-production plants. Management of these plants was in the hands of a cadre of white-collar managers together with a team of engineers and technical workers who were responsible for research and development and for implementing periodic reorganizations of the shop floor. Manual work on the assembly line was carried out by an army of unskilled and semiskilled blue-collar workers who also performed whatever other tasks needed to be undertaken in order to feed and service these operations. In a critical essay in his *Prison Notebooks* written in the early 1930s, Gramsci used the term "fordism" to refer to mass production,[2] in recognition of the key role of Henry Ford in promoting the system, though it was only later in the 1970s that the term together with its critical undertones came widely into use.

The principal manufacturing plants, or lead plants, that dominated the mass-production system invariably lay at the center of extended industrial complexes linking producers together in input-output relationships. These complexes were organized in multiple tiers extending downward and outward from the lead plants and forming a hierarchy in which plant size generally, but by no means always, diminished with functional distance from the lead plant. While lead plants were unequivocally organized along mass-production lines, producers further down the hierarchy were often less routinized and some were oriented to craft and small batch production, like many of the firms that supplied basic operating equipment and components for the assembly line. These hierarchical systems of input-output transactions were labeled as *growth poles* by François Perroux, a term that clearly captures their qualities as composite production systems whose growth (or decline) depended centrally on the fortunes of the central lead plants.[3] Large multiplant corporations provided an institutional framework of ownership and investment that extended across and between different growth poles. These features were conspicuously evident in industries like machinery, construction, chemicals, shipbuilding, and above all, car manufacturing, which, over much of the twentieth century, functioned as the foremost growth pole in a number of different capitalist economies, and most notably of all in the economy of the United States.

It was in the United States that the mass-production system as a whole was brought to its highest pitch of development and where it formed the basis of an enormous surge in prosperity and power over the first three quarters of the twentieth century. The system was subject to periodic downturns that gave rise to high levels of unemployment and social distress, but while its crisis tendencies were never fully tamed, they were considerably moderated after the Second World War as ameliorative government policies were steadily put into effect. The essentials of these policies were derived from two main theoretical sources, one of which was Keynes' *General Theory* (1936) with its advocacy of deficit spending as a counter to recession, the other being the Beveridge Report (1942) which argued for the implementation of far-reaching welfare measures as a means of alleviating the vicissitudes of working-class life.[4] Policy initiatives based on these two approaches underpinned the Long Post-War Boom stretching from the late 1940s to the early 1970s in the capitalist economies of North America and Western Europe.

Mass Production and Urbanization

The implications of these developments for urbanization and the structure of the urban land nexus were enormous. The nineteenth-century factory and workshop economy had already stimulated significant industrial-urban growth, and by the turn of the century two great macro regions each comprising scores of burgeoning manufacturing cities were evidently beginning to take shape. The advent of mass production helped to consolidate these trends by promoting urban growth through its huge demands for labor and its stimulating effects on interurban trade networks. The larger of these two macro regions stretched across much of the northeast of the United States and the eastern provinces of Canada. The Swedish Geographer Sten de Geer identified this region in 1927 as the "North American Manufacturing Belt," reaching from St. Louis in the west through a series of major cities like Chicago, Detroit, and Pittsburgh, to Boston, New York, and Baltimore in the east.[5] De Geer also included in his definition a small group of Canadian cities such as Hamilton and Toronto, with Montreal as a sort of outlier, though he probably should have extended the Canadian segment even further eastward as far as Halifax. An equivalent, but more fragmented Manufacturing Belt could be observed in Western Europe stretching from Glasgow and Birmingham in Britain, through northeastern France, Belgium, southern Holland and the Ruhr region, to Chemnitz and Zwickau in southeastern Germany, with a further eastward extension into Upper Silesia and a small outlier in northwestern Italy.

The cities that developed in the Manufacturing Belts of both North America and Western Europe were the foci of the national-champion industries that functioned over much of the twentieth century as engines of economic growth and development. The structure of these industries had important implications for urban development, because the interlinkages between individual producers in growth-pole systems provided important incentives for at least some of them to agglomerate together in geographic space, and once agglomeration was under way, the tendency was reinforced by emerging external economies of scale and scope. Any agglomeration resulting from these circumstances can be identified as a *growth center*, that is, a cluster of interrelated industries, usually consisting of at least one lead plant together with cohorts of direct and indirect input suppliers but not necessarily comprising a complete growth pole.[6] Growth poles and growth centers thus overlap with one another but are not precisely the same thing. Still, their growth-enhancing potentials—represented on the one side by input-output interdependencies and on the other side by forces of agglomeration—gave rise to massive rounds of large-scale metropolitan development over much of the twentieth century. Nowhere was this more apparent than in Detroit, the car capital of the world, which grew from a population of 285,704 in 1900 to a peak population of 1,849,568 in 1950.

The mass-production system and the large multiplant corporations associated with it also generated huge flows of capital, thereby creating a great demand for commercial and financial service functions to ensure efficient circuits of monetary circulation. Some of these functions were located in the main manufacturing cities, but a definite and intensifying geographic split between commercial and financial services on the one hand, and manufacturing on the other hand, was becoming increasingly apparent. What Jefferson had called "primate cities" like New York, London, Paris, and Berlin had already come to the fore in the nineteenth century[7] and even earlier as specialized business centers, and they now flourished to yet greater extent as their concentrated clusters of banks, stock brokers, financial institutions, and insurance operations grew and diversified in order to meet the needs of the mass-production economy and its offshoots. In spite of this proclivity, the same primate cities also typically functioned as important centers of manufacturing activity as represented by both small-scale craft and fashion industries located in and around core areas and more large-scale capital-intensive industry in intermediate and outer urban zones.

These diverse features of the mass-production system had major impacts on the growth and spread of cities and far-reaching restructuring effects on the urban land nexus. Cities in the United States, in particular, displayed a number of very distinctive trends as the mass-production system evolved from the inter-War years to the post-War years. The urban periphery became steadily more industrialized, intraurban transport facilities were enhanced and extended thus helping to push the suburban edge of cities outward, central business district areas grew in size both laterally and upward as business and financial service employment increased, and working-class residential districts expanded while continuing to fragment along changing racial, ethnic, and national lines. Perhaps the most striking element of this process of readjustment of the urban land nexus was the close relationship between the division of labor in production and the socio-spatial division of residential neighborhoods. On the one hand, while a certain fraction of the upper middle class continued to live in high-rent enclaves close to downtown areas (especially in the old historical cores of European cities), the managerial, professional, and technical cadres forming the new white-collar fraction of the labor force increasingly settled in suburban areas, where a conservative and normative ideology of life focused on home ownership and the nuclear family was being worked out. On the other hand, blue-collar workers, many of them relatively well-paid assembly-line operatives, formed communities that were still mainly concentrated in inner-city areas marked by a distinctive working-class culture, including a degree of political consciousness and class solidarity. Internal divisions within the working class were clearly evident, however, in the formation of specialized immigrant neighborhoods like "Deutschland," "Little Italy," and "Little Poland," in places like Chicago and Detroit and in the emergence of ghettos comprising

African-American migrants from the South who started moving *en masse* into the cities of the Manufacturing Belt in the 1920s and 1930s in order to work on the assembly line. At the same time, the blue-collar suburbs that had already appeared in the nineteenth century were also expanding, as in the case of the small township of Dearborn on what were then the fringes of Detroit and where many large and land-intensive manufacturing plants were located.

Early Theories of Metropolis

The landmark feature of urbanization in the era of mass production was the historical and geographical appearance of the large industrial metropolis. In 1925, Park, Burgess and McKenzie referred to this phenomenon as "the outstanding fact of modern society."[8] Like many other rapidly evolving and disruptive social events, this one, too, engendered theoretical enquiries directed to the search for an understanding of its causes and for insights about what, if anything, might be done to blunt its sharper edges. Accordingly, the first three or four decades of the twentieth century saw the rise of a number of new concepts of metropolitan life and space. Most of these have today faded in the background, but a consideration of their main import is critical for any attempt to understand the main features of urbanization and the urban land nexus in the early and middle decades of the twentieth century.

One of the most influential of the many commentators on the modern metropolis was Georg Simmel, who, in 1903, published an article in German with the resounding title *The Metropolis and Mental Life* in which he proposed that "the individual has become a mere cog in an enormous organization of things."[9] According to Simmel, the rapidly shifting sequences of impressions that constantly bear down on the inhabitants of large cities lead on to the rampant "intensification of nervous stimulation." He then proceeds to enlarge on what he took to be the basic etiology of this alleged condition, claiming that the metropolis, as the seat of money, exchange, and commerce, induces mental attitudes dominated by rationality, calculation, indifference, individualism, and egotism. This diagnosis was shared by many early twentieth-century commentators on the effects of urban life on human consciousness, and it resonated in much of the novelistic literature at that time, as exemplified in the books of Upton Sinclair, Theodore Dreiser, and Sinclair Lewis. A strong echo can be also found in the writings of the Chicago School of Urban Sociology, notably in regard to the portrayal of the inner city as a place of concentrated "social disorganization,"[10] and in Louis Wirth's acerbic view of the effects of density, heterogeneity, and size on urban society.

The research of the Chicago School has already been partially discussed and criticized in Chap. 2, but it is useful here to probe in more detail into some of its purely empirical findings on the city. The pioneering work that Burgess carried out on the spatial organization of the large American metropolis as it took shape in the twentieth century is especially relevant in this context. Burgess' celebrated schematic depiction of the spatial structure of the city, based on the actual case of Chicago, is reproduced in Fig. 4.1. The main feature of this depiction is the representation of intraurban social space as a series of concentric zones characterized by rising socio-economic status as we move from the center of the city to the periphery. Overlying this arrangement is a more detailed pattern of districts and neighborhoods mainly located around the "Loop" (or central business district) and identified either in terms of minority populations, like "Little Sicily" or the "Black Belt," or in terms of deviant social categories like "Vice" and the "Underworld." The Chicago School paid little or no attention to the economic base of the city, apart from an acknowledgment of the existence of a Factory Zone (located within the zone in transition adjacent to the Loop), and they shied away from any attempt to trace out the effects of this base on other aspects of urban reality. Instead, as we have already seen, the structure of the city, from the beleaguered slums at the center to the more upscale suburbs at the periphery, was considered by the Chicago School to be the outcome of an urban "metabolism" based on intergroup relationships of domination and subordination.[11]

In spite of this dubious point of departure, the Chicago school was broadly correct in its view of the internal structure of the large industrial metropolis in the 1920s as a series of concentric zones and specialized socio-spatial nuclei. This view, however, was still far from capturing the full spatial complexity of the city in the inter-War years. In 1939, Homer Hoyt sought to amend the basic Chicago School model by suggesting that the zonal structure of the city was in significant degree being overridden by a sectoral pattern of land uses radiating out from the center (Fig. 4.2). In Hoyt's formulation, which is consistent with remarks made earlier in Chap. 3 about the evolving shape of the urban land nexus, these sectors comprise not only blue-collar and white-collar residential districts but also industrial land use. A further schematization of intraurban space was proposed in 1945 by Harris and Ullman, who claimed that the entirety of

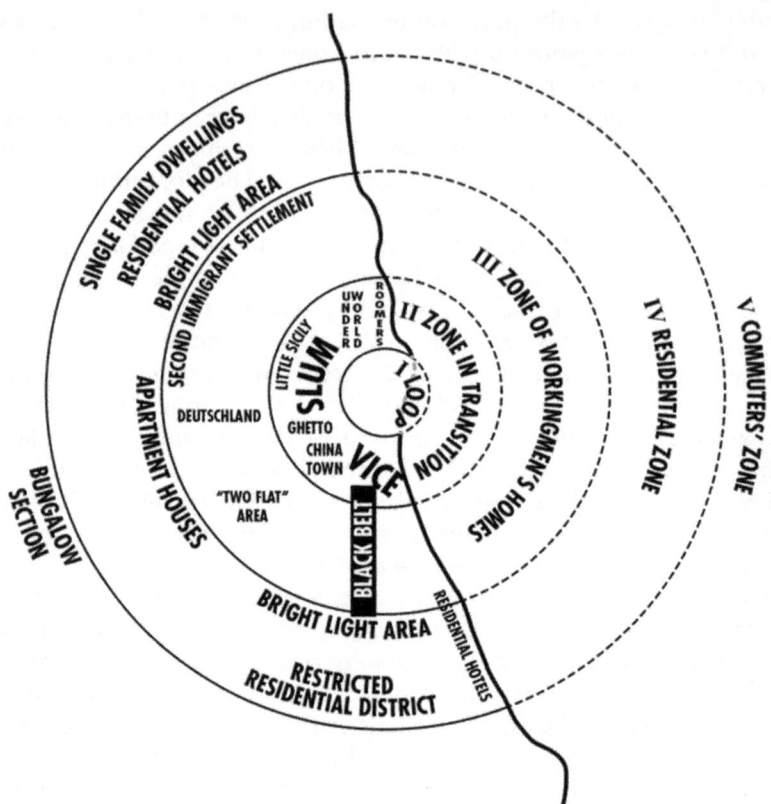

Fig. 4.1 The city as conceived by E. W. Burgess. The figure represents a highly schematized map of the social geography of Chicago. The irregular line drawn approximately from north to south denotes the shoreline of Lake Michigan. Redrawn from the original in E. W. Burgess, "The growth of the city," pp. 47–62 in R. E. Park, E. W. Burgess and R. D. McKenzie, *The City*, Chicago: University of Chicago Press, 1925

land use in the city was arranged in discrete multiple nuclei (Fig. 4.2). The concentric zone model, the sector model, and the multiple nuclei model, each in its own way, capture certain aspects of the formal geography of the mass-production metropolis. Taken together, they also pick up on what might be described roughly as an evolving trend over the twentieth century in which the concentric zone arrangement partly gives way to

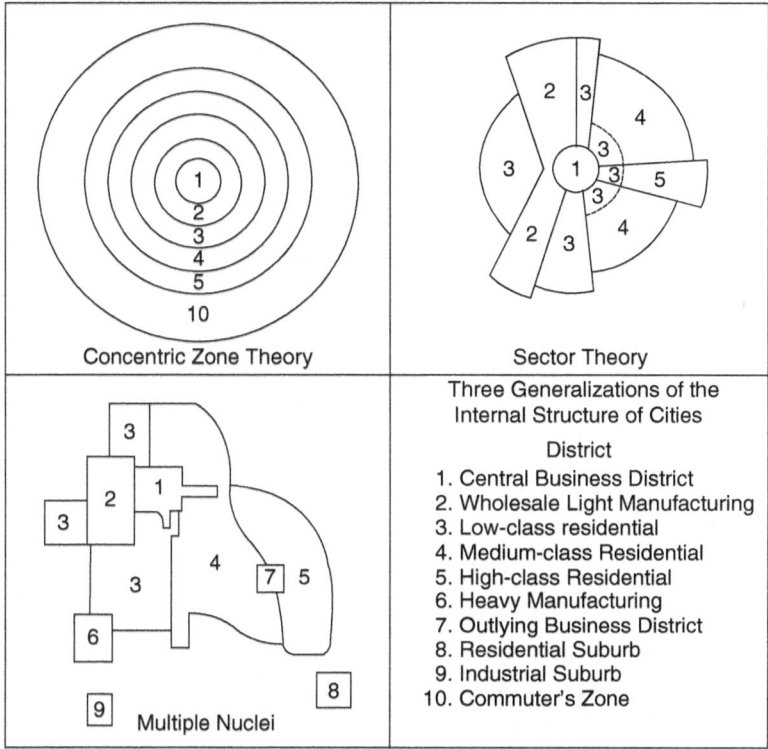

Fig. 4.2 Schematic representations of the city in terms of concentric zones, sectors, and multiple nuclei. Source: C. D. Harris and E. L. Ullman, "The nature of cities," *Annals of the American Academy of Political and Social Science*, 242, 1945, 7–17

the sector model, with diverse multiple nuclei shifting in and out of focus depending on wider changes in class, race, and ethnicity in American society as well as in patterns of intraurban clustering of production units.

Shorn of their biologistic trappings, the ideas of the Chicago School of Urban Sociology, together with amendments by Hoyt and Harris and Ullman, furnish many informative insights into the social geography of the mass-production metropolis in the first half of the twentieth century. As such, they also provided a framework for the empirical and largely atheoretical research in the immediate post-War decades into urban social structure and residential patterns via inductive procedures that came to be known as "social area analysis" and "factorial ecology."[12] Analyses of intraurban *economic* geography were considerably less well developed in the first half of the twentieth century, though a number of scattered offerings about the incidence of industrial activity in large cities contained important insights that would make a more systematic reappearance at a later date.[13]

THE LONG POST-WAR BOOM

While urban theory made only marginal progress over the immediate post-War decades, some very significant stresses and strains were developing in metropolitan areas across the capitalist world at this time. As the Long Post-War Boom lasting from late 1940s to the early 1970s gathered momentum, the mass-production metropolis grew apace, but then faced an accumulation of acute social and political problems as the boom moved into its penultimate stages.

The Core Countries

Large metropolitan areas themselves played a key role in helping to initiate and sustain the Long Post-War Boom. These were the geographic crucibles of the mass-production system. They contained the major lead plants and significant elements of their dependent cohorts of direct and indirect input suppliers, just as they also contained the large pools of the white-collar and blue-collar workers who kept the system going. The relatively subdued shift of manufacturing plants from central to suburban areas that had proceeded in the inter-War years now occurred on a much larger scale. As a corollary, increasing numbers of blue-collar workers participated in reverse commuting patterns involving travel from homes in central city areas to jobs in factories in the suburbs,[14] and many of these workers subsequently took up residence in the suburbs over the 1950s and 1960s. Indeed, the Long Post-War Boom was partly sustained by a virtuous circle of growth constituted by the interrelations between suburbanization, work, and production in the large metropolis. Expanding employment and wages meant that more and more workers were able to purchase housing in the suburbs, and this in turn stimulated increasing demand for cars and other consumer goods such as domestic appliances. The concomitant expansion of the mass-production system encouraged further increases in employment and wages, which incited further suburban expansion and yet further raised demand for cars and other consumer goods in what seemed to many to be an endless upward spiral of progress and prosperity. These were the salad days of American fordism and to a lesser degree of European fordism as well. Against this background, a number of economists in the early 1960s attempted to analyze the formation of intraurban spaces by means of neoclassical models of residential land use.[15] These models essentially sought to account for the structure of the social space of the city as an equilibrium expression of microeconomic decision-making on the part of households searching for residential locations given transport costs, incomes, and preferences about housing-lot size. From these starting points, they provided a reasonable rationale for the observable decline of population densities from the center of the city outward but neglected to qualify this insight with more powerful analytics about the social dynamics of neighborhood formation.

While the large metropolis constituted the spatial and functional core of mass-production society, we cannot fully understand the corresponding logic of urbanization without putting it into the wider regional context of the space-economy of capitalism as a whole. In the 1950s, both Gunnar Myrdal and Albert Hirschman had produced parallel theoretical accounts of the economic geography of fordism by arguing that the space-economy was activated by complementary but unequal forces of convergence and divergence.[16] Convergence, they reasoned, could be understood in terms of a process that Myrdal referred to as "backwash" and Hirschman as "polarization." These terms relate to the agglomerative forces exerted by highly urbanized growth centers or core regions. Given these forces, growth centers function as magnets for capital and migrants originating in much less urbanized and less prosperous peripheral regions, and these centers thus tend to retain their positions of economic leadership over extended periods of time. Divergence, by contrast, corresponds to what Myrdal called "spread" and what Hirschman called "trickle down," as represented by flows of both private and governmental investments from core to peripheral regions. One of the main contributing factors to divergence at this time was the accelerating decentralization of manufacturing branch plants not only from central cities to the suburbs but also and increasingly from core to peripheral regions in search of lower wages, lower land prices, and less unionized workers. Classic examples of this process are the dispersal of branch plants from the US Manufacturing Belt to the Sunbelt and from the Golden Triangle of Italy (Genoa-Milan-Turin) to the Mezzogiorno, over the post-War decades.[17] Both Myrdal and Hirschman were persuaded that backwash or polarization effects would always outweigh spread or trickle-down effects, leading to persistent growth of the core relative to the periphery, though as the Long Post-War Boom came to an end, numerous challenges to this view came increasingly into perspective.

In parallel with these trends, various policy packages based on Keynesian and welfare-statist principles were being constantly fine-tuned (as President Kennedy's economic advisers put it) in order to keep the fordist mass-production system moving smoothly ahead. These packages evolved over the post-War decades into a full-blown policy umbrella designed to curb the cyclical excesses of the mass-production economy and to establish a safety net that would help to maintain the physical and social capacities of the labor force, especially in periods of prolonged unemployment. As Brenner has shown, Keynesian welfare-statist policy was in significant degree translated into practical outcomes by means of explicitly *urban* projects intended to clear away obstructions to growth inherited from the pre-War years and to keep large urban centers operating in a reasonably efficient and socially manageable way.[18] Hence, throughout the 1950s and 1960s, policy-driven programs like urban renewal, intraurban expressway construction, suburban expansion, public housing, and diverse welfare schemes were relentlessly pursued in large urban centers, with significant transformative effects on the urban land nexus. Among these effects, some of the most dramatic involved clearances of slums and other blighted areas in the inner city and the tentacular spread of suburban sprawl as expressways extended outwards and peripheral land was equipped with new infrastructural services. The expanding edges of the metropolis steadily engulfed smaller peripheral communities leading to the notion of the "metropolitan area" as a sort of hybrid phenomenon comprising an original core city surrounded by a widely ranging fringe of suburban municipalities. In addition, physical coalescence of two or more metropolitan areas often came about, as exemplified above all by Jean Gottmann's Megalopolis stretching southward from Boston in the north through New York and Philadelphia to Baltimore-Washington, DC, in the south.[19] Analogous sequences of events could be observed in the 1950s and 1960s in Western European countries, though with distinctive national variations. In Britain and France, for example, clearances of blighted residential areas in the main central cities combined with the generally rising demand for housing led to a peculiar form of decentralization and suburbanization in the shape of new urban development programs (sometimes vaguely but inaccurately associated with the idea of the garden city). In essence, these programs can be seen as substitutes for less-efficient piecemeal modes of suburbanization and housing provision by making it possible to break land development bottlenecks (via state-sponsored land assembly operations) and to achieve significant economies of scale by means of massive coordinated construction programs. Not surprisingly, perhaps, the urban effervescence of the post-War decades led to a great intensification of urban planning activities focused on attempts to rationalize intraurban land use by rearranging spatial patterns of housing and employment relative to new investments in transport facilities. These activities found an ideological echo in the theory of "rational comprehensive planning" reflecting the then current faith in the capacity of planners to achieve overall spatial and functional optimality of the urban land nexus by means of large-scale technocratic systems analysis.[20]

The World Periphery

The period immediately following the Second World War was one of considerable tension and reorganization on the international front. The United States was then the unchallenged hegemon in a world that was becoming rapidly compartmentalized into a threefold division that was categorized over most of the post-War period as the First, Second, and Third Worlds, the latter of these divisions being represented by a heterogeneous collection of countries in Africa, Asia, and Latin America, many of them former colonies and soon-to-be-independent colonies or poor, non-aligned countries that had retained their independence.

The expansion of fordist mass production in the major capitalist countries after the Second World War was accompanied by a surge in the prevailing international division of labor, that is, the exchange of manufactured products from the First World for food and raw materials from the Third World. In the context of an ever-expanding international capitalism, the First and Third Worlds formed an interpenetrating core-periphery system at the world scale, whose early historical origins were identified by Wallerstein as actually going back to the seventeenth and eighteenth centuries.[21] This situation was interpreted by many theorists and political activists in the Third World as one that gave rise to systematically unequal exchange in which the terms of trade were always in favor of the First World, thus locking the Third World into a concomitant condition of dependency.[22] Largely on the basis of what came to be known as the Prebisch-Singer hypothesis, a solution to these problems was sought in a number of different countries by means of autonomous industrialization based on growth-pole development and import-substitution policies.[23] By the early to mid-1960s, countries that followed this prescription, such as Argentina, Brazil, Mexico, Indonesia, Malaysia, South Korea, Taiwan, and Turkey were coming to be known as a club of newly industrializing countries or NICs. Many of the old commercial and entrepôt urban centers in these countries were deeply implicated in these developments and now started to grow with unusual speed in response to both accelerated industrial investment and floods of migrants moving from the countryside to the city.[24]

One of the most successful cities of this sort was São Paulo, which in the post-War years became the most advanced center of the car industry in Latin America, with a large export trade to neighboring countries.[25] São Paulo had a population of 2.3 million in 1950 and 7.9 million in 1970, a more than threefold expansion over only two decades. Urban growth in the NICs was reinforced from the 1960s onward by foreign direct investment as corporations based in the advanced capitalist world diverted branch plant locations away from national peripheries in the core countries and into the global periphery, where they were frequently accommodated in special economic zones adjacent to major urban areas. Even in Third World countries that were not experiencing significant industrialization, the principal or primate cities were subject to rapid population growth as individuals moved in large numbers from agricultural areas in the expectation of improving their lives.[26] This insistent migration combined with elevated birth rates also encouraged the massive build-up of unemployed and underemployed individuals in cities across the Third World leading in turn to high levels of indurated poverty and informal economic activity and the concomitant growth of *favelas, bidonvilles,* and shantytowns.

CRISIS AND READJUSTMENT

The Climacteric

An observer located somewhere in the American Manufacturing Belt and surveying the surrounding scene in the early 1960s would almost certainly have predicted that American economic and urban life would in all likelihood continue to be focused on this region into the indefinite future, despite the signs of new growth in the cities of the Sunbelt. Even when the mass-production system in North America and Western Europe was beginning to shows signs of exceptional stress in the mid-1970s, our observer might well still have considered this to be a temporary and eventually self-correcting anomaly. In fact, the discernible crisis of large industrial cities at this time was just the foretaste of a prolonged period of exhaustion and economic restructuring that also provoked a rearrangement of much of the urban and regional geography of North America and Western Europe.

The crisis itself was partly due to a deepening crisis of stagflation in which stubborn inflationary pressures, combined with high levels of unemployment, made it difficult for central governments to continue to deploy conventional Keynesian welfare-statist policies as instruments of countercyclical stimulus (see Chap. 6). In part it was also due to the rising economic prowess of Japan whose own technologically and culturally distinctive form of industrialization (sometimes referred to as neo-fordism) could churn out mass-produced outputs at significantly lower prices and higher levels of quality than North American and Western European producers, with devastating effects on the ability of these producers to contest markets, even at home. The formerly thriving mass-production cities of the core countries were now faced with massive job loss and physical decay, compounded by the continuing and accelerating decentralization of branch plants to far-flung peripheral locations. In the metropolitan areas that had formerly functioned as the quintessential centers of the Long Post-War Boom, the watchwords now became stagnation and decline, and working-class neighborhoods in inner-city areas, in particular, were exposed to a pervasive syndrome of unemployment, poverty, and dereliction. In the United States, deindustrialization of the cities of the Manufacturing Belt advanced at such a swift pace over the 1970s that the region came to be redesignated as the Rustbelt, and two of its largest metropolitan areas, New York (the financial capital of the American economy) and Detroit (the industrial center), came within a hairsbreadth of bankruptcy.[27] Concurrently, many of those countries that had most energetically pursued import-substitution industrialization policies were falling deeply into debt as they continued to press on with large-scale capital investment programs. The resulting international debt crisis after the mid-1970s now seriously started to compromise import-substitution policies, most notably in the case of Argentina, Brazil, and Mexico, leading to a "lost decade" of diminishing incomes, political uncertainty, and urban disruption.

As these crisis conditions deepened, a number of influential economists and geographers in core countries began to publish exceptionally gloomy accounts of the prospects of cities and regions that had most benefited from economic growth over the period of the Long Post-War Boom.[28] Concomitantly, the deep crisis generated by the downturn helped to promote the rise of a New Right, which came to power under the banner of Ronald Reagan in the United States and Margaret Thatcher in the United Kingdom with mandates to dismantle much of the national policy apparatus of Keynesianism and welfare statism that had been developed in attempts to stabilize the mass-production system and to strengthen its roots in large metropolitan areas. This political change represents a key moment in ushering in the neoliberal ideological climate that still predominates today in economic policy-making, as well as the Washington Consensus with its strictures on aid packages to developing countries. Globalization in its modern guise was now beginning to override the old internationalist system that had prevailed in the post-War decades, and world trade was rapidly reorganizing under the banner of the new international division of labor based on rising exports of industrial products from erstwhile peripheral countries.

Turning Points: Theoretical and Substantive

The puzzling social condition of the mass-production metropolis in the first half of the twentieth century had stimulated the work of the Chicago School on the residential spaces of the city. Sometime in the 1960s, more politically radical thinkers began to turn their attention to issues of how society in general was structured by capitalist class relationships and how these relationships were reflected in configurations of urban life. These considerations stimulated a major reevaluation of urban theory, much of it derived from the pioneering work of the French Marxist sociologist and philosopher, Henri Lefebvre. As early as 1968, in the midst of student protests and the burgeoning anti-War movement, Lefebvre had published a seminal book entitled *The Right to the City*, whose message ran strongly counter to the politically quietistic character of the then-prevailing modes of urban analysis.[29] In this book, which was shortly to become a foundational text for urban theorists, Lefebvre made a forthright case for taking class conflict in capitalist society as the major key to any comprehension of urban dynamics. He advocated, in particular, the right of all to inhabit, use, and make the city, a right that he saw as fundamental to the emancipation of the working class and as the basis of a new more democratic social order. Lefebvre's ideas were directly echoed in the influential research of Manuel Castells, whose book *The Urban Question* was first published in French in 1972. In this publication, Castells attacked the social Darwinist concepts that lay behind the work of the original members of the Chicago School while at the same time sketching out some of the bases for his later analyses of the city as a site of collective consumption and associated social conflict over the allocation of public goods and services.[30] Then, in 1973 David Harvey published *Social Justice and the City*,[31] a book that both criticized mainstream versions of urban theory and explicitly set out to identify an approach to the city in terms of Marxian political economy. In this approach, Harvey laid special emphasis on class struggle around profit, wages, and rent, and on related social clashes over the appropriation of benefits flowing from public investment strategies and planning interventions in the city. These and other books published in the early and mid-1970s opened up urban studies to a new era of theoretical and empirical research that was intent on seeing the city not as an organism or as an equilibrium resulting from microeconomic decision-making or even as just an empirical mosaic of social areas, but as an arena of diverging class interests and political conflict.

These studies appeared toward the end of the Long Post-War Boom and at a time when the economies of North America and Western Europe were facing rapidly deepening crisis conditions. Yet even as the traditional mass-production system was approaching exhaustion, and assessments about its impacts in the core countries were at their most pessimistic, it is evident with the wisdom of hindsight that there were sectors of production in relatively unfamiliar places that were starting to move in quite unforeseen ways and with dramatic implications for the future of urbanization and the structure of the urban land nexus. In particular, by the mid to late 1970s, scattered signs of a new kind of urban and regional dynamism were starting to become evident as incipient clusters of small and medium-sized firms that eschewed the rigidities of mass production and the extreme standardization of outputs made their appearance on the landscape. In an early attempt to understand this phenomenon, Piore and Sabel labeled it "flexible specialization," which they defined in terms of a strategy whereby firms focus on the production of just one kind of output but where the design specifications of the output are continually changing.[32] The sectors actually engaging in this sort of production were quite diverse, but renascent labor-intensive craft industries like shoes, furniture, jewelry, and clothing were conspicuously in the forefront as well as certain high-technology industries, and especially microelectronics.[33] In particular, employment in these sectors was growing rapidly in places far removed from the established centers of mass production, and, as such, they constituted a series of new industrial spaces that functioned as harbingers of a radically changing economic geography of capitalism. Among these new spaces, one of the most emblematic was the so-called Third Italy concentrated in and around Veneto, Emilia-Romagna, and Tuscany. This is a region of small and medium-sized towns that began to expand at a rapid pace in the 1970s based on a diversity of mainly small-scale craft industries including clothing, leather products, shoes, furniture, woolen goods, musical instruments, ceramic tiles, and high-performance cars. Equally, and perhaps even more emblematic, was Silicon Valley in California which was now forging ahead on the basis of semiconductor and computer production, and which swiftly became the classic exemplar of clustered economic development based on high-technology industry.[34]

These changes were portents of what was soon to be referred to as a "postfordist" economic order, which, as it emerged was also becoming intertwined with a multipolar system of globalization. Taken together, these complex outcomes herald the dawn of the third wave of capitalism and the beginning of some remarkable new trends in patterns of urbanization.

NOTES

1. A. Smith, *An Inquiry into the Nature and Causes of the Wealth of Nations*, London: Methuen 1961 (first published 1776).
2. D. Forgacs (ed.) *The Gramsci Reader: Selected Writings 1916–1935*, New York: New York University Press, 2000.
3. F. Perroux, *L'Economie du XXe Siècle*, Paris: Presses Universitaires de France, 1961.
4. J. M. Keynes, *The General Theory of Employment, Interest and Money*, London: Macmillan, 1936; Inter-Departmental Committee on *Social Insurance and Allied Services*, Great Britain, *Social Insurance and Allied Services*, report by Sir William Beveridge, London: H. M. Stationery Office, 1942.
5. S. De Geer, "The American Manufacturing Belt," *Geografiska Annaler*, 9, 1927, 323–359.
6. D. Darwent, "Growth poles and growth centers in regional planning—a review," *Environment and Planning*, 1, 1969, 5–32; see also J. R.

Boudeville, *Problems of Regional Economic Planning*, Edinburgh: Edinburgh University Press, 1966.
7. M. Jefferson, "The law of the primate city," *Geographical Review*, 29, 1939, 226–232.
8. R. E. Park, E. W. Burgess ad R. D. McKenzie, *The City*, Chicago: University of Chicago Press, 1925, p. 47.
9. G. Simmel, "The metropolis and mental life," pp. 47–60 in R. Sennett (ed.) *Classic Essays on the Culture of Cities*, New York: Appleton-Century-Crofts, 1969, (*first published in German in 1903 under the title "Die Großstädte und das Geistesleben"*).
10. R. E. Park, *et al., op. cit.*, 1925.
11. See especially R. E. Park, "Human ecology," *American Journal of Sociology*, 42, 1936, 1–15.
12. K. P. Schwirian, *Comparative Urban Structure: Studies in the Ecology of Cities*, Lexington, MA: Heath, 1974; C-G. Janson, "Factorial social ecology: an attempt at summary and evaluation," *Annual Review of Sociology*, 6, 1980, 433–456.
13. See, in particular, R. M. Haig, *Major Economic Factors in Metropolitan Growth an Arrangement*, New York: Regional Plan of New York and its Environs, 1927; G. C. Allen, *The Industrial Development of Birmingham and the Black Country, 1860–1907*, Hemel Hempstead: Allen and Unwin, 1929; M. Perrin, *Saint-Etienne et sa Région Economique*, Tours: Arrault et Cie., 1937; E. M. Hoover, *Location Theory and the Shoe and Leather Industries*, Cambridge, MA: Harvard University Press, 1937; P. S. Florence, *Investment, Location, and Size of Plant*, Cambridge: Cambridge University Press, 1948; M. J. Wise, "On the evolution of the jewellery and gun quarters in Birmingham," *Transactions of the Institute of British Geographers*, 15, 1949, 57–72; E. M. Hoover and R. Vernon, *Anatomy of a Metropolis*, Cambridge, MA: Harvard University Press, 1959.
14. R. Vernon, "The economics and finances of the large metropolis," *Daedalus*, 90, 1961, 31–47.
15. J. D. Herbert and B. H. Stevens, "A model for the distribution of residential activity in urban areas," *Journal of Regional Science*, 2, 1960, 21–36; L. Wingo, *Transportation and Urban Land*, Washington, DC: Resources for the Future, 1961; W. Alonso, *Location and Land Use: Toward a General Theory of Land Rent*, Cambridge: Harvard University Press, 1964.
16. G. Myrdal, *Economic Theory and Underdeveloped Regions*, New York: Harper and Row, 1957; A. O. Hirschman, *The Strategy of Economic Development*, New Haven: Yale University Press, 1958.
17. R. D. Norton and J. Rees, "The product cycle and the spatial decentralization of American manufacturing," *Regional Studies*, 13, 1979, 141–151;

G. Garofoli, *Economia e Politica Economica in Italia: lo Sviluppo Economico Italiano dal 1945 ad Oggi*, Milan: FrancoAngeli, 2014.
18. N. Brenner, "Urban governance and the production of new state spaces in Western Europe," *Review of International Political Economy*, 11, 2004, 447–488.
19. J. Gottmann, *Megalopolis: The Urbanized Northeastern Seaboard of the United States*, New York: Twentieth Century Fund, 1961.
20. See A. Faludi, *A Reader in Planning Theory*, Oxford: Pergamon, 1973.
21. I. Wallerstein, "The rise and future demise of the world-capitalist system: concepts for comparative analysis," *Comparative Studies in Society and History*, 16, 1974, 387–415.
22. A. Arghiri, *L'Echange Inégal*, Paris: François Maspéro, 1969; A. G. Frank, *Capitalism and Underdevelopment in Latin America: Historical Studies of Chile and Brazil*, New York: Monthly Review Press, 1967.
23. R. Prebisch, The Economic Development of Latin America and Its Principal Problems, New York: United Nations, 1950; H. W. Singer, "The distribution of gains between investing and borrowing countries," *American Economic Review, Papers and Proceedings*, 40, 1950, 473–485.
24. M. Storper, *Industrialization, Economic Development and the Regional Question in the Third World: From Import Substitution to Flexible Production*, London: Pion, 1991.
25. A. J. Scott, "Industrial Revitalization in the ABC Municipalities, São Paulo: Diagnostic Analysis and Strategic Recommendations for a New Economy and a New Regionalism," *Regional Development Studies*, 7, 2001, 1–32; W. Cano *Raízes da Concentração Industrial em São Paulo*, Rio de Janeiro and São Paulo: DIFEL, 1977.
26. This point was articulated in the Harris-Todaro model, which postulates that rural-urban migration in developing countries is governed more by inflated *expectations* about rural-urban income differentials than it is by actual differentials; see J. R. Harris and M. P. Todaro, "Migration, unemployment and development: a two-sector analysis," *American Economic Review*, 60,1970, 126–142.
27. After decades of unmitigated crisis, the city of Detroit finally became formally bankrupt on July 18, 2013.
28. See for example: B. Bluestone and B. Harrison, *The Deindustrialization of America: Plant Closings, Community Abandonment, and the Dismantling of Basic Industry*, New York: Basic Books, 1982; J. Carney, R. Hudson and J. Lewis (eds.), *Regions in Crisis: New Perspectives in European Regional Theory*, New York: St. Martin's Press, 1980; D. B. Massey and R. Meegan, The Anatomy of Job Loss: the How, Why, and Where of Employment Decline, London: Methuen, 1982.
29. H. Lefebvre, *Le Droit à la Ville*, Paris: Anthropos, 1968.

30. M. Castells, *La Question Urbaine*, Paris: Maspéro, 1972.
31. D. Harvey, *Social Justice and the City*, Baltimore: Johns Hopkins University Press, 1973.
32. M. J. Piore and C. F. Sabel, *The Second Industrial Divide: Possibilities for Prosperity*, New York: Basic Books, 1984.
33. A. Amin (ed.), *Post-Fordism: A Reader*, Oxford: Blackwell, 1994.
34. A. Bagnasco, *Tre Italie: la Problematica Territoriale dello Sviluppo Italiano*, Bologna: Il Mulino, 1977; A. Saxenian, *Regional Advantage: Culture and Competition in Silicon Valley and Route 128*, Cambridge, MA: Harvard University Press, 1994; A. J. Scott, New Industrial Spaces: *Flexible Production Organization and Regional Development in North America and Western Europe*, London: Pion, 1988.

CHAPTER 5

Cities in a Globalizing World

Internal and External Relations of the City

The urban land nexus constitutes the vital internal anatomy of the city, but it is also situated within a wider external milieu composed primarily of regional, national, and global linkages to other cities. In a turn of phrase that owes much to Brian Berry, we might say that the urban land nexus represents a system embedded within diverse systems of cities.[1] Some analysts have actually made strong claims to the effect that the city can only be conceptualized in terms of its external environment or its "constitutive outside."[2] There can be no doubt that the external environment influences the form and substance of the city in important ways, and the city's relationships to this environment are assuredly critical to its survival. At the same time, these relationships are assimilated into the reality of the city via the logic and dynamics of the urban land nexus without fundamentally changing its operational significance as the fountainhead of the urbanization process as such. For example, interurban economic competition may result in a given city's loss of critical external markets, and this may then be expressed in a broad decrease in employment as well as in derivative shifts such as population decline, falling land values, land abandonment, neighborhood decay, and so on. Hence, even as the substantive effects of these external influences are etched deeply on the physical appearance of the urban land nexus, its broad functional integrity as a site of historically specific processes of agglomeration and spatial integration remains intact.

© The Author(s) 2017
A.J. Scott, *The Constitution of the City*,
DOI 10.1007/978-3-319-61228-7_5

Still, the multiple external influences channeled through intercity relationships of trade, competition, collaboration, migratory flows, and so on, impinge continually not only on individual cities but also on the shape of the urban system as a whole and leave many traces on its geography and development. Cities are thus always in various states of interaction with one another, and these relationships are variously expressed in recurring statistical and spatial patterns of the urban system as a whole. One of the most pervasive of these patterns is summarized in the model of the urban continuum known as the *rank-size rule*.

THE URBAN CONTINUUM

Any given collection of cities, such as the US urban system or even a perfectly random selection of cities, can be described in statistical terms by ranking all the cities in the set according to their populations such that the largest or primate city is scored one, the second largest is scored two, the third largest is scored three, and so on. The resulting sequence of numbers can then be arrayed in a two-dimensional graph whose horizontal axis is defined by rank and whose vertical axis is defined by some index of population. For present purposes, we define the index of population for any given city with rank r as $p_r = P_r/P_1$, where P_r is the actual population of that city, and P_1 is the population of the largest city in the set. If the values of P_r are equivalent to randomly chosen data points, we would expect the graph of p_r against r to trace out a straight negatively sloping line as r increases. By contrast, when we examine the cities of any given country, the resulting plot of points is usually very different from the random case and often conforms to a negative exponential curve characterized by a steep drop in values of p_r at low levels of r followed by a long trailing tail as r increases. For many countries, this curve can be approximated by the function $p_r = r^{-1}$, in which case the second largest city has half the population of the largest city, the third largest has a population equal to one-third that of the largest city, and so on, though obviously the actual relationships will rarely be quite so precise. This statistical model or rank-size rule roughly describes the arrangement of metropolitan areas relative to rank in the United States today (see Fig. 5.1). It also effectively describes city-size distributions in an enormous variety of other countries and social situations at different historical times and in different geographical contexts.

There is a copious literature dealing with the rank-size rule, going back to the pioneering work of Zipf in 1949.[3] Numerous attempts at

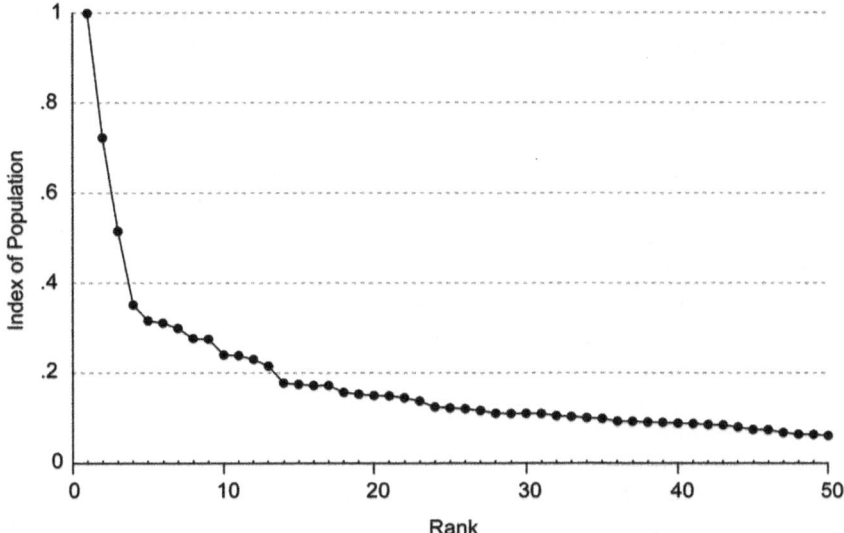

Fig. 5.1 The 50 largest metropolitan areas in the United States arrayed by rank. The population of the largest urban unit (New York-Northeastern New Jersey Metropolitan Area) is coded as one and the populations of all other metropolitan areas are rescaled accordingly. The long tail of the distribution beyond $r = 50$ is not shown. For all 283 metropolitan areas for which data are available, the computed rank-size regression equation is given as $p_r = 3.30 r^{-1.07}$ ($R^2 = 0.97$). The computed equation compares well with the ideal rank-size rule (expressed as $p_r = r^{-1}$) in so far as the regression coefficient is concerned, but it is not a good match in regard to the constant term, whose expected value is unity. Source: United States Bureau of the Census, *American Community Survey*, 2010

constructing explanatory models have been proposed, most of them based on abstract statistical hypotheses like the analysis of Gabaix, which takes off from the dubious assumption that growth rates are constant for all cities.[4] Duranton proposes an alternative approach founded on the more substantive claim that actual city growth is a function of agglomeration economies and diseconomies. Unfortunately, after this promising start, Duranton's analysis then heads off into rather barren territory by suggesting that the basic mechanism underlying the rank-size rule resides in research-driven innovation "shocks" (a claim whose generality is rather obviously undercut by the fact that the rank-size rule also applies to a large number of precapitalist and protocapitalist urban systems).[5] There is indeed little in the way of a substantive explanation of the rank-size rule (and hence no generalizable account of the differing dimensions of the urban land nexus in any given system of cities) that puts the matter in plausible, concrete, and empirically verifiable terms. Even so, and given the frequency with which the rule is observed across systems of cities in many different parts of the world, it is tempting to speculate that the statistical regularities displayed by these systems result from some sort of long-term process of evolutionary convergence within the space-economy as a whole. This process is in all probability related, as Duranton suggests, to the play of agglomeration economies and diseconomies. It may, for example, be shaped in part by some sort of zero-sum relationship governing the creation and intercity distribution of agglomeration economies within a bounded economic system. In any case, the systemic properties of the urban continuum suggest that any question as to the optimal size of any individual city is likely to be rather meaningless, though the recurrent pattern of city-size distributions as revealed by the rank-size rule implies that it might be possible to identify a meaningful overall optimum, such as, for example, one that maximizes the total availability of agglomeration economies, or total economic productivity, subject to appropriate constraints on available resources.

All that being said, there are many country-specific urban systems across the world that do *not* conform to the rank-size rule, and these divergent cases can be observed above all in poor countries, such as the Democratic Republic of Congo, Nicaragua, or the Philippines, where the primate city is unusually large (or "macrocephalic") relative to the next largest city.[6] Several attempts have been made to explain this phenomenon, almost all of which turn on the idea that scarce resources and limited infrastructure impose restrictions on the possibility of significant urban growth beyond one primate city. Since the primate city in these situations is almost always the national capital, it is also likely to be the object of politically preferential investments.[7] If we aggregate all the cities of the world together and draw a corresponding curve of urban population versus city rank, we find that in this instance, too, there is a marked departure from the rank-size rule. The curve is still downward sloping with respect to rank, but as we should expect from an operation that simply combines multiple rank-size distributions together, it is much flatter than it would be in the case of a conventional country-specific system. The same remark applies to the aggregated city-systems of the European Union.[8]

In the light of these observations, we might ask if continued globalization and the ever-increasing integration of global markets will eventually induce a greater tendency on the part of the world's cities as a whole to conform to the rank-size rule. Is it possible that the overall global (or European) urban system may at some future time begin to approximate more closely to this rule?[9] Unfortunately, in view of our deficient knowledge about why and how precisely the rank-size rule operates in empirical reality, there can be no confident response to this question. Alternatively, some analysts have actually predicted that cities will in due course wither away because of the effects of dramatically falling transport costs and instantaneous communication across the globe,[10] though the prospect of this eventuality seems very far distant given the continued significance of agglomeration economies in the structuring of the space-economy and the huge amounts of still-useful physical capital sunk in the urban milieu. A more likely scenario, perhaps, would be to assume continued urban growth for the foreseeable future, but in a rather modified form in comparison with the past, and above all, in a configuration marked by rapidly increasing numbers of very large cities. The 30 largest cities in the world today all range between 10 and 38 million inhabitants according to United Nations data and all the signs suggest that this club of giant cities will continue to grow in size.[11]

Moreover, the current historical period is one in which massive metropolitan aggregates or superclusters are increasingly forming as a consequence of the spatial coalescence of individual metropolitan areas. Several different terms have been devised to designate any supercluster of this sort, including polycentric metropolis, megaregion, and global city-region.[12] Hall and Pain describe this phenomenon as "a new form [comprising] a series of anything between 10 and 50 cities and towns, physically separate but functionally networked, clustered around one or more larger central cities."[13] In the circumstances, it is entirely within the bounds of possibility that we will eventually see some type of overall—but as yet indecipherable—redefinition of the global urban continuum to take account of supercluster formation, possibly in combination with some decay in country-specific rank-size regularities. Certainly, while more or less orderly national urban continua remain strongly inscribed on the landscape of most countries, these are becoming ever more firmly integrated into an explicitly global space of flows and increasingly assertive networks of superclusters, and the long-run effects of these trends will undoubtedly turn out to have major impacts on both local and global patterns of urbanization.[14]

The Geography of Urban Growth and Development

Throughout the history of capitalism, cities have grown and spread with remarkable persistence. Much of this expansion can be ascribed to rising levels of output, productivity, and per capita income in both manufacturing and service systems and the concomitant but selective pressures on significant portions of the capitalist production system to agglomerate in geographic space. A summary view of the relationship between urbanization and per capita income on a country-by-country basis is presented in Fig. 5.2, which shows the clearly strong and positive association between the two variables as well as the sharp contrasts between rich and poor countries. Work published elsewhere indicates that urbanization is also

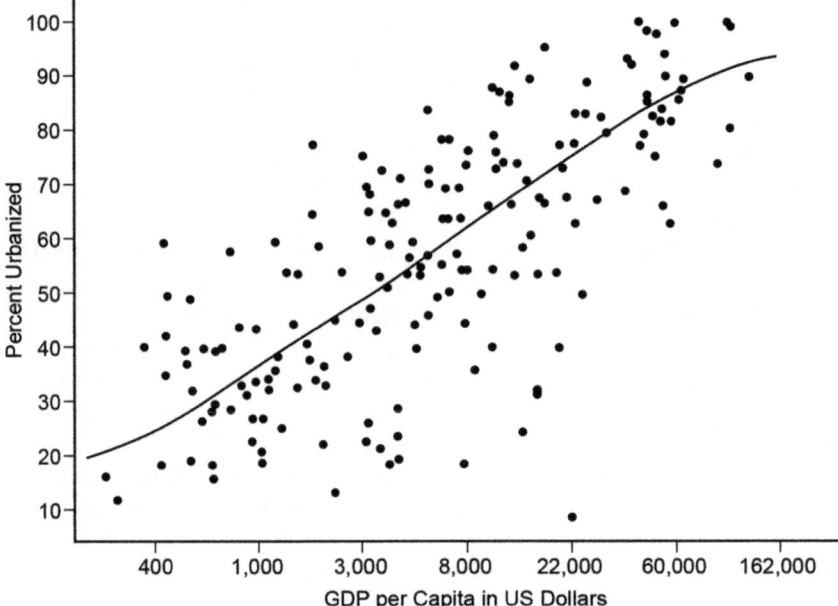

Fig. 5.2 Percentage of total population living in cities in 190 different countries as a function of GDP per capita, 2014. The equation of the curve is given by the logit regression $U_i = 100/[1 + 94.70 \times \exp(-0.57 \times \ln(Y_i))]$ with $R^2 = 0.48$, where U_i is the percentage of the total population living in urban areas for country i, and Y_i is GDP per capita for country i. Source: World Bank, *World Development Indicators*, 2015

significantly influenced in a positive direction by manufacturing activity, literacy levels, and rates of migration from the countryside, and in a negative direction by the rate of agricultural employment and the importance of primary production in the national economy.[15] There are evidently strong causal relationships running from per capita income to urbanization, but causality almost certainly runs in the other direction as well given the influence of agglomeration on economic productivity, competitive advantage, and innovation.[16] A simple counterfactual argument in support of this remark can be adduced by imagining a world in which cities are abolished. The negative consequences of this condition on overall income levels would certainly be enormous given the elimination of agglomeration economies and the ensuing increases in transactions costs.

A somewhat different perspective on urbanization across the world is given by the data in Table 5.1, which sets forth the percentage of the total population living in urban areas from 1955 to 2015 for six major world regions. Levels of urbanization across the six regions have been notably uneven over this entire period of time, though the degree of disparateness has moderated somewhat in more recent years. In 1955, only 31.6% of the population in the world as a whole was living in cities. By far the most urbanized areas at this time were the rich regions of Europe, North America, and Oceania, with the poorer regions of Africa and Asia lagging clearly behind. Latin America, with a relatively high 45.2% of the total population living in cities, occupied an intermediate position between these two ends of the spectrum, largely owing to the growth of urban industry and commerce in several countries of the region after the 1930s and a successful first round of import-substitution policies after

Table 5.1 Percentage of total population living in urban areas by major world region, 1955–2015

Year	Africa	Asia	Europe	Latin America	North America	Oceania	World
1955	16.1	19.3	54.3	45.2	67.0	64.8	31.6
1965	20.6	22.9	60.2	53.3	72.0	69.1	35.6
1975	24.7	25.0	65.4	60.7	73.8	71.9	37.7
1985	28.9	29.8	68.8	67.6	74.7	70.7	41.2
1995	33.1	34.8	70.5	73.0	77.3	70.6	44.7
2005	36.3	41.1	71.7	76.9	80.0	70.5	49.1
2015	40.4	48.2	73.6	79.8	81.6	70.8	54.0

Source: United Nations, *World Urbanization Prospects*

the Second World War, notably in Argentina, Brazil, Chile, Mexico, and Uruguay.[17] Over the succeeding years, urbanization advanced greatly in all major regions of the globe so that by 2015, 54.0% of the total world population was now urbanized. Much of Europe, North America, and Oceania were all by this time close to saturation levels of urbanization, and Latin America had a surprisingly high 80% of its population living in urban areas. By 2015, urbanization had also increased greatly in Africa and Asia, with selected countries like Nigeria, South Africa, China, and South Korea showing particularly large gains due to advancing economic development.

Table 5.2 displays world urbanization data in yet another format. Here, total world population and rates of change are broken down by five different urban categories (identified by population size) and four different years (1950, 1970, 1990 and 2015). Examination of Table 5.2 brings to light three main issues. First, as already shown in Table 5.1, the world's urban population has grown by leaps and bounds since 1950 as indicated by a more than 400% rate of change over this period of time. Second, most of this population is concentrated in cities with under one million inhabitants; however, while these cities accounted for 75.2% of total world urban population in 1950, the percentage had fallen to 58.9% by 2015. Third, and as a corollary, population growth over the last several decades has

Table 5.2 Total world population living in urban areas by different size categories, 1955–2015[a]

Population range	Population in millions				Percentage change			
	1950	1970	1990	2015	1950–1970	1970–1990	1990–2015	1950–2015
>10m	24	55	153	471	131.9	178.8	208.7	1896.0
5m–10m	32	106	157	307	230.0	48.2	95.4	855.9
1m–5m	129	245	459	847	90.0	87.7	84.4	557.6
300th–1m	115	216	359	633	87.2	66.6	76.0	448.9
<300th	447	729	1156	1699	63.2	58.6	46.9	280.4
Total urban population	746	1350	2285	3957	80.9	69.2	73.2	430.1
Urban as a percent of world population	29.6	36.6	42.9	54.0	23.6	17.2	25.9	82.4

[a]m=million; th=thousand. Source: United Nations, *World Urbanization Prospects*

Table 5.3 Number of cities worldwide in different size categories, 1950–2015

Population range	Number of cities				Percentage change			
	1950	1970	1990	2015	1950–1970	1970–1990	1990–2015	1950–2015
>10m	2	3	10	29	50.0	233.3	190	1350.0
5m–10m	5	15	21	44	200.0	40.0	109.5	780.0
1m–5m	71	126	239	428	77.5	89.7	79.1	502.8
300th–1m	229	413	706	1191	80.3	70.9	68.7	420.1
Total	307	557	976	1692	81.4	75.2	73.4	451.1

Source: United Nations, *World Urbanization Prospects*

been most intense for the very large cities in the world, mainly as a result of urban expansion in poorer countries.

Broadly similar developments are revealed in Table 5.3, which presents data on the number of cities worldwide for the same population size categories and years as in Table 5.2. As we would expect in any urban system, the number of cities increases as we descend the hierarchy of population size categories. In addition, and in parallel with the data in Table 5.2, the population of large cities clearly increased in percentage terms more rapidly than smaller cities between 1950 and 2015. In 1950, there were just two urban agglomerations in the world with populations in excess of ten million, that is, New York with a population of 14.9 million and Tokyo with 13.0 million. In the same year, there were 76 cities with populations of between one million and ten million. By 2015, 29 cities had attained populations of ten million or more and as many as 472 had populations between one million and ten million. Since 1980, by far the greater part of this growth has been in the Global South, which now has three times as many cities with populations of a million or more than the Global North. Tokyo, with a population of 38.0 million, is still in the top position in 2015, but Delhi, with a population of 25.7 million, is in the second place followed by Shanghai, São Paulo, Mexico City, and Beijing, all of them in the Global South. New York is currently in the tenth place with a current population of 18.6 million.

These remarks can now be summarized by reference to Fig. 5.3, which shows the geographical distribution of cities with populations of more than one million across the world today. Both North America and Europe contain major clusters of large cities as befits the original homelands of

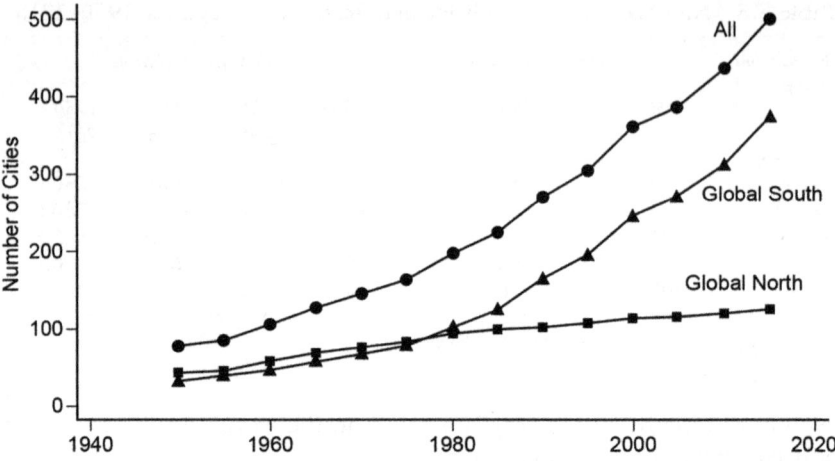

Fig. 5.3 Number of cities worldwide with populations of one million or more, 1950–2015. Source: United Nations, *World Urbanization Prospects*, 2015

capitalist industrialization and urbanization. Yet what is perhaps most striking about Fig. 5.3 is the enormous weight of urban development across the Global South, and especially in Asia (see also Fig. 5.4). Half a century ago, the world map of large cities was overwhelmingly dominated by North America and Europe. Nowadays, as a consequence of the resurgence of cities in other parts of the world, the pattern is tilting perceptibly in favor of the Global South, with two countries above all, China and India, accounting for the lion's share of the change. In China particularly, a great flowering of cities occurred after Mao's death in 1976 when the country was opened up to world markets, leading in turn to rapid national economic growth. In 1976, there were just 17 cities in China with populations over one million; today, there is a total of 106 such cities.[18] Latin America, as already noted, has unusually high overall levels of urbanization, and given the colonial origins of most of the region's cities, these are located mainly in coastal areas. Africa is the least urbanized world region, and most of its large cities—again reflecting the colonial past—are located in coastal areas. In 1950, there were only two cities in Africa with populations greater than one million, that is, Cairo in the extreme north and Johannesburg in the extreme south. However, in recent decades, the pace of change in levels of urbanization in Africa has been second only to that of Asia, and large cities with populations of a million or more are now

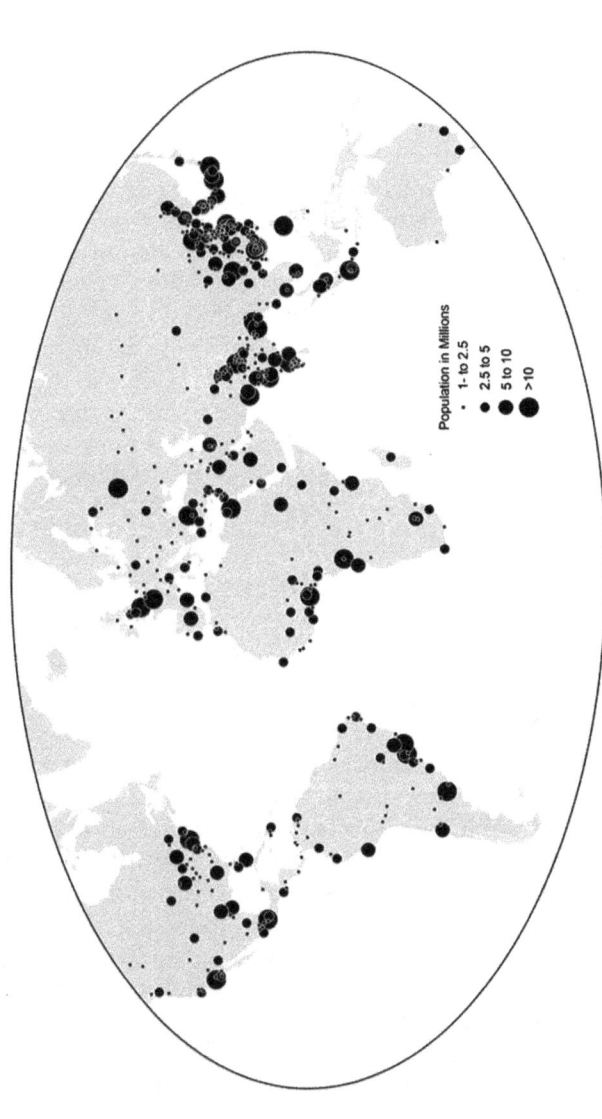

Fig. 5.4 World geographical distribution of cities with populations of one million or more. Source: United Nations, *World Urbanization Prospects*, 2015

developing rapidly in Africa between the tropics in countries like Cameroon, Gabon, Ghana, and Nigeria, largely in response to developmental surges since the early 1980s.

The information set out in Fig. 5.4 is testimony to the extraordinary spread of large-scale urbanization beyond North America and Western Europe in recent decades, and particularly since the rise of globalization after the crisis of fordism in the 1970s. This turn of events has occurred to a significant extent as a consequence of rapid economic expansion and rising per capita income in a number of former Third World countries. Nevertheless, many of these countries continue to be mired in poverty, and whereas income bifurcation is characteristic of cities in both the Global North and the Global South, it is especially manifest in the large cities of the latter. Even in nominally socialist China, urban social inequalities are increasing at a rapid pace.[19] By the same token, slum areas in the large cities of the Global South have exploded in size in recent decades. According to the World Bank, as much as 30% of urban dwellers in low- and middle-income countries currently live in slums, and in the developing countries of sub-Saharan Africa the figure rises to an alarming 55%.[20]

THE GLOBAL MULTIPLEX

In 1966, well before globalization as we now know it had taken hold, Peter Hall published a small book entitled *The World Cities*, in which he proposed the then novel idea that certain major cities like London, Paris, Randstad-Holland, Rhine-Ruhr, Moscow, New York, and Tokyo were coming to function as pivots of the international system.[21] For the next two and a half decades, this notion remained something of an outlier until, in 1982, John Friedmann and Goetz Wolff published their celebrated "world city hypothesis" with its claim that the accelerated internationalization of capital was leading to the formation of a global grid of cities representing the functional and spatial cynosures of "a world system of production and markets."[22] Conjectures about the emergence of a worldwide urban system were pushed further forward by Saskia Sassen in her path-breaking study of New York, London, and Tokyo, published in 1991.[23] In this study, Sassen pointed to the growing importance of global cities as sites of corporate command and control within international capitalism. She also argued that the same cities were becoming increasingly bifurcated in social terms as typified at the extremes by a transnational capitalist class and a low-wage immigrant labor force in manufacturing and service provision.

These are some of the early landmark notions that lie at the origins of what has become a continually deepening and widening flow of academic research on urban growth and change in a steadily integrating world. Like other attempts to formulate ideas about incipient social developments, they have their defects and blind spots. Most notably, perhaps, these early contributions tended to focus unduly on the activities of large corporations at the expense of other dimensions of urbanization in a globalizing world, but they nonetheless represent critical and intellectually productive moments stimulated by the then-dawning realization that the old First World/Third World processes of trade, regional development, and urbanization that had prevailed in the period before the 1980s were being radically restructured on a global scale.

Attempts to construct a theoretical account of the new global capitalist order heralded by these and other forward-looking studies are still very much a work in progress, though some of the main geographical lineaments of this order now seem to be coming into greater focus. The old core-periphery international structure that marked much of post-War capitalism is waning rapidly as a multiplex pattern of cities and countries and more variegated relationships of international development and trade take over more of the global scene. Equally, a new economic dispensation, very different from fordism, and based partly on rapidly evolving digital technologies, is beginning to exert major impacts on the evolutionary development of large cities. By the same token, cities are virtually everywhere subject to deeply polarizing tendencies in their labor market structures, in patterns of social life, and in political dispositions. These trends have by no means swept away all the urban residues of the past, and they differ in detail from place to place, but they certainly do represent major currents in the world today, and they provide important clues about the lineaments of a new twenty-first-century urbanism that seems to be coming increasingly into view. The chapters that follow will deal in some detail with these trends, but in the interim, I offer a few introductory comments about the global geography of cities that appears to be taking shape today.

Consider Fig. 5.5, which displays in diagrammatic form some basic spatial patterns in the contemporary world. The key element of the figure is a system of global city-regions, representing the largest and the most complex urban units in the world today. Each city-region is defined at a minimum as a central core made up of a large metropolitan area combined with a surrounding hinterland or urban field comprising territory that is strongly tied to the core. The hinterland itself may comprise satellite urban

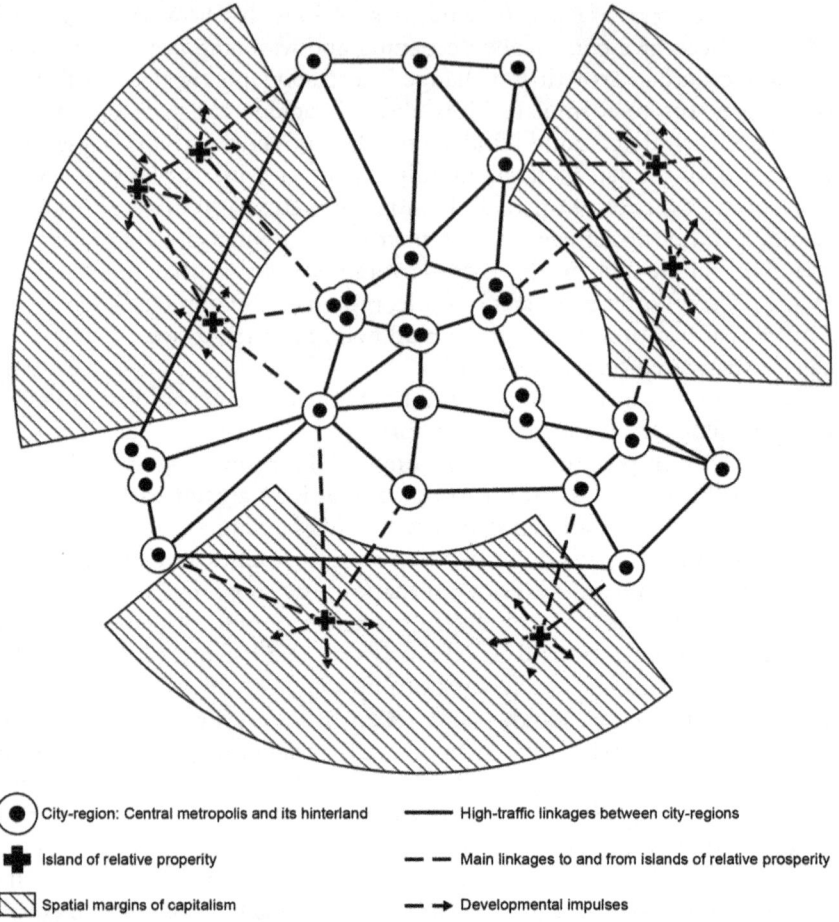

Fig. 5.5 The global multiplex of city-regions within the world system: a schematic representation

settlements. In addition, as shown in Fig. 5.4, individual city-regions may coalesce to form amoeba-like manifolds, or agglomerations within agglomerations, sometimes extending over a range of hundreds of miles. In these cases, the urban land nexus takes on the semblance of multiple polarized land-use systems that overlap and interpenetrate with one another. Between these city-regions lie interstitial spaces occupied by sundry types of land uses and landscapes, together with multitudes of small and medium-sized urban centers. Many of these centers retain traditional features in their social life and physical form, but large numbers of them are also increasingly articulated with major city-regions and through them with world capitalism. Figure 5.4 also shows high-traffic linkages representing flows of goods, services, and people between global city-regions. These linkages include the commodity chains based on subcontracting and other input-output relationships that now increasingly tie urban areas in different parts of the world together in geographically fragmented production networks controlled by corporate entities.[24]

Beyond the multiplex of global city-regions lie the spatial margins of capitalism. These are shown in Fig. 5.4 as three spatially disconnected swaths of territory that represent the retreating residues of the old-world periphery. The margins are no doubt where traditional styles of life and urbanization are most likely to be found in today's world. However, the margins also harbor large cities, or what are referred to in Fig. 5.5 as islands of relative prosperity, with dynamic and increasingly competitive economies, though also usually with a large underclass of unemployed and underemployed migrants from the countryside. These islands of relative prosperity are directly linked into the global economy and are subject to large-scale transformation as capitalist, social, and property relations progressively take hold on their internal organization. They also generate developmental impulses that radiate spatially outward, helping to foster economic growth in surrounding territories, and thus contributing further to the geographic retreat of the margins. As they develop, these islands eventually accede to the condition of full-blown city-regions and become integrated as major nodes into global capitalism, thus following in the footsteps of Hong Kong, Singapore, and numerous other cities of the former Third World that have already shifted from peripherality to global-city status. One city that seems currently to be on the point of making this transition is Accra, Ghana, which, as Grant and Nijman have written, is now growing apace on the basis of its dynamic manufacturing, producer services, and financial sectors.[25] Other possible contenders for global city-region status in intertropical Africa are Dakar, Lagos, and Nairobi.

Large city-regions are a relatively novel phenomenon, and Harrison and Hoyler have recently referred to them as a distinctive "new urban form."[26] As we move more deeply into the twenty-first century, they are becoming increasingly widespread and are in some instances attaining gargantuan dimensions. Southern California is one such city-region, extending for some 450 miles from north to south and 300 miles from east to west with a total population of some 22 million. Even more dramatic instances at the present time are represented by the three great urban regions of eastern China, namely, Beijing-Tianjin-Tangshan, the Yangtze River Delta focused on Shanghai, and the Pearl River Delta anchored at its western and eastern ends by Guangzhou and Hong Kong, respectively.[27] Each of these Chinese city-regions has anywhere from 120 to 140 million inhabitants. As yet these regions are far from operating as fully integrated urban units, and they remain extremely fragmented in administrative terms. Nevertheless, considerable policy efforts are now being invested in efforts to link their component parts together by means of upgraded transport infrastructure in the attempt to build more functionally coherent entities and to create unprecedented regional competitive advantages for Chinese industries.[28]

According to the World Bank, 80% of global GDP today is generated in cities,[29] and we can be fairly confident that a not-insignificant proportion of this amount comes from large city-regions, most of them no doubt in the Global North, but also, and to a rapidly increasing degree, in the Global South. The selected set of 42 large global cities alone (15 of them in the South) that make up the current Global Power City Index published by the Mori Memorial Foundation in Tokyo generate as much as 11% of the world's GDP.[30] In the twenty-first century, city-regions constitute the basic drivers of the global economy in terms of production, employment, and innovation, and there is every likelihood that they will continue to consolidate their position in this regard over the future decades.

Point Counterpoint

Much of the preceding commentary focuses on worldwide patterns of urbanization dominated by a system of global city-regions that are separated from one another by a wide variety of interstitial spaces including large numbers of small and medium-sized towns. Several different currents in the contemporary urban studies literature take issue with a number of different points of emphasis in this narrative, and above all with its overarching search for theoretical generality. Hence it is apposite here to confront at least some of the arguments proposed by these alternative voices.

Post-colonial urban theorists, in particular, are apt to be highly skeptical of work that they see as being aligned with a "world cities" analytical agenda. Protests in this regard have been raised against so-called metrocentricity, or an emphasis on large, successful, economically dynamic cities at the expense of cities that lie more toward the margins of the world system.[31]

Likewise, Robinson refers to a "regulating fiction" by which the same emphasis is supposed to conjure up pejorative assessments of the cities in the Global South.[32] Many post-colonial theorists are also critical of studies that fail to give due weight to the particularities of individual cities.[33] Robinson, for example, castigates much of the extant literature of urban studies for its alleged undue neglect of these particularities and above all of those many cities in the Global South, which, as she says, lie "off the map." She has also been much concerned to establish the principle that cities are invariably "ordinary," in the sense that there can be no privilege accorded to given cities on the basis of some special criterion of judgment, such as size, or function, or location.[34] The preferred approach of Robinson and many other post-colonial theorists to the investigation of cities entails an inductive comparativism that insists on the unique and irreducible identity of every individual city. In addition, Robinson along with Roy and others, is deeply distrustful of theoretical generalizations about cities, especially where they involve the application of (allegedly Eurocentric) concepts developed in the Global North to situations in the Global South.[35]

Post-colonial scholars are quite right to complain about the relative neglect of the cities of the Global South in the scholarly literature and to call for a more cosmopolitan urban geography. They are also right to insist that individual cities differ from one another—often greatly—in regard to their internal composition. As I have tried to demonstrate in Chap. 2, however, it is incorrect to assert that different cities are absolutely incommensurable with one another. To the contrary, there are many commonalities across cities that can be accommodated within the concept of the constitution of the city that is offered here. This concept is far from encompassing the totality of urban reality, though it does claim to offer the tools whereby we can distinguish between those things that are properly urban and those that are not. More importantly, there is nothing in this concept that is in principle at odds with a focus on diversity and comparative methodologies. As for possible Eurocentric bias, the most effective response to this putative line of critique is quite simple. If theories that emanate from one cultural or geographical situation are intrinsically invalid when applied in another then presumably we simply retreat into our own respective solitudes. If, on the other hand, a theoretical construct can be shown to be misconceived on grounds other than its own solipsism, then in principle, its errors of commission or omission can be demonstrated and corrected by means of appeals to empirical evidence and reasoned argument. I readily offer the ideas presented here for potential disconfirmation by those who are skeptical of their relevance to an understanding of urbanization at large.

There is, in addition, a strong epistemological case to be made for *not* treating every city in every investigation as equally "ordinary," or deserving of attention, for the excellent reason that (analytically and politically) meaningful research always and necessarily entails selective or evaluative decisions that highlight significant aspects of the question in hand. In this light, any attempt to make sense of many of the most pressing human predicaments and opportunities in the current conjuncture cannot avoid emphatic reference to the sheer magnitude and complexity of the city-regions and urban megaregions of the world (in both the Global North and the Global South) and their ever-intensifying status as economic engines and political actors on the global stage. It is scarcely reasonable in any case, to relegate these exceptionally significant places to the status of "ordinary" sites of urban life in the twenty-first century.[36] Contrary to what is often implied in the literature, propositions like this in no way necessarily silence, or deform, or obscure the role that small cities or any other forms of human settlement play in the contemporary world. Bunnell and Maringanti (echoing Robinson) write that "global-city research reproduces hierarchies of attention that serve to drop most cities in most regions of the world off the map."[37] The point, however, is that paying "attention" to one thing rather than to another is often no more than innocent silence. Culpable or constructed silences (i.e. that by reason of their ontological or epistemological commitments actively impede our ability to perceive or to understand other situations) are, of course, another matter. In the absence of any demonstrated culpability of this sort, it is far from clear why or how consideration of one empirical category of cities impedes consideration of other empirical categories of cities.

These remarks now bring us back to the concept of planetary urbanism, which has already been discussed in Chap. 2. Here, I shall simply reiterate one main point in response to the concept as formulated by Brenner and Schmid. Recall that this idea goes well beyond the suggestion that cities are densely scattered over much of the contemporary world, or that the majority of the world's population is concentrated in cities. To the contrary, it is centrally devoted to the proposition that the urban in the twenty-first century is now spread out in a continuous, laminated film across the surface of the globe.[38] This intentional conceptual deliquescence of the urban—as the term is commonly understood—and its reassignment to the level of geographic space as a whole has been endorsed by like-minded analysts who have argued that the city is a purely ideological construct.[39] If my own arguments about agglomeration and the formation of the urban land nexus are correct, it follows that the city is a territorially finite social entity organized around a unique and dominant center of gravity and endowed with *sui generis* internal relationships and synergies that distinguish it from the rest of society. By the same token, the city always has an ontological identity that differentiates it from its external spatial milieu, even if these two domains of geographic reality also interact continuously with one another. When we consider that this external milieu is constituted out of diverse regional elements such as forests, tracts of commercial agriculture, pastoral grasslands, banana plantations, fishing grounds, mining camps, deserts, and so on, it becomes even more of a stretch to claim that it has been transformed into an overarching urbanism, unless the urban is simply dissolved away by assimilating it (with considerable loss of analytical traction) into a more encompassing conceptual abstraction like, say, the space-economy of global capitalism. True enough, global capitalism contains the urban as one distinctive element of the space-economy, but no value added whatever is to be obtained, either in analytical terms or from the perspective of practical policy-making, by conflating them indiscriminately within the oxymoron of planetary urbanization.

Notes

1. B. J. L. Berry, "Cities as systems within systems of cities," *Papers in Regional Science*, 13, 1964, 147–163.
2. The view that the city is defined by its external relationships is strongly developed in A. Amin and N. Thrift, *Cities: Reimagining the Urban*, Cambridge: Polity, 2002. Roy, drawing on Mouffe, writes about the "constitutive outside" of the city as critical to any understanding of the urban, and, mysteriously, of its "undecidability"; see A. Roy, "What is urban about critical urban theory?" *Urban Geography*, 37, 2016, 810–823.
3. G. K. Zipf, *Human Behavior and the Principle of Least Effort: An Introduction to Human Ecology*, Cambridge, MA: Addison-Wesley, 1949.
4. X. Gabaix, "Zipf's law for cities: an explanation," *Quarterly Journal of Economics*, 114, 1999, 739–767.
5. G. Duranton, *City Size Distributions as a Consequence of the Growth Process*, CEP Discussion Paper 550, Centre for Economic Performance, London School of Economics and Political Science, 2002.
6. The Canadian urban system is also an exception to the rank-size rule. The difference in population between Canada's two largest cities, Toronto and Montreal, is much less than it would be if the strict rank-size rule applied. This state of affairs reflects the function of these two cities as major foci relative to English and French Canada, respectively. The Canadian exception was actually more marked in the past than it is today.

7. K. Junius, "Primacy and economic development: bell shaped or parallel growth of cities?" *Journal of Economic Development*, 24, 1999, 1–22; J. R. Short and L. M. Pinet-Peralta, "Urban primacy: reopening the debate," *Geography Compass*, 3, 2009, 1245–1266; A. F. Ades and E. L. Glaeser, "Trade and circuses: explaining urban giants," *Quarterly Journal of Economics*, 110, 1995, 195–227; J. C. Davis and J. V. Henderson, "Evidence on the political economy of the urbanization process," *Journal of Urban Economics*, 53, 2003, 98–125.
8. A. J. Venables, "European integration: a view from geographical economics," *Swedish Economic Policy Review*, 12, 2005, 143–169.
9. Cf. K-H. Midelfart, H. G. Overman and A. J. Venables, "Monetary union and the economic geography of Europe," *Journal of Common Market Studies*, 41, 2003, 847–868.
10. Cf. A. R. Winger, "Finally, a withering away of cities," *Futures*, 2, 1997, 251–256.
11. United Nations, Department of Economic and Social Affairs, Population Division, *World Urbanization Prospects* (2014 revision).
12. R. Florida, T. Gulden and C. Mellander, "The rise of the mega-region," *Cambridge Journal of Regions, Economy and Society*, 1, 2008, 459–476; J. Harrison and M. Hoyler, "Megaregions: foundations, frailties, futures," pp. 1–28 in J. Harrison and M. Hoyler (eds.) *Megaregions: Globalization's New Urban Form?* Cheltenham: Edward Elgar, 2015; A. J. Scott, J. Agnew, E. W. Soja and M. Storper, "Global city-regions," pp. 11–32 in A. J. Scott (ed.) *Global City-Regions: Trends, Theory, Policy*, Oxford: Oxford University Press, 2001.
13. P. Hall and K. Pain, *The Polycentric Metropolis: Learning from Mega-City Regions in Europe*, London: Earthscan, 2006, p. 3.
14. E. Brown, B. Derudder, C. Parnreiter, W. Pelipessy, P. J. Taylor and F. Witlox, "World city networks and global commodity chains," pp. 15–41 in B. Derudder and F. Witlox (eds.) *Commodity Chains and World Cities*, Oxford: Wiley-Blackwell, 2010.
15. J. V. Henderson, "The urbanization process and economic growth: the so-what question," *Journal of Economic Growth*, 8, 2003, 47–71; R. L. Moomaw, "Urbanization and economic development: a bias toward large cities?" *Journal of Urban Economics*, 40, 1996, 13–37.
16. Any attempt to establish a fully identified model of the interrelationships between rates of urbanization and GDP per capita would not only need to consider many other independent variables but would also need to proceed on the basis of a simultaneous equations model. For further commentary on these issues see: R. C. Allen, *Capital Accumulation, Technological Change and the Distribution of Income During the British Industrial Revolution*, Discussion Paper No 239, Department of Economics,

University of Oxford, 2005; D. E. Bloom, D. Canning and G. Fink, "Urbanization and the wealth of nations," *Science*, 319, 2008, 772–775; M. Spence, P. Clarke Annez and R. M. Buckley (eds.), *Urbanization and Growth*, Washington, DC: The International Bank for Reconstruction and Development and the World Bank on Behalf of the Commission on Growth and Development, 2009.
17. A. Gilbert, *The Latin American City*, London: Latin American Bureau, 1994; A. Portes, B. R. Roberts, and A. Grimson, *Ciudades Latinoamericanas: Un Análisis Comparativo en el Umbral del Nuevo Siglo*, Buenos Aires: Prometeo Libros, 2005.
18. J. Friedmann, *China's Urban Transition*, Minneapolis: University of Minnesota Press, 2005.
19. F. Wu, "Emerging Chinese cities: implications for global urban studies," *Professional Geographer*, 68, 2016, 338–348.
20. World Bank, *World Development Indicators*, http://www.data.worldbank.org/data-catalog/world-development-indicators
21. P. Hall, *The World Cities*, London: Weidenfeld and Nicolson, 1966.
22. J. Friedmann and G. Wolff, "World city formation: an agenda for research and action, *International Journal of Urban and Regional Research*, 6, 1982, 309–344.
23. S. Sassen, *The Global City: New York, London, Tokyo*, Princeton, NJ: Princeton University Press, 1991.
24. P. J. Taylor, *World City Network: A Global Urban Analysis*, London: Routledge, 2004.
25. R. Grant and J. Nijman, "The re-scaling of uneven development in Ghana and India," *Tijdschrift voor Economische en Sociale Geografie*, 95, 2004, 467–481.
26. J. Harrison and M. Hoyler, *op. cit.*, 2015.
27. J. Bie, M. de Jong and B. Derudder, "Greater Pearl River Delta: historical evolution towards a global city-region," *Journal of Urban Technology*, 22, 2015, 103–123; Z. Xu "Globalization and the megaregion: investigating the evolution of the Pearl River Delta in a historical perspective," pp. 175–199 in J. Harrison and M. Hoyler (eds.) *op. cit.*, 2015; Y. Zheng, T Chen, J. Cai and S. Liu, "Regional concentration and region-based urban transition: China's mega-urban region formation," *Urban Geography*, 30, 312–333.
28. J. Xu and A. G. O. Yeh, Re-building regulation and re-inventing governance in the Pearl River Delta, China," *Urban Policy and Research*, 30, 2012, 385–401.
29. http://www.worldbank.org/en/topic/urbandevelopment/overview
30. Global Power City Index, *Yearbook 2016*, Institute for Urban Strategies, The Mori memorial Foundation.

31. T. Bunnell and A. Maringanti, "Practising urban and regional research beyond metrocentricity," *International Journal of Urban and Regional Research*, 34, 2010, 415–420.
32. J. Robinson, "Global and world cities: a view from off the map," *International Journal of Urban and Regional Research*, 26, 2002, 531–554.
33. See, in particular, A. Roy, "The 21st-century metropolis: new geographies of theory," *Regional Studies*, 43, 2009, 819–830; A. Roy, "Slumdog cities: rethinking subaltern urbanism," *Journal of Urban and Regional Research*, 35, 2011, 223–238; E. Sheppard, H. Leitner and A Maringanti, "Provincializing global urbanism: a manifesto," *Urban Geography*, 34, 2013, 893–900.
34. J. Robinson, *Ordinary Cities: Between Modernity and Development*, London: Routledge, 2006. See also: J. Robinson, "Cities in a world of cities: the comparative gesture," *International Journal of Urban and Regional Research*, 35, 2011, 1–23.
35. A. Roy, *op. cit.*, 2009 and 2011.
36. Cf. P. J. Taylor, *Extraordinary Cities: Millennia of Moral Syndromes, World-Systems and City/State Relations*, Cheltenham: Edward Elgar, 2013.
37. Bunnell and Maringanti, *op. cit.*, 2010, p. 417.
38. N. Brenner and C. Schmid, "The urban age in question," *International Journal of Urban and Regional Research*, 38, 2014, 731–755; N. Brenner and C. Schmid, "Towards a new epistemology of the urban," *City*, 19, 2015, 151–182.
39. See, for example, H. Angelo and D. Wachsmuth, "Urbanizing urban political economy: a critique of methodological cityism," *International Journal of Urban and Regional Research*, 39, 2015, 16–27.

CHAPTER 6

The Third Wave

Since the 1980s, capitalism has evidently been moving into the formative phase of a third historic wave of development that is bringing in its train major changes in economic and social structure as well as in patterns of urbanization. On the one hand, as revealed in Tables 5.1, 5.2, and 5.3, there has been a clear resurgence of metropolitan growth not just in the old-established capitalist countries but also in many parts of the former world periphery. On the other hand, extreme forms of income polarization are becoming more marked in cities everywhere. At the same time, an overarching process of global economic integration is bringing all cities into closer and more systemic relationship with one another, as manifest above all in the evolving worldwide mosaic of city-regions and their dependent hinterlands (Fig. 5.5). In view of these changing circumstances, four fundamental questions now need to be addressed: What are the principal features of this third wave of capitalist development? What conditions have brought it forth? Why and how is it reshaping so much of contemporary life? What are its effects on urbanization processes, and specifically, on the functions and configuration of the urban land nexus? In the search for answers to these questions, I shall lay out a broad schematic view in this chapter of how capitalism is being radically reshaped in the twenty-first century by significant new trends in technological development, human capital formation, and the organization of geographic space, and in the succeeding three chapters, I shall attempt to trace out the principal effects of these trends on basic patterns of urbanization.

Conceptual Preliminaries

The broad socio-economic framework of capitalism can be identified in the first instance in terms of two interlocking features. On the one hand, firms deploy capital and labor in processes of production, thereby generating the physical wealth of society and relevant income shares. On the other hand, the legal and constitutional order governing these arrangements rests on the imperative of private property and the privileged status of individual decision-making and behavior. *A fortiori*, these features also represent key categories in any meaningful approach to the analysis of cities in capitalism. Since profits and wages are inversely related to one another at any given moment in time,[1] it follows that firms (i.e. the owners of capital) and workers (the sellers of labor) are inescapably caught up in an agonistic relationship over distribution, as manifest historically in periodic outbreaks of open struggle between the two sides. Competition between firms for the sale of their products, combined with selective purchasing behavior by workers in their role as consumers, brings markets into being. By the same token, firms are engaged in an endless search for competitive advantage, which means in turn that they have powerful incentives to divert their profits, either directly (via outlays on internal assets) or indirectly (via banking and financial institutions) into new investments. As a consequence, capitalism is marked by round after round of capital accumulation and—notwithstanding intermittent business downturns—generally positive rates of economic growth. The different pressures and strains brought on by these processes are played out in complex sequences of technological, social, and economic change, much of it with important impacts on the urban land nexus.

In spite of the endemic volatility of capitalist society, there are extended periods of time, as we learned in Chap. 3, when relatively stable regimes of accumulation or waves of capitalist development come into being.[2] Any given regime or wave can to a large extent be identified by reference to four main structuring elements that provide a relatively coherent framework of production, work, and market activity, namely

- a central ensemble of sectors with relatively high levels of performance in terms of employment, growth, and innovation;
- a set of basic technologies (e.g. water power, electromechanical contrivances, digital systems);

- a system of labor relations and labor market norms (e.g. collective bargaining, lifetime employment, casualization); and
- rules of market competition and exchange (e.g. *laissez-faire*, oligopoly, monopolistic competition).

We might also add a fifth element to this list, namely, the spatial and locational propensities of productive activity (e.g. agglomeration, dispersal, or globalization). However, neither in principle nor in practice can any regime of accumulation survive in the absence of a further structural layer comprising institutions of governance, or, in another vocabulary, a *mode of social regulation*.[3] We have previously noted the significance of regulatory institutions as a condition of subsistence of the urban land nexus, but the argument can now be made more broadly by reference to the congenital incapacity of capitalism to reproduce itself purely on the basis of atomized decision-making and market competition in a regime of private property. These operational conditions are incapable of dealing with the systemic externalities and other market breakdowns that occur pervasively in capitalism. Indeed, many of capitalism's most threatening vulnerabilities arise, precisely, out of socially toxic outcomes (such as recession, financial crisis, or environmental degradation) engendered directly by atomistic decision-making and market competition. The survival of capitalism is therefore always dependent on ancillary institutions of governance and collective order capable of remedial action in regard to these sorts of irrationalities and crises. Competitive markets themselves require an infrastructure of enforceable legal arrangements in order to operate in a well-ordered fashion. For these reasons, every capitalist regime of accumulation is associated in practice with an array of institutions and foci of political authority whose function is to find ways as best they can of dealing with recurrent problems that cannot be resolved effectively by social mechanisms based purely on market relations.

These remarks now help us to outline some of the main ingredients of the third wave that is currently gathering momentum. As fordism has waned, many new and dynamic sectors of production, from high-technology manufacturing to cultural industries have moved into leading positions within the capitalist economic system, and many older sectors, from cars to financial services, have been radically transformed by recent technological shifts. These shifts themselves are of paradigmatic significance, founded as they are on the widespread digitization of production and salient modifications of human capital requirements in production. Labor markets in the advanced capitalist countries have become very much more flexible and competitive and for the same reasons more stringent than they were in the fordist era when unionization was widespread. Labor market conditions are even harsher in different cities of the erstwhile Third World, where huge and growing concentrations of impoverished individuals eke out a living in the informal sector. Markets for almost all kinds of products and services are also becoming intensely competitive, and this trend is reinforced by the relentless expansion of international trading relationships. In addition, the geographical bases of the third wave are simultaneously local and global, in the sense that large diversified city-regions function as the principal specialized foci of the economy while at the same time being linked in complex interactions with one another across the entire world. Beyond the spatial hinterlands of these city-regions lie disparate spaces together with small and medium-sized urban centers at many different levels of economic development and cultural autonomy, but even these are more or less articulated with global capitalism. Modes of regulation of this still-materializing regime of accumulation differ widely from country to country, though all of them generally partake of one version or another of "neoliberalism." This is a term that has been somewhat abused by overextension,[4] but it is helpful as a way of designating the much wider exposure of all segments of society to market discipline than was the case in classical fordism, and, concomitantly, the broad retreat in the more advanced capitalist countries from state-mandated welfare support of the unemployed, the disabled, and the destitute.

From Late Capitalism to Post-Fordism

The Collapsing Second Wave

Until the late 1960s and early 1970s, the fordist regime of accumulation and the Keynesian welfare-statist mode of social regulation that had been politically woven into and around it worked with such efficacy that the post-War years are often referred to as the golden age of capitalism.[5] By the mid-1970s, however, fordism was showing definite signs of exhaustion. Domestic markets for mass-produced goods were becoming saturated so that sales came to depend only on sluggish periodic replacement demands. Japanese firms, especially car producers, were now also making serious competitive incursions into American and European markets, thus compounding the effects of domestic oversupply. These negative trends were reinforced in the United States by increasing instability in macroeconomic arrangements as reflected in the uncoupling of the dollar from the gold standard in 1971 and rising deficits in governmental finances. The fiscal crisis was compounded by the oil shock of 1973, the mounting budgetary burden of the Vietnam War, and rapidly accelerating inflation. As the 1970s wore on, a number of Third World countries, most especially in Latin America where import-substitution policies were still prevalent, steadily succumbed to an exacerbated debt crunch leading to a so-called lost decade of stagnation and decline.

Under the multiple stresses they were subjected to in the 1970s and early 1980s, the mass-production economies of North America and Western Europe endured an acute restructuring crisis with notably disastrous effects on established centers of fordist industry. Formerly thriving manufacturing cities were now faced with massive job losses and decline, and the endemic process of geographic dispersal to low-wage locations, which had always been a feature of the economic geography of fordism, was now becoming a routine. Moreover, industrial dispersal was by this time bypassing domestic peripheries in favor of countries where abundant cheap labor was available and where political conditions were favorable to foreign capital. The concomitant development of special economic zones, export processing platforms, and maquiladoras in these countries made them yet more attractive to foreign direct investment and to subcontracting operations controlled from the Global North thus intensifying the crisis in the core. The resulting transformation of the long established Manufacturing Belts of North America and Western Europe into declining rust belts signaled the demise of what had been for the greater part of a century a relatively stable configuration of economic and urban geography comprising the powerhouse of world capitalism.

This turn of events also did much to erode confidence in conventional theoretical and analytical accounts of urban and regional development and helped to ignite a rebirth over the 1970s of Marxian and *Marxisant* investigations into the spatial foundations of capitalist society. Among the research offerings that came forward on urban and regional issues at this time were several notably pessimistic studies of job losses and industrial plant closures in the large manufacturing cities of North America and Western Europe. So marked were the economic depredations associated with these crisis conditions in the United States that Bluestone and Harrison, two influential observers of the scene, proclaimed that a long-term process of deindustrialization had set in and could only be reversed by means of a radical reform of capitalist social and property relations as a whole.[6] Recession and rising unemployment in Western Europe were stimulating equally gloomy accounts of the future prospects of traditional industrial regions of Britain, France, Germany, and the Low Countries.[7] And despite the early successes of import-substitution strategies, many analysts, above all in Latin America, became increasingly convinced that the Third World would remain stubbornly locked into a state of economic dependency and underdevelopment so long as a capitalist order prevailed.[8] This was a time when radical economists, with Ernest Mandel perhaps most forcefully in the lead, were actively promoting the idea that the then-current situation could best be described in terms of "late capitalism," with the distinct imputation that the end was nigh.[9]

The Post-Fordist Moment

Meanwhile, alternative and somewhat more prescient narratives about the prospects of capitalist society and the development of cities and regions were emerging from a variety of sources. One of the more remarkable pronouncements on the future of capitalism, both in terms of foresight and intellectual range, was Daniel Bell's *The Coming of Post-Industrial Society*, published in 1973,[10] just a year after the original German edition of Mandel's book on late capitalism. Bell perhaps laid too much emphasis on the prospective wholesale evacuation of manufacturing from capitalism, and he undoubtedly went astray in predicting the deepening and widening of bureaucracy as one of the key features of his "post-industrial" society, but he was prophetic in his claim that science, cognitive values, information, and intellectual labor would come to play a major role in the economy of the future. In a memorable passage, Bell writes "The concept of post-industrial society emphasizes the centrality of theoretical knowledge as the axis around which new technology, economic growth, and the stratification of society will be organized" (p. 112). He also alludes to "the rise of a new class," a theme that was to be rehearsed a few years later by Alvin Gouldner, who pointed to the mounting significance of intellectuals and technocrats in a cosmopolitan society marked by secularization, rationality, critical discourse (communication via reasoned argument as opposed to the exercise of authority), and the waning of the patriarchal family.[11] Many of the changes anticipated by Bell and Gouldner were already identifiable in the 1970s in various corners of advanced capitalist society. They were especially apparent in segments of the economy where, in contrast to declining fordist industry, employment growth and the reagglomeration of productive activity were actively occurring. Some of these segments, such as finance, banking, and business services were expanding in core areas of large metropolitan areas, while others were colonizing diverse new industrial spaces, as, for example, in the US Sunbelt where clusters of technology-intensive industries were springing up, and in the so-called Third Italy, where many small and medium-sized towns were experiencing new growth on the basis of rejuvenated craft production systems.[12]

Silicon Valley in the Bay Area of California was the canonical case of resurgent agglomeration and economic growth during the climacteric of fordism in the 1970s. Although the origins of this peculiar industrial cluster can be traced back to the mid-1950s and even earlier, the first published allusion to Silicon Valley, as such, was in a series of three articles written by Don C. Hoefler in 1971 for the trade magazine *Electronic News*.[13] These pointed to the region's growing importance as the epicenter of the semiconductor and computer industry, which itself was one of the drivers pushing the American economy beyond fordism. In 1983, AnnaLee Saxenian published a landmark paper drawing attention to the developmental dynamics of Silicon Valley specifically as an agglomerated production system imbricated within a supporting structure of urban land uses.[14] Subsequent work by various scholars showed how the agglomeration processes underpinning Silicon Valley's economic vibrancy could be analyzed in terms of an efficient social division of labor, a fluid local labor market for engineers and technicians, and a revolving system of interfirm transactional relationships that sustained high levels of information exchange and innovation.[15]

The renaissance of the Third Italy was also pivotal in shaping ideas about the world that was emerging as fordism approached its final years in the 1970s. Up to this time, the economic geography of Italy had usually been portrayed in terms of a bipartite division of the country into the North (focused on the so-called Golden Triangle of Genoa-Milan-Turin), where large-scale fordist manufacturing was concentrated, and the South or *Mezzogiorno*, a region of peasant agriculture and a prime destination for manufacturing branch plants decentralizing from the metropolitan areas of the North. Bagnasco showed as early as 1977 that there was also a "Third Italy" comprising much of the northeast and center of the country. This was an area that harbored many traditional small and medium-sized towns—including the *quattrocento* centers of Florence, Venice, and Bologna—that had been bypassed by fordist industrialization. In spite of the deepening economic crisis in other parts of Italy, the economy of this region was starting in the 1970s to expand on the basis of numerous small-scale, labor-intensive craft or artisanal industries producing high-quality products with a strong fashion and design element, such as shoes, jewelry, leather goods, clothing, ceramics, and furniture.[16] As Bagnasco and other Italian commentators like Becattini,[17] Fuà,[18] Garofoli,[19] and Brusco[20] pointed out, much of the success of craft industry in the Third Italy was due to an organizational model based on the vertical disintegration of production combined with the concentration of firms and workers in specialized industrial districts. Piore and Sabel's *The Second Industrial Divide*, published in 1984, proposed that the peculiar model of industrialization then occurring in the Third Italy represented a foretaste of a new (or reemerging) species of capitalism.[21] Piore and Sabel also came up with the term "flexible specialization" to describe this model, which they characterized as one in which production processes—in contrast to the giantism and rigidities of classical fordist enterprise—are focused on small-batch operations and a constantly shifting spectrum of variations on a particular kind of output (e.g. shirts, gloves, or electronic components).

Concurrently with the appearance of these new spatial formations in the advanced capitalist economies, and even as the crisis of import substitution was reverberating through parts of the Third World, an alternative model of development based on export-oriented industrialization was being pioneered in the world periphery. More precisely, this model was being actively promoted in what were then coming to be known as the Asian Tigers (Hong Kong, Singapore, South Korea, and Taiwan). As in the case of Silicon Valley and the Third Italy, this model, too, was heavily dependent on the formation of specialized industrial districts in both large and small urban centers. In contrast to the quest for economic autarchy that had been the driving imperative of import-substitution policies, export-oriented industrialization focused on attempts to carve out viable niches in the international division of labor, and such was its success that the model spread widely to other low- and medium-income countries, where it has become one of the mainstays of national economic development strategies over the last few decades.[22]

Mass production has by no means disappeared from capitalist society, but after the late 1970s, the diffusion of the model of economic development typified by Silicon Valley, the Third Italy, and the export-oriented industrialization programs of the then-peripheral countries—together with an unprecedented expansion of business and financial services in large cities—marked the early stages of a radically transformed economic geography of capitalism. Along with these changes came a steady shift from the relatively rigid managerial structures that had hitherto prevailed in large firms to the more flexible arrangements that became much more characteristic of production activities after the mid-1970s. To an ever-increasing extent, too, the diverse operating units within multiplant corporations now behaved as quasi-autonomous profit centers, each ensconced in a locational niche where it could benefit from the competitive advantages of the surrounding milieu. Some of these units thus gravitated to the specialized industrial districts that were simultaneously materializing across the globe and where they could readily tap into dense local reservoirs of information and skills to supplement their in-house capacities for innovation and cutting-edge production.

These many crosscurrents of change in the occupational, sectoral, and geographic dimensions of capitalism together with the rapid development of electronic technologies over the 1970s and early 1980s made it clear that the old world of modernist fordism had not just become stalled in a prolonged crisis but was in fact being rapidly superseded. In conjunction with this transformation, the term "post-fordism" began to appear with increasing frequency after the mid to late 1980s as a means of identifying the regime of accumulation that seemed to be in an incipient stage of development, at least in the advanced capitalist countries.[23] The seeds of a new mode of social regulation were also being planted at this time as Thatcher in Britain and Reagan in the United States set about dismantling the Keynesian welfare-statist policy measures that had kept fordism on a reasonably even keel. In their place, various reforms were introduced with the objective of radically opening up society to the full blast of market forces. This shift of political atmosphere, at first referred to as "neoconservatism," directly paved the way for the far-reaching neoliberalism that has prevailed in capitalist countries over the last two or three decades. The reforms implemented by Thatcher and Reagan were spearheaded by assaults on the old trade unions and a significant restructuring of labor markets in the interests of enhanced competition. They also included a significant retreat from government-sponsored social programs of all kinds. There was now a shift toward privatization as the answer to pervasive governmental fiscal crises and a strong reaffirmation of "individual responsibility" as a basic principle of social existence. Different countries pursued this agenda in different ways and at different rates of change, but the end result always pointed in the same direction, namely, to intensified market forces and to what Beck called the "risk society."[24] The stage was now set for the consolidation of the formative stage of the third wave of capitalism, and for major worldwide readjustments in patterns of urban development.

Toward Cognitive-Cultural Capitalism

Digitization Takes Command[25]

Many analysts in the mid-twentieth century thought of fordism as a definitive model of industrialization that would continue to expand in a more or less uninterrupted historical progression due to continual improvement of electromechanical technologies and ever-increasing scale and efficiency in production units. Similarly, the later Schumpeter argued that falling marginal costs in the mass-production system would eventually drive it to a point where large vertically integrated monopolistic corporations would dominate the whole economy.[26] These were perfectly logical projections deduced from the central dynamics of fordism, but, as it happens, the deviousness of history almost always outstrips our theoretical powers of prediction.

Among the major factors promoting the eventual efflorescence of the third wave of development were the advances being made in digital technologies of calculation, data storage, and communication, beginning with the emergence of computers and the invention of the transistor as early as the 1940s. Over the 1950s, 1960s, and 1970s, improvements in these technologies relied to a very significant extent on military funding rather than on their commercial applications, and their social impacts were relatively restrained. By the 1980s, however, steep reductions in the costs of computing and automation were being realized and digital technologies began to diffuse with remarkable rapidity across the whole domain of industry and commerce and even to intrude into social life. These developments helped to spur the creation of many new industries and to stimulate the restructuring of more traditional sectors of production.

As Levy and Murnane point out, computers have contradictory effects on labor processes depending on the nature and complexity of the work to be performed.[27] On the one hand, computers and computer-driven machinery represent a ready *substitute* for standardized work and for work that follows algorithmic routines, no matter whether the relevant tasks consist of manual operations (like repetitive assembly, fabricating, and sorting procedures) or mental tasks (like accounting, calculating, and record keeping). Once a computer is properly programmed, it can perform work tasks like these virtually endlessly and with extreme accuracy and rapidity. Digital technologies are therefore taking the place of many different kinds of repetitive or formulaic labor processes in the advanced capitalist economies, and various types of occupations (e.g. print setters, switchboard operators, draftsmen, and typists) are now effectively vanishing from factories and offices. On other hand, computers also *complement* human labor by enhancing the selective capacities and operational powers of the individual worker as well as by making huge amounts of information available at the touch of a button. Even where work calls for human skills that cannot easily be replicated in digital technologies, like creativity, imagination, empathy, ethical judgment, leadership, negotiating abilities, critical thinking, social perceptiveness, cultural sensitivity, and so on, computers often provide critical assistance by making it possible to experiment with alternative solutions, to communicate more effectively, and to access large pools of data. Artisanal work, too, can benefit significantly from digital technologies by reason of their power to enhance craft skills and to search out possibilities for more expressive treatment of physical materials.

As these contending currents of substitution and complementarity work themselves out, employment in routine forms of labor—both manual and mental—is steadily diminishing, leading to high levels of unemployment among unskilled and semiskilled workers, while the number of workers in non-routine jobs is mounting rapidly. At the same time, it is important to note that while non-routine jobs are often well paid and socially prestigious, many of them lie at the opposite end of the scale. Some of these low-grade non-routine jobs are occupied by neophytes or aspirants who have not yet accumulated sufficient experience, skill, or reputational capital to enable them to climb to higher levels of the employment ladder. More importantly for the argument that follows, other non-routine jobs coincide with the run-of-the-mill service occupations that abound in third-wave capitalism and that have become one of the mainstays of the employment systems of large cities today.

Human Capital Issues

Partial but reasonably persuasive evidence in support of these arguments about technological change and occupational readjustment in

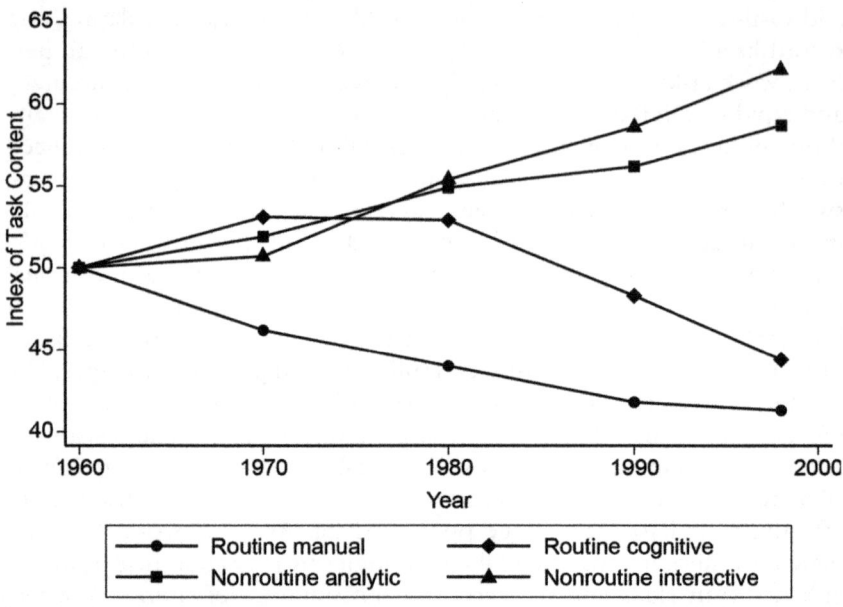

Fig. 6.1 US labor force characteristics, routine and non-routine task content, 1960–1998. Redrafted with modifications from: D. H. Autor, F. Levy and R. J. Murnane, "The skill content of recent technological change: an empirical exploration," *Quarterly Journal of Economics*, 118, 2003, 1279–1333

the contemporary economy is adduced in Fig. 6.1. The figure is based on calculations by Autor *et al.*, who offer measures of the incidence of routine manual, routine cognitive, non-routine analytic, and non-routine interactive classes of work in the American economy between 1960 and 1998, that is, from the precomputer era to a time when digital technologies had made very significant inroads into the workplace.[28] Over this designated period, the incidence of routine manual tasks in the US labor force fell continuously and precipitously, while routine cognitive tasks first of all increased slightly from 1960 to 1970 but then also declined sharply. By contrast, both non-routine analytic and non-routine interactive tasks grew strongly and consistently from 1960 to 1998. Unfortunately, the data do not allow us to refine the analysis in order to distinguish between changes due to computerization and changes due to other factors. For example, some of the decline of routine tasks is unquestionably a consequence of offshore movement of blue-collar jobs, while at least some of the rise of non-routine tasks can probably be ascribed to growing market demand (e.g. for personal services) without any particular reference to technological shifts. Even so, Hicks and Devaraj estimate for the period from 2000 to 2010 that as much as 88% of job losses in American manufacturing can be ascribed to automation.[29]

Complementary indications of the effects of digital technologies on occupational change in the United States are presented in Fig. 6.2, which refers to variations in the labor force in five main occupational groupings between 1980 and 2010. The five groupings are: (a) blue-collar workers (operators and fabricators); (b) clerical and allied occupations (secretaries and stenographers, records-processing personnel, telephone operators, and office clerks); (c) sales occupations (insurance sales, retail cashiers); (d) service occupations (housekeepers, guards, waiters, janitors, and porters); and (e) managers and professionals (a category that includes a great variety of non-routine administrative, scientific, medical, legal, vocational, and artistic occupations). The first four of these categories are for the most part low-wage occupations while the fifth primarily represents middle- to high-wage occupations. All five of them have diagnostic value in the present context, for despite the fact that each of them exhibits a degree of internal heterogeneity, they enable us to make some further assessments of shifts in the incidence of routinized and non-routinized work in advanced capitalist society. We consider each occupational category in turn. First, blue-collar occupations commonly entail routinized manual work focused on operations like machine minding and assembly-line maneuvers. Work of this sort is highly susceptible to automation, and predictably, the labor force in these occupations in the United States fell in absolute terms by 24.7% between 1980 and 2010. Second, clerical and allied occupations comprise a range of routine tasks such as filing, sorting, and accounting, and non-routine tasks such as administrative support and reception work. Unsurprisingly, then, the directions of employment change in these occupations are mixed, with the number of workers increasing in absolute numbers by 30.2% between 1980 and 2010, but then falling as a percentage of the total labor force from 16.1% to 14.1%. Third, employment in sales occupations increased modestly from 9.7% to 11.1% of the labor force from 1980 to 2010. Much of this growth has been in the retail segment, where, despite the automation of certain operations, face-to-face interaction with customers remains a critical part of the job. Fourth, service personnel, from housekeepers to waiters, are apt

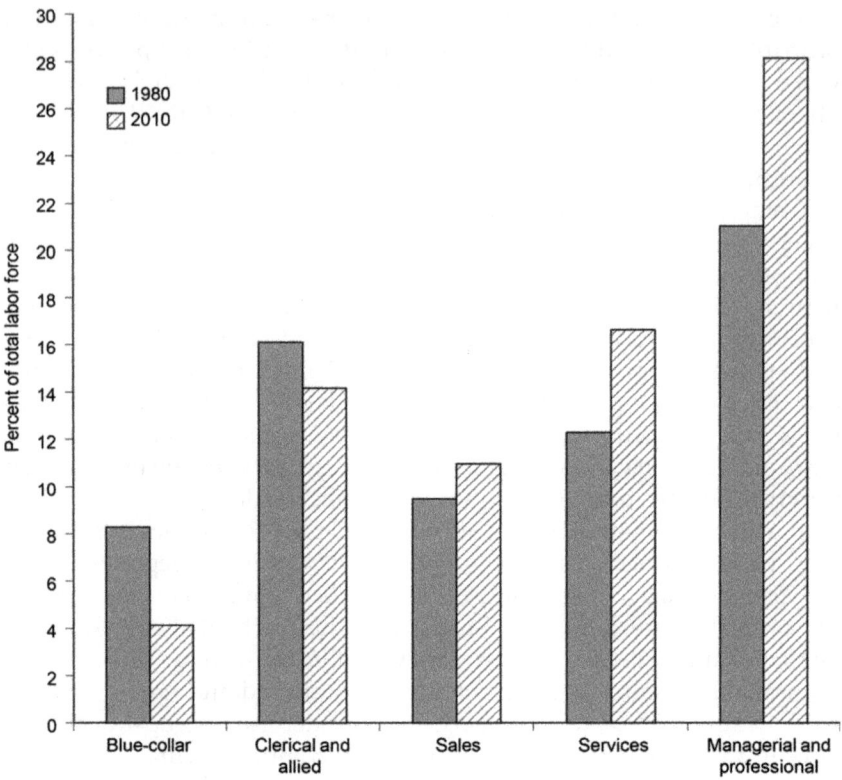

Fig. 6.2 Workers in the labor force in selected occupational groupings as a percentage of the total labor force in the United States, 1980 and 2010. Groupings are defined in terms of the IPUMS OCC1990 classification of occupations, and each pair of groupings has been standardized with respect to its detailed internal occupational composition. See text for further definition of occupational groupings. Source: *Integrated Public Use Microdata Series: Version 6.0*, University of Minnesota, 2015

to face workloads that are predominantly non-routine, and even though wage levels in these occupations are relatively low, the work generally entails interpersonal relationships and irregular sequences of actions that resist automation. Symptomatically, the labor force in service occupations increased appreciably from 12.3% to 16.6% of the total US labor force in the 1980–2010 period. Fifth, the number of individuals in managerial and professional occupations (which coincide with a great variety of non-routine administrative, scientific, medical, legal, vocational, and artistic pursuits) expanded at about the same rate as service occupations from 21.2% to 28.2% of the labor force.

Again, then, the overall body of evidence is consistent with the claim that automation has been selectively eliminating routine jobs in recent decades while non-routine jobs have tended to grow. These remarks are corroborated by parallel shifts in the incidence of human capital in the US labor force. Human capital is a complex, multidimensional phenomenon for which meaningful concrete measures are notoriously difficult to obtain. One variable, however, is widely used as a proxy, namely, the percentage of the labor force with a bachelor's degree or equivalent, and fortunately, excellent information on this yardstick is readily available. In 1980, the percentage of the labor force of the United States with a bachelor's degree or equivalent was 17.7%; by 2010, figure was equal to 29.7%. These changes represent a growth in terms of numbers of workers of almost 150%, and they are testimony to a conspicuous increase in the intellectual capacities of the labor force. Moreover, for the 283 metropolitan areas recorded in the American Community Survey in 2010, the simple correlation between the percentage of the total labor force with a bachelor's degree or equivalent and the magnitude of the labor force as a whole (in logarithms) was 0.41, indicating that workers' endowments of human capital increase significantly as metropolitan size increases.

The information set forth in these paragraphs points strongly to major structural changes in occupational composition, job content, and human capital in the American economy since the demise of fordism in the late 1970s and early 1980s. These changes can be ascribed for the most part to the shift from a dominantly mechanical-electrical technological paradigm to one based on digitization and flexible labor processes, though other factors such the assignment of blue-collar work to low-wage countries and changes in structures of demand have also certainly played a role. Intensifying robotization will eventually have even deeper impacts on occupations and work. Already, effective medical diagnosis can be carried out by computers, a turn of events that will undoubtedly have long-run consequences for the organization of the medical profession and the geography of medical service provision. Similarly, three-dimensional printing, still in its infancy, will in all likelihood generate important changes in manufacturing procedures by making it possible to synthesize sequences of complex processes into a single composite operation. Three-dimensional printing will also allow for considerable dispersal of productive activity to places otherwise lacking in locational advantages, though higher-level functions like conception, design, and programming will doubtless remain concentrated in just a few large cities. More experimental technologies, from self-driving cars through virtual reality to artificial intelligence will have even further impact on the organization of the economy and urban development. Even now, the "smart city" is becoming a concrete reality as new electronic technologies are embedded in the urban land nexus thus increasingly reconfiguring urban interaction systems into webs of automated flows and information exchanges by means of intelligent highways, computerized utility grids, GPS systems, and, for better or worse, more intensive social surveillance.

A Prospective View

The early stages of the third wave of capitalist development, as we have seen, were commonly labeled by observers over much of the 1980s and 1990s as a "post-fordist" conjuncture.[30] A signal problem with this terminology is that it refers explicitly only to an antecedent situation as opposed to what is concretely the actual state of affairs. Accordingly, as the incipient third wave started to gather momentum, a number of alternative designations were proposed in attempts to capture more overtly something of its inner essence. Terms such as "flexible accumulation,"[31] "knowledge economy,"[32] "cognitive capitalism,"[33] and "cybercapitalism,"[34] among others, thus started to appear with increasing frequency in the literature after the 1980s and especially after the late 1990s. These designations all allude to important aspects of the third wave, but I prefer to employ the term "cognitive-cultural capitalism" in reference to the situation that is now unfolding, unevenly but discernibly, in capitalist societies everywhere. To be sure, complex structures of knowledge and digital technologies need to be recognized as fundamental components of contemporary capitalism, but the more obvious active social face of the way things are today is presented by the dimensions of cognition and culture in the practice of work. These dimensions are especially evident in the sectoral, occupational, and human capital composition of twenty-first-century capitalism, and in the new division of labor with its distinctive focus on flexible or discretionary decision-making and action in the sphere of production. The notion of a "cognitive-cultural" capitalism, then, captures very explicitly the centrality of non-routine cerebral and expressive forms of work (with or without computers) in *both* high-skill sectors ranging from technology-intensive industry to musical performance *and* in many of the low-skill service activities that have expanded apace over the last few decades.

Divisions of Cognitive and Cultural Labor

In a study of the changing nature of work in the 1990s, Robert Reich averred that "we are living through a transformation that will rearrange the politics and economics of the coming century."[35] Reich argued that a class of workers, somewhat akin to Bell's and Gouldner's new class, and whom he designated as "symbolic analysts," was moving aggressively into a position of prominence in the advanced capitalist economies. He described these workers as being highly qualified, and often highly paid, and engaged in occupations calling for sophisticated levels of intellectual engagement and human interaction. Reich also pointed to a growing class of low-wage workers whose jobs relate to what he called "in-person service provision." These workers, such as hospital attendants, domestic helpers, waiters and waitresses, supermarket checkout clerks, hotel receptionists, gardeners, and security personnel are rarely formally qualified but are expected to display definite capacities for flexibility and intercommunication in their jobs. For example, child minders are called upon to expend considerable emotional energy in dealing with their charges, janitors must know how to go on in an often unpredictable tangle of building layouts and variable sequences of tasks, and hotel clerks are required to manage complex human relations issues in dealing with a great variety of clients.

Subsequent to Reich's analysis of the changing nature of work, Richard Florida produced a study of what appeared to be a newly forming social category that he labeled the "creative class." Florida identified this class in statistical terms as comprising all individuals with the equivalent of a bachelor's degree or better.[36] As such, and despite the different nuances of the terms "creative" and "symbolic," the creative class can be more or less equated to Reich's symbolic analysts. The overall argument proposed by Florida has been much disparaged for its rather breathless celebration of the imputed creative powers of this social fraction and above all for his claims about its alleged capacities for triggering urban renaissance. There can be no doubt that Florida (like Reich) was correct in pointing to the increasing importance of advanced forms of human capital based on the mental and intuitive capacities of workers in leading-edge capitalist production activities. However, Florida gave scant attention to what was happening in the lower reaches of society below his creative class, whereas Reich was quite explicit about the erosion of the blue-collar working class and the increasing incidence of low-wage service providers in advanced capitalism.

The social structure of capitalism today is in fact becoming ever more deeply polarized. At the same time, it differs in several important respects from the white-collar and blue-collar division that characterized the fordist regime.[37] This state of affairs is especially marked in the large metropolitan areas of the advanced capitalist countries. The skilled and highly qualified workers who constitute the prestigious upper tiers of the contemporary labor force in these areas can no longer be simply conflated with the bureaucratic white-collar fraction typical of fordism. To an even lesser extent can they be cast as a troop of conformist organization men.[38] Rather, the upper tier of the labor force now constitutes a new class fraction made up of men and women endowed with markedly varied forms of human capital and whose work is increasingly performed within non-hierarchical project-oriented teams focused on constantly varying input-output configurations. We may designate the members of this fraction as "high-level cognitive-cultural workers" in recognition of their function as suppliers of labor with strongly developed intellectual and affective content.[39] Running parallel to this trend is the growth of a second fraction composed of low-wage service workers, or what I shall occasionally and more polemically refer to in this book as a "new servile class." This fraction has been steadily taking the place of the old blue-collar labor force as the subordinate class in the main urban centers of contemporary capitalism. The primary social function of this class is to provide low-cost service labor in support of the social reproduction of life in the large cities of third-wave capitalism. This function has two main facets, first, to satisfy the "in-person" needs of the upper tier of the labor force, and second, to maintain the physical and organizational fabric of the city, including its buildings, its hard infrastructure, its transport operations, and many of its security and public service arrangements. Since most of these activities must be carried out at the point of consumption and therefore cannot be assigned to offshore production sites, low-wage service workers are found in large numbers precisely in the most dynamic and prosperous metropolitan areas of the third wave.[40] Some service activities are nevertheless marked by internal economies of scale and can be packaged into composite units and efficiently dispatched to distant production sites. This is common in the case of call centers or "digital workshops" set up by American and British telecommunications companies in the Caribbean, India, and the Philippines, where fluent English-speaking workers can be hired at low wages. Other examples are provided by the offshore back-office functions and customer-service operations of large banking and financial institutions and other corporate entities that—like their counterparts in manufacturing sectors—are apt to seek out cheap labor pools in the Global South as locations for many of their operations.

These cheap labor pools are hence very much a part of the new global capitalism, and their ranks have swollen greatly as the large cities of Africa, Asia, and Latin America have been pulled ever more intensely into the orbit of international production and trade. In these cities, the low-wage workers in more or less regular employment fade imperceptibly into large masses of economically and politically marginalized individuals whose collective presence in the urban land nexus is indicated by the slums and shantytowns that abound in these parts of the world. The very success of these cities as globalizing economic centers in contemporary capitalism makes them magnets for the poor and the disenfranchised who pour into their overflowing slum communities from small towns and depressed agricultural areas in the wider national arena. Even in China, where the *hukou* household registration system imposes strong constraints on resettlement, rural migrants still crowd in large numbers into urban areas.[41] These communities constitute complex social ecosystems revolving around informal housing and precarious, small-scale, labor-intensive economic activities such as recycling waste materials, petty commodity production, delivery services, street hawking, and whatever forms of bricolage may bring in a small irregular return. The insecurities of life in these enclaves are typically exacerbated by ambiguous property rights that leave residents persistently vulnerable to expropriation by private developers and city authorities. Their residents in effect lie mostly outside of formally constituted society and outside the main circuits of modern capitalism, but they are articulated with this other world not only on account of the subcontracting work and services that they export to more prosperous parts of the city,[42] but also by virtue of the labor they supply to the workshops and factories that often locate in these enclave areas to take advantage of the low-cost workforce and lax enforcement of environmental regulations.[43]

Equal Partners?

The final years of the second wave of capitalist development saw the collapse of the old international order with its strategic blocs of nations forming the First, Second, and Third Worlds. As the cognitive-cultural regime of accumulation has emerged at the forefront of contemporary life, an alternative geopolitical order has appeared in the guise of a multifaceted mosaic of city-regions, nations, and supranational entities, intimately intertwined with one another at the global scale. In spite of the recurrent crises and severe social polarization that have attended the rise of this regime, the current period has been one of mounting overall prosperity for many countries (albeit with an extremely uneven distribution of the wealth) and widespread urban growth as a corollary.

Large city-regions, linked together in a worldwide network of social and economic relationships, constitute the main geographical anchors and the global nerve centers of this new order. To an ever-increasing degree, the key economic functions of these city-regions revolve around a core of administrative, managerial, professional, technical, and creative sectors set within a penumbra of low-wage labor-intensive supporting activities. For one thing, as Sassen has argued, major city-regions comprise important concentrations of corporate headquarter offices that sit at the top of a hierarchy of global investment operations, production processes, value chains, and international subcontracting relationships.[44] For another thing, they are also critical nuclei of basic financial operations (including stock markets, insurance brokerage, and international banking functions), business services (including consultancies, advertising, law, and accounting), and, to an ever-increasing degree, cultural production for national and world markets (including film, television programming, music, electronic games, social media, architectural services, and fashion). In line with this general vocation, more and more city-regions today are resorting to assertive branding campaigns in their efforts to consolidate their flagship status in the global economy and as a means of facing up to steadily rising competition for inward flows of capital investments and skilled labor.[45]

Useful sidelights on these propositions can be gleaned from a scrutiny of the comparative performance of different city-regions around the globe as centers of advanced international business activities. A helpful set of measures in this regard is provided by the *Worldwide Centers of Commerce Index* published by MasterCard,[46] which ranks 75 major global cities on their receptiveness and adaptability to international business operations.

The ranking is constructed by reference to five main measures of cities' participation in the new economy, that is, the quality of their financial and banking services, their openness to commercial transacting, their position within global airline networks, their capacities for knowledge creation and dissemination, and their livability. These measures in turn break down into more detailed variables involving 43 indicators and 74 subindicators. As might be expected, the leading cities in the MasterCard Index are located in the advanced capitalist countries, with London, New York, and Tokyo in the top three positions, but five cities of the Global South (or perhaps more tellingly the ex-Third World), namely, Singapore, Hong Kong, Seoul, Taipei, and Shanghai are also highly ranked, with Singapore at fourth place and Hong Kong at sixth. Eleven other Asian cities (including Bangkok, Mumbai, Kuala Lumpur) are listed, as are seven Latin American centers (including Santiago, Mexico City, São Paulo). On the African continent, only Cairo and Johannesburg are recorded in the Index, but rapid accession of other African cities to equivalent status can be expected and has undoubtedly occurred since the Index was last published. Indeed, the Index has not been revised since 2008, and it is hence now somewhat outdated, which means that it almost certainly offers an understated view of the degree of incursion of the new economy into the cities of the Global South. The point is that in spite of the special problems of mass poverty, overcrowding, and inadequate infrastructure that they face, many major city-regions in low- and middle-income countries are now being assimilated into the world economy as significant centers of leading-edge production and innovation, and, by the same token, as dynamic equal partners with the cities of the more advanced capitalist countries in the global system of cognitive-cultural capitalism. Notwithstanding a prevailing view in the literature to the effect that all cities are equally "ordinary" and hence are all equal in their claims to our attention,[47] these city-regions stand out as the praetorian guard of what Baldwin calls "the Great Convergence" of the twenty-first century.[48]

NOTES

1. This feature is revealed with exceptional clarity in Ricardian models of the capitalist economy. See especially, P. Sraffa, *Production of Commodities by Means of Commodities*, Cambridge: Cambridge University Press, 1960.
2. R. Boyer, *La Théorie de la Régulation: Une Analyse Critique*, Paris: Algalma, 1986.

3. A. Lipietz, "New tendencies in the international division of labor: regimes of accumulation and modes of social regulation," pp. 16–40 in A. J. Scott and M. Storper (eds.) *Production, Work, Territory: The Anatomy of Industrial Capitalism*, Boston: Allen and Unwin, 1986.
4. P. Le Galès, "Neoliberalism and urban change: stretching a good idea too far?" *Territory, Politics, Governance*, 4, 2016, 154–172; M. Storper, "The neo-liberal city as idea and reality," *Territory, Politics, Governance*, 4, 2016, 241–263.
5. S. A. Marglin, *Lessons of the Golden Age of Capitalism*, Helsinki: WIDER, 1988.
6. B. Bluestone and B. Harrison, *The Deindustrialization of America*, New York: Basic Books, 1982.
7. F. Blackaby (ed.) *De-industrialization*, London: Heinemann, 1978; D. Massey and R. A. Meegan, "The geography of industrial reorganization: the spatial effects of the restructuring of the electrical engineering sector under the Industrial Reorganization Committee," *Progress in Planning*, 10, 1979, 155–237; A. Jacquemin, "Le phénomène de désindustrialisation et la Communauté Européenne," *Revue Economique*, 30, 1979, 985–999; J. Carney, R. Hudson and J. Lewis, *Regions in Crisis: New Perspectives in European Regional Theory*, New York: St. Martin's Press, 1980.
8. E. Arghiri, *L'Echange Inégal*, Paris: François Maspéro, 1969; F. H. Cardoso and E. Faletto, *Dependency and Development in Latin America*, Berkeley: University of California Press, 1979; A. F. Frank, *Dependent Accumulation and Underdevelopment*, New York: Monthly Review Press, 1979.
9. E. Mandel, *Late Capitalism*, London: Verso, 1973 (German original published in 1972).
10. D. Bell, *The Coming of Post-Industrial Society*, New York: Basic Books, 1973.
11. A. Gouldner, *The Future of Intellectuals and the Rise of the New Class*, New York: Seabury, 1979.
12. See: A. J. Scott, *New Industrial Spaces: Flexible Production Organization and Regional Development in North America and Western Europe*, London: Pion, 1988.
13. D. C. Hoefler, "Silicon Valley USA," *Electronic News*, January 11, pp. 1, 4–5, January 18, pp. 1, 4–5, January 25, pp. 4–5.
14. A. Saxenian, "The urban contradictions of Silicon Valley," *International Journal of Urban and Regional Research*, 17, 1983, 237–261.
15. A. J. Scott and D. P. Angel, "The U.S. semiconductor industry: a locational analysis," *Environment and Planning A*, 19, 1987, 875–912; D. P. Angel, "High-technology agglomeration and the labor market—the case of Silicon Valley," *Environment and Planning A*, 23, 10, 1991, 1501–1516;

A. Saxenian, *Regional Advantage: Culture and Competition in Silicon Valley and Route 128*, Cambridge, MA: Harvard University Press, 1994.
16. A. Bagnasco, *Tre Italie: La Problematica Territoriale della Sviluppo Italiano*, Bologna: Il Mulino, 1977.
17. G. Becattini, "Dal settore industriale al distretto industriale. Alcune considerazioni sull'unità di indagine dell'economia industriale," *Rivista di Economia e Politica Industriale*, No. 2, 1979, 7–21.
18. G. Fuà, "Rural industrialization in later developed countries: the case of northeast and central Italy," *Banca Nazionale del Lavoro Quarterly Review*, December, 1983, 351–377.
19. G. Garofoli, "Lo sviluppo delle aree periferiche nell'economia italiana degli anni settanta," *L'Industria*, No. 3, 1981, 391–404.
20. S. Brusco, "The Emilian model: productive decentralisation and social integration," *Cambridge Journal of Economics*, 6, 1982, 167–184.
21. M. J. Piore and C. Sabel, *The Second Industrial Divide*, New York: Basic Books, 1984. The second industrial divide can be approximately equated to the discontinuity between the second and third waves of capitalist development as discussed in the present book.
22. Nowhere is the connection between export-oriented industrialization and industrial district formation more evident than in Southern China today. See: B. Christerson and C. Lever-Tracy, "The Third China? Emerging industrial districts in rural China," *International Journal of Urban and Regional Research*, 21, 1997, 569–588.
23. One of the earliest published references to the term occurs in J. Hirsch, "The trend towards postfordism—the present reformation of capitalism and its political consequences," *Argument*, 27, 1985, 325–342. See also A. Amin (ed.) *Post-Fordism: A Reader*, Oxford: Blackwell, 1994.
24. U. Beck, *Risk Society: Towards a New Modernity*, London: Sage, 1992.
25. I am of course here echoing the celebrated study by S. Giedon, *Mechanization Takes Command: A Contribution to Anonymous History*, New York: Oxford University Press, 1948, a book that documents the utilitarian, impersonal, and stereotyped excesses of the mass production system.
26. J. A. Schumpeter, *Socialism, Capitalism and Democracy*, New York: Harper and Brothers, 1942.
27. F. Levy and R. J. Murnane, *The New Division of Labor: How Computers are Creating the New Job Market*, Princeton: Princeton University Press, 2004.
28. D. H. Autor, F. Levy and R. J. Murnane, "The skill content of recent technological change: an empirical exploration," *Quarterly Journal of Economics*, 118, 2003, 1279–1333.
29. M. J. Hicks and S. Devaraj, *The Myth and the Reality of Manufacturing in America*, Ball State University, Centre for Business and Economic Research, 2015.

30. A. Amin, *op. cit.*, 1994.
31. D. Harvey, "Flexible accumulation through urbanization: reflections on American post-modernism in the American city," *Antipode*, 19, 1987, 260–286.
32. H. Etkowitz and L. Leydesdorff (eds.) *Universities and the Global Knowledge Economy: A Triple Helix of University-Industry-Government Relations*, London: Pinter, 1997.
33. Y. Moulier Boutang, *Le Capitalisme Cognitif, Comprendre la Nouvelle Grande Transformation et ses Enjeux*, Paris: Editions Amsterdam, 2007; E. Rullani, "Le capitalisme cognitif: du déjà vu?" *Multitudes*, 2, 2000, 87–94; C. Vercellone, "From formal subsumption to general intellect: elements for a Marxist reading of the thesis of cognitive capitalism," *Historical Materialism*, 15, 2007, 13–36.
34. J. Laxer, *The Undeclared War: Class Conflict in the Age of Cyber Capitalism*, Toronto: Viking, 1998; N. Dyer-Witheford, *Cyber-Marx: Cycles and Circuits of Struggle in High Technology Capitalism*, Urbana-Champaign: University of Illinois Press, 1999.
35. R. B. Reich, *The Work of Nations: Preparing Ourselves for 21st-Century Capitalism*, New York: Knopf, 1991.
36. R. Florida, *The Rise of the Creative Class*, New York: Basic Books, 2002.
37. In addition to the works already cited, see: F. S. Levy and R. J. Murnane, *The New Division of Labor: How Computers are Creating the Next Job Market*, Princeton: Princeton University Press, 2004; A. Toscano, "From pin factories to gold farmers: editorial introduction to a research stream on cognitive capitalism, immaterial labour, and the general intellect," *Historical Materialism*, 15, 2007, 3–11; A. J. Scott, *A World in Emergence: Cities and Regions in the 21st Century*, Cheltenham: Edward Elgar, 2012.
38. W. H. Whyte, *The Organization Man*, New York: Simon and Schuster, 1956.
39. "Immaterial labor" has also been offered by a number of continental theorists as a possible term. See, for example, A. Negri and M. Lazzarato, "Travail immatériel et subjectivité," *Futur Antérieur*, 6, 1991, 86–89. See also A. Corsani, M. Lazzarato and A. Negri, *Le Bassin de Travail Immatériel (BTI) dans la Métropole Parisienne*, Paris: L'Harmattan, 1996.
40. Cf. M. Gatta, H. Boushey and E. Appelbaum, "High-touch and here-to-stay: future skills demands in US low wage service occupations," *Sociology—The Journal of the British Sociological Society*, 43, 2009, 968–989. D. H. Autor and D. Dorn provide an equivalent formulation with their remark that services cannot stored and transported; see their paper "The growth of low-skill service jobs and the polarization of the US labor market," *American Economic Review*, 103, 2013, 1553–1597.

41. M. Sun and C. C. Fan, "China's permanent and temporary migrants: differentials and changes, 1990–2000," *Professional Geographer*, 63, 2011, 92–112; S. Swider, "Reshaping China's urban citizenship: street vendors, chengguan and struggles over the right to the city," *Critical Sociology*, 41, 2015, 701–716.
42. B. C. Arimah, "Nature and determinants of linkages between informal and formal sector enterprises in Nigeria," *African Development Review*, 13, 2001, 114–144; M. Mukim, "Coagglomeration of formal and informal industry: evidence from India," *Journal of Economic Geography*, 15, 2015, 329–351. See also: P. Rey, Y. Duroux and C. Bettelheim, *Sur l'Articulation des Modes de Production*, Paris: Ecole Pratique des Hautes Etudes, Centre d'Etudes de Planification Socialiste, 1971.
43. J. Nijman, "India's urban future: views from the slum," *American Behavioral Scientist*, 59, 2014, 406–423.
44. S. Sassen, *The Global City: New York, London, Tokyo*, Princeton, NJ: Princeton University Press, 1991.
45. A-V. Anttiroiko (ed.) *The Political Economy of City Branding*, London: Routledge, 2014.
46. MasterCard Worldwide, *Worldwide Centers of Commerce Index*, 2008, http://docplayer.net/2937087-Insights-worldwide-centers-of-commerce-index.html
47. Cf. J. Robinson, *Ordinary Cities: Between Modernity and Development*, New York: Routledge, 2006.
48. R. E. Baldwin, *The Great Convergence: Information Technology and the New Globalization*, Cambridge, MA: Belknap Press, 2016.

CHAPTER 7

Mainsprings of Resurgence

The Flexible City

One of the remarkable features of the urban land nexus in the twenty-first century is the way in which it has accommodated and adapted to the flexible production relations of the cognitive-cultural economy. We have already seen how the search for spatial efficiency in regard to interfirm linkages and local labor markets encourages the agglomeration of economic activities. We have also seen how, once this search triggers the clustering of firms and workers, the skeletal outlines of the urban land nexus come into view, and competitive advantages of different sorts start to flow forth. This developmental logic has always played a major role in the formation of cities in capitalism, but it has assumed a special kind of importance within the framework of cognitive-cultural capitalism where flexibility of production processes and labor market configurations are key foundations of firms' competitive strategies in the new economy. The resilient texture of the urban land nexus helps to potentiate exactly these types of economic arrangements and likewise to sustain the revivified processes of innovation and entrepreneurship that have been unleashed in the last few decades.

Linkages and Labor Markets

Classical fordism was characterized by relatively inflexible organizational structures focused on large capital-intensive units of production typified by high levels of vertical integration, the routinization of manufacturing processes, and large-batch production runs. Interunit linkages were generally bulky in scale and relatively stable in regard to their substantive content, and the main labor force comprised large complements of unionized blue-collar workers. Much of the cognitive-cultural economy, by contrast, has been evolving in opposite directions. One of the main elements of this alternative evolutionary pathway has been the proliferation over these last few decades of small disintegrated production units engaged in flexibly specialized manufacturing and service activities with variable input-output relationships and forming dense specialized agglomerations. Another important element consists of big "systems houses," meaning plants that produce large-scale outputs in strictly limited batches, such as space equipment or lavish feature films. Because of their variable, and frequently quite detailed, input needs together with their specialized labor demands, systems houses are often locationally anchored in these same agglomerations where they have access to pertinent suppliers and subcontractors and reserves of appropriate labor.

Even in the age of the Internet, many of the interfirm linkage networks that characterize the new economy can still only be efficiently effectuated at the local level. This may be either because these networks involve intense personal contact where face-to-face negotiating procedures entailing exchanges of tacit knowledge are in play, or because interfirm dealings are so specialized and their substantive content so varied that survival depends on high levels of mutual proximity among different participants in order to reduce the risk of a failure to complete buy or sell orders. These interdependencies between agglomeration processes and linkage flexibility are exemplified by many high-technology sectors where a research-driven, constantly changing production environment means that firms must be able to call incessantly on a varying congeries of specialized suppliers. Other examples can be found in cultural sectors where cutting-edge firms often interact with one another on the basis of continual and tightly wrought exchanges that are rich in symbolic but often ambiguous content that can only be mediated by personal contact. Nowhere is this more apparent that in the film, television, and media complex of contemporary Hollywood.

Similarly, local labor market structures in cognitive-cultural capitalism are now considerably more malleable and less institutionally constrained than they were some decades ago. In the fordist economy, both the upper and lower tiers of the labor force had a reasonable expectation of steady employment within the same firm over a comparatively extended period of time. White-collar workers enjoyed substantial stability of employment over the business cycle; blue-collar workers were selectively (depending on seniority) subject to lay-offs in periods of economic downturn but were systematically recalled when economic activity recovered. Moreover, in the immediate post-War decades, the wages of American blue-collar workers were among the highest in the world. Many kinds of high-level cognitive-cultural workers in the new economy of the twenty-first century are still able to command a degree of durability of job tenure, and their levels of remuneration are of a high order on average, but even workers in this privileged stratum of the labor force are now facing conditions of rising employment instability. The low-wage service segment of the work force has been particularly affected by the flexibilization of labor markets in recent decades, as reflected in the precipitous decline of job security for individuals employed in this segment, together with a distinct attenuation of their bargaining power with respect to wages.

These changing labor market conditions are manifest, as well, in the shifting character of the employment relation in contemporary capitalism. Temporary and part-time work contracts are increasingly common at all levels of the labor market. These trends have been accompanied by a notable expansion of the so-called gig economy where individuals offer their services as on-call workers or independent freelancers in sectors as varied as retail sales, transport services, entertainment, personal care, and construction. By the same token, temporary work agencies acting as information-bridging channels have increased greatly in number everywhere. Workers themselves have come up with diverse strategies for coping with the challenges posed by these circumstances. More qualified types of cognitive-cultural workers, for example, tend to be inveterate networkers, especially in the early stages of their careers. They are prone to spend large amounts of time in formal and informal organizations outside their normal working hours in building relationships with allied workers so as to consolidate their reputations, maintain their stocks of useful knowledge, and keep abreast of new employment opportunities.[1] Low-wage service workers also rely to a high degree on interpersonal networks as a means of obtaining information about employment opportunities. In many instances, these networks are rooted in particular racial, ethnic, or cultural groups.[2]

According to Krueger and Katz, alternative employment arrangements (i.e. temporary and part-time work) accounted for 10% of the American labor force in 2005, rising to just under 16% in 2015, of which as many as

32.4% had a bachelor's degree or better.³ These alternative arrangements are especially adapted to the requirements of the new economy by providing widening options for flexible staffing in firms that are themselves subject to chronic instabilities and by making it possible for private individuals to avail themselves of short-term or irregular in-person services. Moreover, labor market flexibility generally increases as a positive function of city size. This relationship reflects the relative facility with which workers and employers in large urban centers can find a new job or employee, respectively, in contrast to the situation in small urban centers or rural areas where local pools of workers and jobs are limited in size. Hence, as Jayet and others have pointed out, workers' bouts of employment and unemployment in large and densely developed centers tend to alternate more frequently than in less densely developed areas where periods of employment are liable to be more extended and where periods of unemployment between jobs are more prolonged.⁴

Agglomeration and functional flexibility in general are hence deeply intertwined with one another in the urban land nexus, and this relationship is especially intense in the context of cognitive-cultural capitalism. Agglomeration enlarges the possibilities for the flexibilization of production activities, input-output relations and labor markets, and flexibility in turn represents one of the linchpins of the competitive advantages of contemporary cities. At least some part of the resurgence of large urban areas since the demise of fordism can be attributed to these deepening synergies in the geography of the new economy.

The Creative Field of the City

Innovation. Peter Hall has shown in enormous empirical detail that cities have always been places where novel ideas and initiatives tend to flourish pell-mell across many different social domains including the economy, modes of cultural expression, and the realm of political ideas.⁵ In this respect, the structures and dynamics of cognitive-cultural capitalism have once more combined with the logic of the urban land nexus to amplify the resulting outcomes. Even in fordism, cities were major generators of cutting-edge developments in all spheres of life, though in the domain of the economy innovation processes were in varying degree shaped and circumscribed by the peculiar emphasis on top-down in-house research and development and on the search for stable oligopolistic scale effects in production as distinct from "creative destruction" wrought by vigorous entrepreneurial action. Top-down, in-house research and development and oligopolistic producers still exist in capitalism, though they are complemented in large measure today by much more finely grained patterns of innovation and entrepreneurship. Nowadays, these activities are deeply enfolded in the logic of the urban land nexus, which, in this regard, functions as a *creative field*, that is, a web of generative spatial relationships constituted by the intersection of intraurban space and the flexible operations of the cognitive-cultural economy.[6]

At the outset, the dense aggregation of many different but interlinked production activities in cities is eminently conducive to repeated exchanges of information in ways that often have cumulatively significant impacts on learning and hence on innovation. Numerous analysts have commented on this phenomenon, going back to Rogers and Larsen's *Silicon Valley Fever*, first published in 1984, which focused attention on the organizational networks and informal gatherings of entrepreneurs and engineers in the Valley and the ways in which the information passed backward and forward in these contexts forms an essential component of the Valley's intensely innovative environment.[7] In a study of design-intensive ceramic tile production in Sassuolo, Italy, Russo has also shown how industry representatives spend considerable time in transactional interactions with one another leading to the continual generation of new knowledge and insights and hence to intermittent improvements in the details of manufacturing processes and product design.[8] More generally, studies that draw on patenting data in order to analyze innovation processes reveal that the development of new methods and products depends significantly on the existence of localized clusters of individual specialists who influence one another through their formal and informal interactions. Many of the same studies also point to the existence of a strong positive correlation between city size and industrial patenting activity.[9] Of course, in a world of digital communication technologies, information spillovers and interpersonal networks also have widely ranging extra-local dimensions, and there is mounting evidence that far-flung business ecosystems are increasingly functioning as sites of innovative stimuli.[10] Even so, much empirical research continues to show that the urban milieu is a fertile hub of information spillovers, especially in view of the importance of face-to-face communication in which tacit knowledge can be most effectively transmitted. Of notable relevance in this context is the analysis of Noteboom, who has pointed to the influence of the social and cultural milieu on the effectiveness of knowledge diffusion.[11] Thus, exchanges of information that is already well understood by all parties are unlikely to lead to learning; and conversely, only mutual incomprehension is apt to result from exchanges involving high levels of novelty and unfamiliarity. In contrast to these two sets of circumstances, the effects of information transmission on learning and innovation will tend to be optimized where transactions involve intermediate doses of novelty mixed with some degree of familiarity. A roughly similar kind of argument might be made in regard to urban communities. Some of these are marked by an overwhelming uniformity of culture and ideas so that innovation is subdued or stifled; some divide into non-communicating solitudes, putting barriers around the flow of information; yet others are composed of a varied, fluid, and intermingled mix of individuals where many new ideas, both big and small, are freely generated and find a receptive audience. Partial evidence in favor of the first part of this argument is offered in the study by Bautès and Valette of a community of religious painters in Rajasthan, India, where innovative gestures are largely absent because entrenched traditions and norms impose strict limits on artistic experimentation beyond historically established protocols.[12] However, even in places where receptivity and spontaneity run rife, innovation is rarely if ever an unconstrained or open-ended process, but one that is engendered and shaped by underlying realities and imperatives. Flows of innovations do not generally spring out of thin air but out of concrete social and economic imperatives. This means that in the specific case of any given industrial cluster, innovations will tend to be shaped by the needs and opportunities specific to that cluster and its constituent cohort of firms. I stress this point because some versions of creative-class theory seem to assume that innovations emerge in purely unmediated form from the minds of gifted individuals in abstraction from the practical realities of place.[13]

Entrepreneurship. When we speak about innovation in the economic sphere, we are usually referring to changes or improvements in process and product configurations. The notion of innovation, however, also relates directly to issues of entrepreneurship and new firm formation.

The conventional theory of entrepreneurship is for the most part quite aspatial, and much of it, following the pioneering work of Schumpeter in his book *The Theory of Economic Development*, is focused on issues of psychosocial motivation, and above all, the propensity to take risks.[14] This sort of approach is entirely justifiable, but in addition, entrepreneurial processes are strongly shaped by and in turn reshape the creative field of the city. In the cognitive-cultural economy of the twenty-first century, these relationships are of particular significance because the reassertion of vertical and horizontal disintegration in clusters of producers provides numerous opportunities for entrepreneurial action. Some entrepreneurs, of course, get their start in a purely fortuitous way, but in a series of articles, Klepper has shown how the process in general can be most effectively analyzed in terms of multiple rounds of spin-offs from already existing producers. Klepper has also documented empirical instances of this process in industries and places as different from one another as semiconductors in Silicon Valley, the rubber tire industry in Akron, Ohio, clothing in Dhaka, Bangladesh, and even the early car industry in Detroit.[15] Clusters act as breeding grounds of the entrepreneurial urge in two separate but related ways. First of all, any given unit of production in any given cluster offers very specific types of practical experience to its employees, and direct previous experience is a critical resource for would-be entrepreneurs. Second of all, the same employees are optimally positioned to observe and to exploit the concrete opportunities for new firm formation within the multilayered and networked structure of the cluster as a whole. Provided that other conditions (such the availability of capital) are reasonably supportive, some of these employees may find it possible to build on these twofold advantages and to set up in business by finding a profitable niche for themselves within the existing network of economic relationships either by replacing production units that have expired or by extending the horizontal or vertical division of labor. Not all of these entrepreneurial initiatives can be expected to remain within the spatial orbit of the source cluster, but the dense agglomeration economies in and around the cluster will provide strong incentives for new entrepreneurs to stay in the local area.[16]

Thus, so long as external markets do not collapse and new and more competitive production locales do not arise elsewhere, many clusters have a propensity to reproduce themselves via continual entrepreneurial effort and are often surprisingly long-lived through many different generations of firms. To take just one example, the Hollywood film industry has existed for over a century at a high level of competitive performance in a constantly shifting swirl as firms come and go and as corporate reorganizations occur.[17] The structured entrepreneurial energies in productive clusters thus help to maintain and extend the urban economy, and, in combination with the wider innovative potentials of the city to stimulate and reinforce new bursts of urban expansion. The current period of history is one in which these expansionary conditions appear once again to be operating, selectively but widely, in active mode.

Specialization and Competition

Chamberlinian Competition

There has always been a tendency in capitalism for some products to take on identifying characteristics specific to the firm or place of origin. Vuitton handbags are an example of the former case; Bollywood films are an example of the latter. In the new economy, these types of product identity have assumed unusual and rising importance. Of special interest in the present context is the role of place-specific product identity and its roots in agglomerations of interdependent firms. Urban agglomerations that foster this kind of identity are usually characterized by two core sets of conditions, both of which tend to promote a common industrial atmosphere. One of them is a relatively unstable and variable pattern of intra-agglomeration linkages requiring significant personal intermediation and hence information exchange. The other is based on shared pools of habituated workers endowed with agglomeration-specific skills, sensibilities, and cultural reference points, such as a specialized body of scientific and technical know-how or a set of distinctive styles and design motifs. In a few cases, a unique physical resource base may also have some effect, and specialized agricultural districts given over to products such as wine or cheese are especially liable to reflect this circumstance. Conditions like these will then be apt to leave tangible traces on the form or function of end-of-the-pipe outputs. Vivid illustrations of this point can be observed in the product characteristics of firms in geographic contexts like the electronics industry of Silicon Valley and the aerospace complex of Toulouse,[18] or the business and financial service hubs of New York, London, Tokyo, Shanghai, and São Paulo,[19] or foci of cultural production such as Bollywood in Mumbai and the entertainment industry hotbed of Seoul, South Korea.[20] The craft industry clusters of northeast and central Italy are another example of production centers whose outputs are stamped with place-specific styles, idioms, and functional properties, and in the case of the high-performance car-manufacturing center of Modena, all three of these qualities combine together to put a unique imprint on local products.

The idiosyncrasies that demarcate the place-specific origins of particular products represent a type of product differentiation that allows firms to contest markets on the basis of quality and reputation as well as price. Moreover, while competitors may be able to imitate some of these idiosyncrasies, they are rarely, if ever, able to reproduce all the resonances (in terms of the technical or cultural aura) that adhere to the original models.[21] This type of situation was characterized by Chamberlin in the 1930s as *monopolistic competition*, which he described as a form of rivalry between firms in any given sector, but where (in contradistinction to *laisser-faire*) at least some of these firms are able to distinguish their output from that of their competitors on grounds other than price alone.[22] At the time when Chamberlin published his ideas, monopolistic competition was seen by most economists as something of a curiosum. However, with the rise of the cognitive-cultural economy and the insistent reassertion of product differentiation, the notion of monopolistic (or oligopolistic) competition has taken on new significance, especially given the increasing number of urban agglomerations in different parts of the world whose unique traditions, cultures, design ideologies, skills, residues of tacit knowledge, practical know-how, and so on, imbue local products with inimitable qualities. Hence, whereas interfirm competition continues to intensify as globalization proceeds further forward, the changing modalities of production in the new economy mean that this competition is increasingly monopolistic in the Chamberlinian sense. Indeed, this type of product differentiation or branding, along with more formal assertions of exclusive product origins such as trademarks, copyright, and geographical indications has become one of the hallmarks of the twenty-first-century economic order. The monopolistic and oligopolistic advantages that derive from Chamberlinian competition are also one of the prime reasons why the earnings of capitalist firms increasingly involve a significant element of rent over and above normal profits.

Developments like these, in combination with the re-agglomeration of production, have undoubtedly helped to strengthen localized competitive advantages and to facilitate market extension of favored production locales. By the same token, they have contributed significantly to the resurgence of many urban centers in recent decades. Even as recently as the 1990s, several pundits proclaimed that distance was effectively dead and that cities would henceforth steadily lose much of their reason for being.[23] Contrary to this view, cities have continued to grow by leaps and bounds in the twenty-first century as sectors as diverse as advanced electronics, biotechnology, aerospace, software, banking, finance, business services, advertising, design consulting, fashion industries of all kinds, film and television production, media, music, video games, architecture, tourism, and many more have pursued strategies of flexible production and monopolistic competition (both firm- and place-based), and have flourished in urban settings in self-reinforcing cycles of intensifying competitive advantage. This is not to say that contemporary capitalism has moved entirely in this direction. Many sectors in today's economy continue to exhibit technologies, organizational structures, and labor processes that would not have been out of place in earlier historical rounds of development, and many of these sectors still account for much productive activity around the world, especially in low-wage national and global peripheries. All the same, the most radical stimuli to urban growth and development over the last few decades are rooted in production and exchange processes peculiar to the new cognitive-cultural economic order. This state of affairs is palpable in large global city-regions around the world, but it is also evident in numerous small and medium-sized towns and even some rural areas where new forms of dynamism based on traditional crafts and art forms, organic agriculture, regional cuisine, the revalorization of heritage, festivals, local environmental assets, tourism, and so on, have flourished greatly of late.[24]

Global Connections

The webs of economic interaction and the place-specific resources contained in individual cities are all simultaneously bound up in overlapping networks of trade and other forms of economic and social interaction that extend across the entire globe. These force-fields of relationships are in part straddled and created by transnational firms, which by reason of their spatially dispersed structure are able to exploit and combine the unique competitive advantages of different places. These are firms, as Dunning has shown, that seek to combine ownership or firm-specific assets (such as a legally protected brand or an established reputation) with locational or place-specific advantages that lower the cost or enhance the quality of their products.[25] In many, if not most cases, they achieve this fusion by internalizing production within a single structure of proprietorship spread out over different holdings or branch plants at different locations, though they also sometimes dispense with specific physical facilities by subcontracting work to independent production units in collaborative relationships and partnerships. Much commercial and technical know-how is transmitted through these interconnections thus helping to upgrade the competitive advantages of particular agglomerations. Strategic alliances concerning activities like research and development also make it possible to achieve beneficial combinations of firm- and place-specific advantages. These organizational strategies clearly describe important aspects of large transnational corporations like Apple, Procter and Gamble, Toyota, or Verizon with their far-flung operational sites, including administrative offices, research and test facilities, manufacturing plants, and distribution centers. However, medium-sized and even quite small firms are also often able to establish an effective presence in sundry cities and countries on account of the availability of cheap, rapid, and reliable communications and travel facilities. The net result is a multiplication of the synergistic powers of place as the competitive advantages of different locations are jointly exploited within the institutional framework of multi-establishment, multinational firms and their various appendages.

Some revealing information in this respect has been brought to light by the research carried out by Peter Taylor and his collaborators on the internationalization of producer service firms.[26] Taylor and Catalano, in particular, present an invaluable data set that identifies different facilities owned by 100 different firms (in advertising, banking and finance, insurance, law, and management consultancy) in 315 cities in all parts of the world.[27] The data reveal that these firms favor important financial and business centers for their operations (including headquarters offices) with the top five cities being London (where the 100 firms own 368 different facilities between them), New York (357), Hong Kong (253), Tokyo (244), and Paris (235). However, the same firms are also spread out over an exceptionally wide-ranging set of cities in different countries, where they offer their specialized services while reaping specific forms of local knowledge to supplement their more broadly based expertise. For illustrative purposes, a representative range of cases from this data set is provided in Table 7.1, which sets forth cross-tabulated data on five selected major producer service firms and the top 15 cities in which they own facilities.

These organizational structures, woven into global patterns of production, trade, and investment testify to the interlocking relationships that tie the cities of the modern world together and that reflect and in many instances reinforce the peculiar competitive advantages of individual nodes within the system. This remark is exemplified by the film and television programming industry today. Contrary to many earlier predictions, Hollywood, despite its dominant global role in the supply of filmed entertainment products, has failed to eradicate competing production centers in the rest of the world. Rather, film and television programming

Table 7.1 Selected transnational producer service firms, showing the top 15 cities ranked from top to bottom in order of the number of facilities belonging to each firm[a]

Allen & Overy	Allianz	Asatzu-DK	J P Morgan	SEMA
(Law)	(Insurance)	(Advertising)	(Banking and finance)	(Management consulting)
London (HQ)	London	Tokyo (HQ)	New York (HQ)	Paris (HQ)
Amsterdam	Singapore	Beijing	London	London
Hong Kong	Brussels	Taipei	Tokyo	Madrid
Milan	Munich (HQ)	Hong Kong	Los Angeles	Stockholm
Frankfurt	Hong Kong	Singapore	San Francisco	Singapore
Paris	Shanghai	Seoul	Chicago	Brussels
Madrid	Paris	London	Singapore	Hong Kong
Singapore	Amsterdam	Bangkok	Brussels	Beijing
Bangkok	Madrid	Shanghai	Hong Kong	Buenos Aires
Luxembourg	Milan	Guangzhou	Madrid	Atlanta
Moscow	São Paulo	Ho Chi Minh City	São Paulo	Rome
New York	Istanbul	Kuala Lumpur	Frankfurt	Kuala Lumpur
Prague	Luxembourg	Frankfurt	Mexico City	Cologne
Tokyo	Zurich	New York	Sydney	Hamburg
Warsaw	Vienna	Paris	Melbourne	Manchester

[a] HQ headquarters city; based on data from P. J. Taylor and G. Catalano, *World City Network: The Basic Data*, GAWC Data Set 11, http://www.lboro.ac.uk/gawc/datasets/da11.html

agglomerations in places as far apart as Mexico City, Bogotá, Mumbai, Hong Kong, Tokyo, Shanghai, Seoul, Bangkok, and Lagos (now reputed to be one of the largest film production centers in the world), not to forget the traditional film industries of Europe, are not only generally thriving but are also in many cases successfully contesting international markets on the basis of their distinctive competitive advantages rooted in place-specific know-how, cultures, and aesthetic idioms.[28] Equally significant is the fact that Hollywood production companies increasingly see fit to implant their own facilities in many of these agglomerations in order to tap into local pools of talent and to engage in coproduction deals with local investors and entrepreneurs.[29]

In more general terms, the main sources of growth and prosperity in the new economy coincide with large urban centers, each of which is endowed with its own unique amalgam of agglomeration economies and yet is simultaneously imbricated in networks of competition, collaboration, and institutional authority that span the globe. These cities are also the privileged haunts of what Sklair calls the "transnational capitalist class" comprising a cosmopolitan and ostentatiously wealthy elite occupying positions of influence and power in the global economy.[30]

Radiant Cities?

The Creative City

The terms *creativity* and *innovation* overlap in a number of different ways, but it is useful for present purposes to draw a crucial distinction between them. We can think of creativity as a mental process that generates fundamental insights, intuitions, and imaginative gestures. Innovation can be defined in a more restricted way to signify the concrete realization or implementation of a creative impulse (for not all creative impulses lead on to actual innovations).

The urban land nexus has always fostered creativity and innovation by reason of its internal heterogeneity in combination with the intense and continual interaction between all the different behavioral units out of which it is composed. The emergence of the cognitive-cultural economy has greatly magnified these properties of the urban land nexus, and it is hence not surprising to find that sometime in the 1990s, as the new economy started to flourish, the notion of the "creative city" burst onto both the academic and the policy scenes.[31] The growing importance of cultural industries in the urban economic mix also played a major role in the initiation of this idea, and all the more so in view of the intensity of their creative content. A degree of crystallization of the notion that cities are progenitors of creative activity was prompted by Richard Florida's writings concerning the formation of a "creative class" in contemporary capitalism and its concentration in large cities.[32] Florida also made the claim that cities with diverse populations and abundant amenities like parks, museums, art galleries, theaters, and exclusive restaurants were especially attractive to individuals endowed with high levels of human capital. On this basis he suggested that municipal policy-makers could encourage the inward migration of creative individuals by investing in amenities like these. According to Florida, the expanding pool of talent in any city that followed this prescription would then stimulate local economic development, though the precise mechanisms underlying this supposed relationship remained unspecified.[33]

Faced with this alluring and relatively inexpensive policy formula, municipal officials in many urban centers began to declare their commitment to developmental agendas based on the notions of the creative city and the creative class, often with a special emphasis on promoting the arts and the cultural economy. This agenda was, and continues to be, especially seductive to policy-makers in cities that experienced deindustrialization in the later years of fordism. Early commitments to the agenda were made in the 1990s by Vancouver, Toronto, and Cologne, and in succeeding years by large and small cities all over the world including not only prominent urban centers like Buenos Aires, Barcelona, and Shanghai but also such disparate and unlikely places as Sudbury, Canada,[34] Milwaukee, USA,[35] Huddersfield, UK,[36] and Darwin, Australia.[37] Today, UNESCO's Creative City Network comprises 116 members from 54 countries, including Brazzaville, Dakar, Kinshasa, and Lubumbashi in sub-Saharan Africa, and the list continues to grow. The specific policy objectives of these different cities vary widely, but a composite normative vision of what is at stake can be roughly assembled from various policy documents and academic publications. The goals alluded to in these sources include such specifics as an employment base comprising dynamic new-economy industries, high levels of environmental quality, a unifying symbolic identity in the guise of a striking global brand, and a thriving cultural milieu with particular emphasis on the arts, iconic architecture, and periodic festivals. To be sure, a vibrant pool of talented and qualified labor constantly refreshed by new migrants drawn in by the amenities of the city also ranks highly on this list of desiderata. This "creative cities script" to use Peck's felicitous phraseology,[38] is highly synthetic, but it nonetheless captures some of the main themes that have now entered into the ever-broadening but often extremely problematical discussion on the creative city.

There is, in fact, much wishful thinking in this rather overblown script, and equally, much about which it is disconcertingly silent. It lays out policy aims that cater above all to the predilections of the upper fractions of urban society but that essentially underplay the needs and aspirations of the lower fractions. By the same token, public investments in pursuit of these aims can almost certainly be counted on to provide disproportional benefits to the already well off (including property owners) in comparison with the rest of urban society. Small wonder that popular political movements in large cities everywhere have rather consistently turned their backs on these kinds of policy advocacies in favor of goals that address issues more directly relevant to the concerns of low-wage workers, the unemployed, and the destitute. Even groups of artists (who, on the basis of narrow self-interest, would seem to have much to gain from creative-city policies) in urban centers as far apart as Hamburg and Toronto have been active in the call for reconsideration of some of the more overtly regressive and philistine policy initiatives intended to bring creative-city ideas into concrete realization. As I will argue at a later stage, there are grounds for particular skepticism in regard to one of the key propositions of much extant creative-city theory, namely, the notion that a durable process of urban growth and development can be unleashed simply on the basis of free-floating talent irrespective of other urban conditions and, most of all, irrespective of the existing productive capabilities of the city. Equally doubtful is the proposition that talented individuals can be motivated in any significant degree to migrate to a given city on the basis of its amenities without reference to the more fundamental issues of employment and wages.

Despite these objections to much of the creative-city theory as currently formulated, there nevertheless remains a specific sense in which we can talk quite meaningfully about the mobilization of creativity and innovation in the city of cognitive-cultural capitalism, especially by reference to the organization of the urban land nexus. Note, however, that I mean by the term "creativity" not some mysterious act of communication with the transcendental, or some revolutionary break with the past, but rather a very concrete and continuing process of individual and collective discovery (usually small in scale) resulting in periodic adjustments of and increments to acquired intellectual and social capital. Clusters of cognitive-cultural industries, from high-technology production to fashion and film, are one obvious site of this sort of activity for all the reasons set out at earlier stages in the discussion. Burgeoning infrastructures devoted to entertainment, the arts, and other cultural amenities in modern cities are also often thought to enhance local creative capacities, though the validity of this particular point presumably depends very much on the wider social context. In the same way, the urban landscape itself might be seen as influencing the creative ambience of the city. Certainly, in many of the cities of cognitive-cultural capitalism, a renewed engagement with imaginative and playful architectural experimentation has been closely associated with attempts to foster creativity and innovation. The most obvious expression of this engagement can be found in the central business districts of major global cities where avant-garde buildings signed by star architects, from the Guggenheim Museum in Bilbao, through the Burj Khalifa in Dubai, to the Petronas Towers in Kuala Lumpur function as a means of amplifying the vibrancy of the urban milieu. Equally, selected retail areas, especially in central cities, are increasingly subject to what is often referred to as "disneyfication" in order to frame the urban environment with particular kinds of cultural stimuli while simultaneously facilitating upscale shopping experiences and arousing consumer desires. Even old, rundown industrial buildings are frequently harnessed for "creative" redevelopment, as exemplified in numerous cities by the widespread recycling of derelict factories and warehouses to serve as art centers and galleries, music venues, boutique retail outlets, and to provide space for small entrepreneurs in sectors like design, media, and fashion.

Labor Mobility, Skills, and Urban Growth

A widely circulating idea with strong affinities to creative-city theory is that we are now living in an era of "consumer cities" in which the old driving forces of urban development based on productive activity have given way before a new kind of urbanization that reflects above all the consumption behavior of mainstream society.[39] It is far from my intention here to argue against the role of urban residents at large in shaping the constitutive elements of the city (see Chaps. 8, 9, and 10), or to deny those numerous aspects of city life that resonate with the everyday tastes and preferences of the citizenry, but I certainly do want to offer a critique of one important aspect of this general approach. This concerns the formulation, advanced by Florida and a number of academic economists, of what amounts to a consumer-sovereignty theory of the growth and development of cities in the more advanced capitalist countries in the twenty-first century. More specifically, this formulation turns on the idea that I have already mentioned to the effect that the creative class is preeminently attracted to cities rich in amenities.[40] Policy-makers, it is said, can therefore substantially increase the representation of the creative class in the labor force of any given city by providing a copious supply of these amenities. Appealing natural conditions, and especially warm winters, are also alleged to have a positive influence on the choices made by the creative class in regard to place of residence. On the latter grounds, cities in the Sunbelt of the United States are supposed to have a special pull on migratory flows. The theory then suggests that once a city has put together an irresistible package of amenities, along with whatever natural assets it may possess, the creative class can be expected to converge upon it, whereupon waves of economic energies will be unleashed thus leading to desirable forms of growth and development.

As it happens, certain themes within this narrative have been subject to debate well before discussions of consumer cities appeared on the horizon, going back to a paper published by Muth in 1971 in which he posed the question: do workers follow jobs or do jobs follow workers?[41] A subsequent steady stream of statistical analysis around this question turns out to be remarkably inconclusive, which is perhaps not surprising given the variations from one study to the next in the types of workers subjected to analysis, in the methodologies and research designs pursued, and in the geographical contexts selected for study.[42] Theoretical reflection, however, suggests that claims about jobs following workers, who in turn are attracted by amenities, need to be treated with great caution.[43] In spite of the fact that amenities can assuredly be taken as making a positive contribution to the quality of urban life, it is difficult to see what kind of utility-maximizing calculus, to use the language of neoclassical advocates of the people-first, jobs-later account, would induce skilled workers to place superior value on amenities as opposed to employment and income. Most skilled workers have invested considerable resources and time in acquiring their qualifications and experience, and it is surely a stretch of the imagination to believe that they would be willing, except under special circumstances (such as retirement[44]), to squander these assets by moving to places that are rich in amenities but poor in jobs. Rather, we may expect them to put a high premium on places with economies that are already able to make use of and adequately remunerate their specialized skills. If there is a causal link in this circle of relationships, the likelihood is that it runs from prosperous cities to an abundant supply of amenities rather than the other way around.

All of this being said, proponents of the people-first, jobs-later argument also point to the strong migratory flows from the northeast of the United States to the Sunbelt in recent decades, together with the consistently high positive correlation between the growth of cities and average winter temperatures, as clear evidence that amenities (in this case, climate) exert a major influence on population movements and patterns of urban development.[45] Examination of the historical geography of the United States, however, suggests strongly that this correlation actually reflects a pure contingency without any meaningful causal substance. Right at the start, the argument fails signally to account for the timing of these shifts. Over the twentieth century and down to the 1960s, the economy of most of the Sunbelt was relatively stagnant and in-migration was restrained, notwithstanding any climatic advantages that the region may be presumed to have. Over this same period, the Manufacturing Belt attracted constant inflows of migrants, many of whom actually originated in the Sunbelt. Concomitantly, the cities of the Manufacturing Belt expanded apace. After the Second World War, these patterns of migration and settlement began to change radically. On the one side, and to repeat, the decentralization of standardized branch plants from cities in the Manufacturing Belt to low-wage labor pools in the South intensified greatly as fordism began to encounter its own internal weaknesses, especially after the 1960s. On the other side, much new urban economic development in the Sunbelt was generated by the post-War development of electronics and aerospace industrial agglomerations in places like Santa Clara County, Los Angeles, Orange County, San Diego, Phoenix, Colorado Springs, Dallas-Fort Worth, and elsewhere.[46] The science-based industries at the core of these agglomerations did not for the most part exist before the Second World War, and as they began to take on concrete sectoral identities in the 1940s and 1950s, they were clearly averse to locating in the old industrial spaces of the Manufacturing Belt, with the signal exception of the Boston-New York-New Jersey area where many of these industries originated. A new window of locational opportunity that was no longer harnessed to the agglomeration economies of fordist industry was opening up. The Sunbelt offered locational opportunities unencumbered by the gritty, rough-edged industrial conditions of the cities of the northeast, and perhaps most significantly of all, unencumbered by a working class with a strong traditional culture of unionization. The locational choices of these new industries were also partly a response to a deliberate federal policy of allocating defense spending so as to ensure a wide geographic distribution of recipients. These developments established the basis for the formation of dynamic new production centers and set the stage for the economic resurgence of the Sunbelt. After the 1960s, the shifting character of American urban fortunes became even more pronounced as employment in the Manufacturing Belt collapsed and the new industrial spaces in the former periphery continued to gather expansionary momentum. To put the matter in a wider perspective, the migratory movements that occurred after the 1960s from the Manufacturing Belt to the Sunbelt were no more due to a search for warm winters than the current massive migration from western and central China to the burgeoning city-regions of Beijing, Shanghai, Guangzhou, and other major centers of the eastern coastal region is due to a preference for a monsoon climate.[47]

These arguments can now be summarized in a general statement about the growth of cities in terms of a path-dependent dynamic in which capital, labor, and geographic space come into mutual temporal relationship with one another. We know from earlier comments in this book that productive agglomerations are possessed of a sort of genetic code rooted in networks of specialized but complementary firms. So long as external markets are able to absorb increments of output, these networks are also characterized by a time-dependent recursive development process revolving around innovative activity and entrepreneurial effort in a structured sequence of interdependencies. New workers can be expected to migrate into the agglomeration to take advantage of expanding employment opportunities while the local supply of habituated labor will also undoubtedly attract new firms. However, these are not equally balanced chicken-and-egg relationships. To the contrary, as argued at length in earlier chapters, the dynamics of agglomerated development and growth are principally governed by the collective energies of the production system. Without a supply of labor, production would, of course, clearly collapse, but without production, there would be no process of agglomeration and hence no overall pattern of concentrated growth and development. In this complex play of factors and forces, labor is evidently an indispensable but subdominant variable. Moreover, there is a supplementary reason why labor (skilled or otherwise) cannot be a *primum mobile* of agglomerated production. Without some effective mechanism for filtering out specific types of human capital, the in-migration of workers to any given place is quite unlikely to result in the kind of specialization that is one of the familiar features of clustered economic development. It strains credulity, for example, to imagine that a self-sustaining inflow of electronics engineers might have been the sole or even the prime factor sustaining the emergence, subsequent development, and industrial character of the semiconductor- and computer-producing agglomeration of Silicon Valley (whose amenities, apart from sunshine, are even today extremely modest). Like other agglomerations across the world, Silicon Valley's inner developmental motor resides in its overall constellation of functionally interrelated production units. When the motor is running smoothly in this or any other agglomeration, specialized labor is continually drawn in as part of the path-dependent logic of development; and when the motor fails, unemployment and outflows of population to other places are the predictable consequence.

The basic lesson of all of this for policy-makers concerned with local economic growth is that they are well advised to pay primary attention to issues of job creation and only subsequently to labor supply, and to treat amenities as a promising source of collective self-esteem but assuredly not as a fundamental means of leveraging economic gains.

Notes

1. A. J. Scott, "Multimedia and digital visual effects: emergence of a local labor market," *Monthly Labor Review*, March, 1998, 30–38.
2. A. Ahmad, "Connecting with work: the role of social networks in immigrants searching for jobs in Finland," *European Societies*, 13, 2011, 687–712; R. Waldinger, "The immigrant niche in global city-regions: concept, patterns, controversy," pp. 299–322 in A. J. Scott (ed.) *Global City-Regions: Trends, Theory, Policy*, Oxford: Oxford University Press, 2001.
3. A. B. Krueger and L. F. Katz, "The rise and nature of alternative work arrangements in the United States, 1995–2015," http://krueger.princeton.edu/sites/default/files/akrueger/files/katz_krueger_cws_-_march_29_20165.pdf (accessed June 25, 2016).
4. H. Jayet, "Chômer plus souvent en région urbaine, plus longtemps en région rurale," *Economie et Statistique*, 153, 1983, 47–57. See also: B. O. Pettman, *Labor Turnover and Retention*, New York: Wiley, 1975.
5. P. Hall, *Cities in Civilization*, London: Weidenfeld and Nicolson, 1998.
6. A. J. Scott, "Cultural economy and the creative field of the city," *Geografiska Annaler*, Series B, *Human Geography*, 92, 2010, 115–130.
7. E. Rogers and J. K. Larsen, *Silicon Valley Fever: Growth of High-Technology Culture*, New York: Basic Books, 1984.
8. M. Russo, "Technical change and the industrial district: the role of inter-firm relations in the growth and transformation of ceramic tile production in Italy," *Research Policy*, 14, 1985, 329–343.
9. A. B. Jaffe, M. Trajtenberg and R. Henderson, "Geographic localization of knowledge spillovers as evidenced by patent citations," *Quarterly Journal of Economics*, 108, 1993, 577–598; see also: N. Sedgley and B. Emslie, "Do we still need cities? Evidence on rates of innovation from count data models of metropolitan statistical area patents," *American Journal of Economics and Sociology*, 70, 2011, 86–108; and M. Feldman and D. F. Kogler, "Stylized facts in the geography of innovation," pp. 381–410 in B. H. Hall and N. Rosenberg, *Handbook of the Economics of Innovation*, Vol. 1, Amsterdam: Elsevier, 2012.
10. See, for example, P. Sunley, S. Pinch, S. Reimer and J. Macmillen, "Innovation in a creative production system: the case of design," *Journal of Economic Geography*, 8, 2008, 675–698.

11. B. Noteboom, "Innovation, learning and industrial organization," *Cambridge Journal of Economics*, 23, 1999, 127–150. See also: I. Nonaka, "A dynamic theory of organizational knowledge creation," *Organization Science*, 5, 1994, 14–37.
12. N. Bautès and E. Valette, "Miniature painting, cultural economy and territorial dynamics in Rajasthan, India," pp. 207–223 in A. J. Scott and D. Power (eds.) *Cultural Industries and the Production of Culture*, London: Routledge, 2004.
13. See, for example, R. Florida, *The Rise of the Creative Class*. New York: Basic Books, 2002; idem., *Cities and the Creative Class*, London: Routledge, 2004.
14. J. A. Schumpeter, *The Theory of Economic Development: An Inquiry into Profits, Capital, Credit, Interest, and the Business Cycle*, Cambridge, MA: Harvard University Press, 1934 (original German edition first published in 1911).
15. S. Klepper, "The origin and growth of industry clusters: the making of Silicon Valley and Detroit," *Journal of Urban Economics*, 67, 2010, 15–32; G. Buenstorf and S. Klepper, "Why does entry cluster geographically? Evidence from the US tire industry," *Journal of Urban Economics*, 68, 2011, 103–114; S. Klepper, "Nano-economics, spinoffs, and the wealth of regions," *Small Business Economics*, 37, 2011, 141–154.
16. C. Armington and Z. J. Acs, "The determinants of regional variation in new firm formation," *Regional Studies*, 36, 2002, 33–45; R. Sternberg, "Regional dimensions of entrepreneurship," *Foundations and Trends in Entrepreneurship*, 5, 2009, 211–340.
17. A. J. Scott, *On Hollywood: The Place the Industry*, Princeton: Princeton University Press, 2005.
18. M. Castells and P. Hall, *Technopoles of the World: The Making of Twenty-First-Century Industrial Complexes*, London: Routledge, 1994; A. J. Scott and J-M. Zuliani, "L'industrie de l'informatique à Toulouse: développement, structure, enjeux," *Revue d'Economie Régionale et Urbaine*, 3, 2007, 339–364.
19. N. Thrift and A. Leyshon, "A phantom state? The de-traditionalization of money, the international financial system and international financial centres," *Political Geography*, 13, 1994, 299–327.
20. A. J. Scott, *op. cit.*, 2005; M. Lorenzen and F. A. Täube, "Breakout from Bollywood? The roles of social networks and regulation in the evolution of Indian film industry," *Journal of International Management*, 14, 2008, 286–299.
21. A. J. Scott, "The changing global geography of low-technology, labor-intensive industry: clothing, footwear and furniture," *World Development*, 34, 2006, 1517–1536.

22. E. Chamberlin, *The Theory of Monopolistic Competition*, Cambridge, MA: Harvard University Press, 1933.
23. F. Cairncross, *The Death of Distance: How the Communications Revolution will Change our Lives*, Cambridge, MA: Harvard Business School Press, 1997; R. O'Brien, *Global Financial Integration: The End of Geography*, London: Pinter, 1992.
24. See, for example, D. Bell and M. Jayne, "The creative countryside: policy and practice in the UK rural cultural economy," *Journal of Rural Studies*, 26, 2010, 209–218; C. Gibson and J. Connell, "Cultural industry production in remote places: indigenous popular music in Australia," pp. 243–258 in D. Power and A. J. Scott (eds.) *Cultural Industries and the Production of Culture*, London: Routledge, 2004; A. J. Scott, "The cultural economy of landscape and prospects for peripheral development in the twenty-first century: the case of the English Lake District," *European Planning Studies*, 18, 2010, 1567–1589.
25. J. H. Dunning, *Multinational Enterprises and the Global Economy*, Reading, MA: Addison-Wesley, 1992.
26. See, for example, P. J. Taylor, B. Derudder, M. Hoyler and P. Ni, "New regional geographies of the world as practised by leading advanced producer service firms in 2010," *Transactions of the Institute of British Geographers*, 38, 2013, 497–511; B. Derudder, P. J. Taylor, F. Witlox and G. Catalano, "Hierarchical tendencies and regional patterns in the world city network: a global urban analysis of 234 cities," *Regional Studies*, 37, 2003, 875–886.
27. P. J. Taylor and G. Catalano, *World City Network: The Basic Data*, GAWC Data Set 11, http://www.lboro.ac.uk/gawc/datasets/da11.html
28. A. J. Scott, "Hollywood and the world: the geography of motion-picture distribution and marketing," *Review of International Political Economy*, 11, 2004, 33–61.
29. A. J. Scott and N. Pope, "Hollywood, Vancouver and the world: employment relocation and the emergence of satellite production centers in the motion picture industry," *Environment and Planning A*, 39, 2007, 1364–1381.
30. L. Sklair, *The Transnational Capitalist Class*, Oxford: Wiley-Blackwell, 2001.
31. C. Landry and F. Bianchini, *The Creative City*, London: Demos, 1995; C. Landry, F. Bianchini, R. Ebert, F. Gnad and K. R. Kunzmann, *The Creative City in Britain and Germany*, Berlin and London: Anglo-German Foundation for the Study of Industrial Society, 1996.
32. R. Florida, *op. cit.*, 2002; *idem.*, *op. cit.*, 2004.

33. Even though he is not, strictly speaking, a creative city theorist, E. L. Glaeser has also been a strong proponent of the idea that urban amenities (or what he calls "playground effects") exert a decisive influence on the migratory movements of skilled workers; see, for example, *The Triumph of the City: How Our Greatest Invention Makes Us Richer, Smarter, Greener, Healthier, and Happier*, New York: Penguin, 2011; see also: T. N. Clark, R. Lloyd, K. K. Wong and P. Jain, "Amenities drive urban growth," *Journal of Urban Affairs*, 24, 2002, 493–515.
34. J. Paquette, "De l'enthousiasme à l'horizontalité: Sudbury, ville créative," *Cahiers de Géographie du Québec*, 53, 2009, 47–61.
35. J. Zimmerman, "From brew town to cool town: neoliberalism and the creative city development strategy in Milwaukee," *Cities*, 25, 2008, 230–242.
36. P. Chatterton, "Will the real creative city please stand up?" *City: Analysis of Urban Trends, Culture, Theory, Policy, Action*, 4, 2000, 390–397.
37. S. Luckman, C. Gibson and T. Lea, "Mosquitoes in the mix: how transferable is creative city thinking?" *Singapore Journal of Tropical Geography*, 30, 2009, 70–85.
38. J. Peck, "Struggling with the creative class," *International Journal of Urban and Regional Research*, 29, 2005, 740–779.
39. E. L. Glaeser, J. Kolko and A. Saiz, "Consumer city," *Journal of Economic Geography*, 1, 2001, 27–50.
40. Cf. E. L. Glaeser et al., *op. cit.*, 2001; M. D. Partridge, "The duelling models: NEG vs amenity migration in explaining US engines of growth," *Journal of Economic Geography*, 89, 2010, 513–536.
41. R. Muth, "Migration: chicken or egg?" *Southern Economic Journal*, 37, 1971, 295–306.
42. J. van Dijk, "Do jobs-follow-people or people-follow-jobs? A meta-analysis for Europe and the US," plenary lecture at the 20th congress of the *Portuguese Association for Regional Development*, University of Évora, Portugal, July 10–11, 2014.
43. The discussion here is based on M. Storper and A. J. Scott, "Rethinking human capital, creativity, and urban growth," *Journal of Economic Geography*, 9, 2009, 147–167. The reader is advised to consult this article for a detailed exposition of the argument.
44. In fact, in a study of the migratory patterns of engineers in the United States, it was found that the only statistically significant exception to the finding that workers follow jobs concerned retirees. See A. J. Scott, "Jobs or amenities? Destination choices of migrant engineers in the USA," *Papers in Regional Science*, 89, 2010, 43–63.

45. See, for example, E. L. Glaeser and J. M. Shapiro, "Urban growth in the 1990s: is city living back?" *Journal of Regional Science*, 43, 2003, 139–165; P. E. Graves, "Migration and climate," *Journal of Regional Science*, 20, 1980, 227–237.
46. A. J. Scott and D. P. Angel, "The U.S. semiconductor industry: a locational analysis," *Environment and Planning A*, 19, 1987, 875–912.
47. A. J. Scott, *op. cit.*, 2010.

CHAPTER 8

Social Differentiation and Forms of Life

THE STRATIFICATION OF URBAN SOCIETY

The Widening Divide

Heterogeneity was one of the three variables that Louis Wirth singled out in 1938 as a fundamental descriptor of modern urban society.[1] Social heterogeneity remains an intrinsic feature of cities in the twenty-first century, and, if anything, has probably become even more entrenched since Wirth produced his celebrated analysis. The precise forms that this heterogeneity takes vary enormously, depending on the broad social and property relationships that prevail in any given society. A varying palette of sociocultural types can thus be found in cities everywhere, though we can also usually identify a prevalent twofold class division cutting through these different types, notwithstanding the often and increasingly ambiguous political alliances on each side of the divide.

Much has been made in recent years about the condensation of a new plutocracy—the so-called one percent—in contemporary capitalist society, and much political protest has been justifiably directed at the spectacular level of social inequality signified by this situation. Still, as reprehensible as this asymmetrical concentration of wealth may be, and in spite of its insistent documentation in the media, it tends to obfuscate the much more pervasive social divide in urban society between high-wage, cognitive-cultural workers on the one hand and low-wage workers (especially low-wage service workers) on the other. This divide is becoming increasingly accentuated as the cognitive-cultural economy continues to consolidate its hold over the urban production system and associated labor market relationships.

In the period of fordism, income discrepancies between white- and blue-collar workers were substantial but relatively subdued compared to the situation in advanced capitalist cities today.[2] Consider Fig. 8.1, which shows frequency distributions of individual wage and salary incomes (in constant 2010 dollars) for the total labor force in 139 metropolitan areas of the United States for the years 1950 and 2010. The 139 metropolitan areas in this and subsequent figures and tables represent the maximum

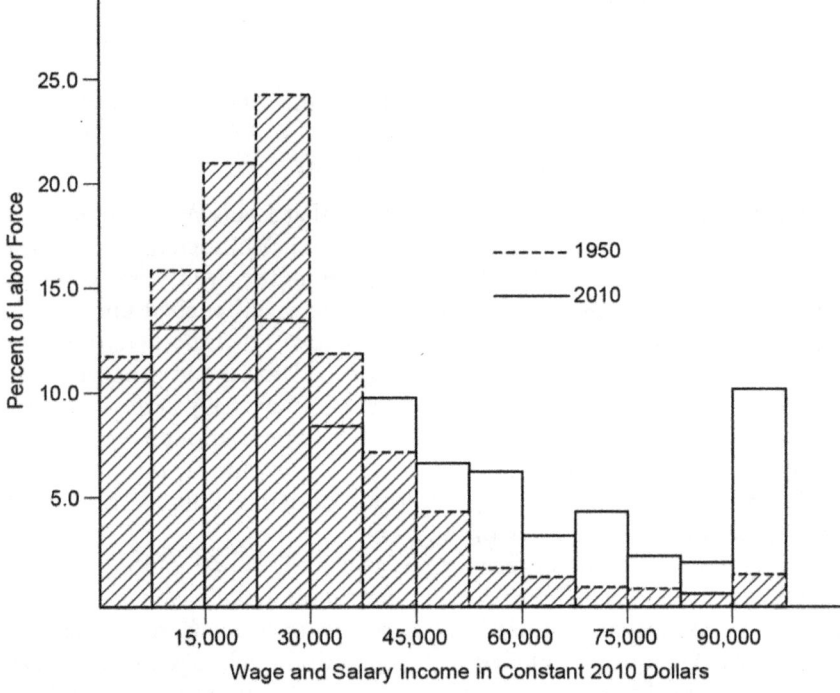

Fig. 8.1 Wage and salary income in constant 2010 dollars for the labor force in US metropolitan areas, 1950 and 2010; data presented in the figure are based on the 139 metropolitan areas that appear in *both* of the years 1950 and 2010 in US Department of the Census sources; workers with zero income in any year are omitted from the analysis. Source: Integrated Public Use Microdata Series (IPUMS-USA)

number of paired cases that can be extracted from US Department of Census sources for *both* of the years 1950 and 2010.[3] Figure 8.1 plainly displays the great increase in real income disparities from 1950 when fordism was still dominant in American cities to 2010, by which time the cognitive-cultural economy accounted for a sizeable share of total employment.

The companion data presented in Table 8.1 show wage and salary incomes (again in 2010 constant dollars) at different percentile levels of the labor force in 1950 and 2010 together with the percentage change in income for each percentile. In 1950, workers at the 90th percentile earned just over six times more than workers at the 10th percentile. In 2010, they were earning 13 times more. What is most striking about the data shown in Table 8.1 is the small increase over the 1950–2010 period in income for workers at the low end of the scale (a change of just 1.7% for workers at the 10th percentile) compared with the very substantial increase that has occurred at higher levels of income (152.6% for workers at the 95th percentile). Furthermore, two-income families have become much more prevalent today than they were in 1950, and disparities in terms of total family incomes are even more extreme than those that we observe in the case of individual wage and salary incomes. Thus, in 1950, families at the

Table 8.1 Wage and salary income of employed workers in US metropolitan areas by percentile, 1950–2010[a]

Percentile	Wage and salary income		Percent change
	1950	2010	
10	6,788	6,900	1.7
20	11,313	13,400	18.5
30	15,838	20,667	30.5
40	19,458	26,000	33.6
50	22,173	33,000	48.8
60	24,888	40,100	61.1
70	28,508	52,000	82.4
80	33,033	65,000	96.8
90	41,178	90,000	118.6
95	47,513	120,000	152.6

[a] Data presented in the table are based on the 139 metropolitan areas that appear in *both* of the years 1950 and 2010 in US Department of the Census sources; incomes for 1950 are converted to 2010 constant dollars; workers with zero income in any year are omitted from the analysis. Source: Integrated Public Use Microdata Series (IPUMS-USA)

top 90th percentile of total family income earned 7.2 times more than families at the 10th percentile, but by 2010, the ratio had increased massively to 20.4.

These deepening income inequalities in cities in the United States and elsewhere are intimately bound up with diverse other dimensions of social differentiation, including occupation, ethnicity, race, and gender in ways that leave palpable traces on the urban land nexus, as will be shown in Chap. 9. In addition, incomes vary widely as a function of city size. Median incomes in North America and Western Europe, for example, are typically higher in large cities than they are in smaller ones. Guilluy has recently called attention to the privileged position of large metropolitan areas or what he refers to as the "new citadels," where a liberal "new bourgeoisie" (surrounded by the myrmidons who serve its needs) profits disproportionately from global capitalism.[4] In small towns and rural communities in peripheral areas beyond these citadels, we find a rather distinct type of social formation with many similarities to the old working class, but negatively affected by globalization and facing declining prospects of meaningful and remunerative work, and nowadays much given to populist right-wing political sentiments.

Occupational Structures and Social Differentiation

In fordist capitalism, labor markets in core metropolitan areas were typically divided into what Reich, Gordon, and Edwards called "primary" and "secondary" segments, distinguishable from one another in terms of the levels of job security, pay, and benefits that they offered.[5] These segments were more or less equivalent to white-collar managerial, professional, and technical workers on the one side, and a composite group comprising blue-collar workers and low-wage white-collar workers such as file clerks and typists on the other. Workers in the former segment were employed in diverse management and technical positions, ranging from the bureaucratic and supervisory control of production, through top-down corporate research and development, to the provision of advanced social and financial services for society at large. Workers in the latter segment mainly carried out manual labor on the factory floor and served in subordinate positions in the bureaucracy of corporate capitalism.

Since the crisis of fordism in the 1970s, much of this old occupational structure in American and other cities has been significantly modified in favor of the dominant bipartite arrangement of cognitive-cultural capitalism as discussed at various points in previous chapters. It is an extremely difficult task to track this shift in detail on the basis of official statistics, but I shall offer a preliminary analysis by examining employment changes in seven broad occupational categories in US metropolitan areas for 1950 and 2010 (see Table 8.2). A few words about the construction of Table 8.2 are essential at the outset. Employment data for the occupational categories used in the table are obtained by aggregating statistics for more detailed occupational titles as given by the 1990 occupational classification provided by IPUMS-USA.[6] However, only those titles that remain unchanged from 1950 to 2010 are used in this exercise, and these are shown in the Appendix to this chapter. We must bear in mind that this manner of proceeding almost certainly leads to an underestimate of the recent growth of core cognitive-cultural workers in the US economy, for the 1990 occupational classification omits many new job titles that have emerged of late years, most notably in the fields of computer systems analysis and software development.[7] That being said, the conclusions drawn below are strengthened rather than weakened by this bias. We must

Table 8.2 Employment levels by occupational category in US metropolitan areas, 1950–2010[a]

Occupational category	Employment 1950	Percent of total	Employment 2010	Percent of total	Percent change 1950–2010
Managerial and professional occupations	6,223,575	18.9	23,800,000	34.1	282.4
Sales occupations	2,878,520	8.7	9,895,153	14.2	243.8
Administrative support occupations	5,538,564	16.8	7,965,650	11.4	43.8
Service occupations	3,729,367	11.3	13,900,000	19.9	272.7
Precision production, craft and repair occupations	4,942,004	15.0	6,495,916	9.3	31.4
Operators, fabricators, and laborers, except transport occupations	7,830,390	23.8	4,089,914	5.9	−47.8
Transport occupations	1,824,403	5.5	3,711,555	5.3	103.4
Total	32,966,823	–	69,858,188	–	111.9

[a]Data presented in the table are based on the 139 metropolitan areas that appear in *both* of the years 1950 and 2010 in US Department of the Census sources. See the Appendix to this chapter for a full definition of the seven occupational categories

bear in mind, as well, that the substantive nature of the work in any given occupational category is subject to change over time, though this circumstance, too, probably works in favor of the present analysis. Note that the occupational data presented in Table 8.2 represent aggregates over the 139 metropolitan areas (as already defined) for both of the years 1950 and 2010. These data are fully consistent with the notion that the social stratification of American cities has moved decisively away from a fordist configuration and is now more aligned with the division of labor peculiar to the cognitive-cultural economy. Three detailed points need to be made in elaboration of this remark.

First, workers in prestigious managerial and professional occupations increased by an impressive 282.4% over the period from 1950 to 2010, that is, more than twice as fast as the expansion of the labor force as a whole over the same period. In the 1950s, a large proportion of the workers in these occupations would be classifiable as regular white-collar employees in diverse kinds of hierarchically organized administrative positions. With the rise of the cognitive-cultural economy, managerial and professional workers are more likely to be engaged in much more open-ended and innovative styles of operation, not only in the worlds of industry, commerce, and finance but also in new or restructured sectors such as software development, architecture, social media, film production, and fashion.

Second, employment in three occupational categories that to a significant, though very imperfect, degree coincide with what I have earlier characterized as the "new servile class" at the low-wage and low-prestige end of the labor market also increased rapidly from 1950 to 1960. These categories, namely, sales, services, and transport occupations, expanded by 243.8%, 272.7%, and 103.4%, respectively. By far the majority of workers in sales occupations are engaged in relatively poorly-paid retail trade though some sales workers (e.g. in corporate offices) are more clearly aligned with managerial and professional occupations; the service occupations break down into more detailed divisions like housekeepers, bartenders, kitchen workers, cooks, janitors, and porters; and transport occupations (in metropolitan areas) are mainly concerned with the operation of bus, subway, taxi, and delivery services. All of these occupations are necessary elements of support systems for the cognitive-cultural economy and its more privileged representatives in metropolitan areas.

Third, the remaining occupational categories in Table 8.2 make up a further composite group comprising administrative support occupations together with two nominally blue-collar categories: (a) precision production, craft and repair occupations; and (b) operators, fabricators, and laborers. These are all occupations that have performed relatively poorly in

American metropolitan areas as the cognitive-cultural economy has grown. Employment in administrative support occupations and precision production, craft, and repair occupations grew by just 43.8% and 9.3%, respectively, from 1950 to 2010; these percentages are far below the rate of growth of the labor force as a whole, and employment actually declined in both of these occupations in the ten largest metropolitan areas. In addition, employment of operators, fabricators, and laborers fell sharply across the board from 1950 to 2010. A large part of the poor record of these three main occupational categories in recent decades can be accounted for by the fact that automation is eliminating significant elements of their human substance from the economy while decentralization of significant swaths of manufacturing activity to low-wage countries has also eroded much of their presence in the large metropolitan areas of advanced capitalism.

These contrasting trends in occupational structure in American metropolitan areas reveal that the labor force has been significantly reshaped in comparison to what it looked like in the 1950s. The four occupational categories most closely associated with the upper and lower tiers of the labor force in the new economy of the twenty-first century (i.e. managerial and professional, sales, service, and transport occupations) represented 44% of all workers in the 139 metropolitan areas in 1950. By 2010, they constituted the overwhelming majority of workers, with 73.5% of the total.[8] The remaining three occupational categories indicated in Table 8.2 (i.e. administrative support occupations, precision production, craft and repair occupations, and operators, fabricators, and laborers) declined collectively from 55.6% of the labor force to 26.5%. For some of the detailed occupations that make up these latter three categories, the substantive character of the work involved has changed little over the last several decades; in other cases, it has been reconstructed in ways that make it more clearly aligned with the new economy, a point that contributes positively to the general argument offered here.

Human Capital Variations

The claim that cities in the advanced capitalist societies have evolved away from fordism and are now consolidating their role as centers of cognitive-cultural production (with corresponding transformative effects on the urban land nexus) leads on the allied claim that significant qualitative changes in intraurban stocks of human capital have also come about, and more specifically, that human capital assets relating to practical skills and manual work have declined in major cities while assets like analytical, cognitive, relational and multicultural aptitudes have increased. Unfortunately, any attempt to test these statements directly faces the immediate problem that only recently has it become feasible to construct city-specific measures of these different types of human capital, and significant time depth in these measures reaching back to the fordist period is impossible to achieve.[9] For present purposes, therefore, we must find a readily available proxy variable, and probably the best way forward in these circumstances is to consider levels of educational attainment. In particular, changes in the percentage of the workforce with a bachelor's degree or equivalent would seem to offer a means of assessing at least some of the expected shift in the intellectual qualities of the urban labor force. This measure is an approximate and in several respects ambiguous gauge of human capital, but being easily obtainable over an extended time period, it is frequently resorted to in research by urban economists and geographers on issues of urban development.[10]

Figure 8.2 provides a view of the relationship between the percentage of the workforce with a bachelor's degree or equivalent and the logarithm of population in American metropolitan areas for each of the years 1950 and 2010. Both of the graphs shown in Fig. 8.2 are based on the standard 139 metropolitan areas. The difference between the two graphs is conspicuous. In 1950, only 2.0% of the metropolitan labor force in the United States had achieved a level of education equivalent to a bachelor's degree or better, and this percentage was remarkably constant across metropolitan areas of different sizes. Indeed, the correlation between the percentage of the labor force with a bachelor's degree or better and the logarithm of metropolitan population in 1950 was a statistically insignificant 0.08. By 2010, the percentage of the total labor force with a bachelor's degree or better had risen to 22.0%, and the values of this variable also now varied noticeably across US metropolitan areas as revealed by a highly significant correlation of 0.42 with the logarithm of population.[11] Even though we cannot standardize for changes in the average quality of a bachelor's degree since the 1950s, the rather dramatic shift revealed by these remarks is entirely consistent with the rise of the cognitive-cultural economy and its observable concentration in large cities.

Table 8.3 displays a corresponding body of data where the percentage of the labor force with a bachelor's degree or equivalent is cross-tabulated three different ways, namely, by year, by two classes of metropolitan areas (the ten largest and all others), and by the seven broad occupational categories already identified in Table 8.2. In 1950, even in managerial and professional occupations, the incidence of workers with advanced educational qualifications was

THE STRATIFICATION OF URBAN SOCIETY 163

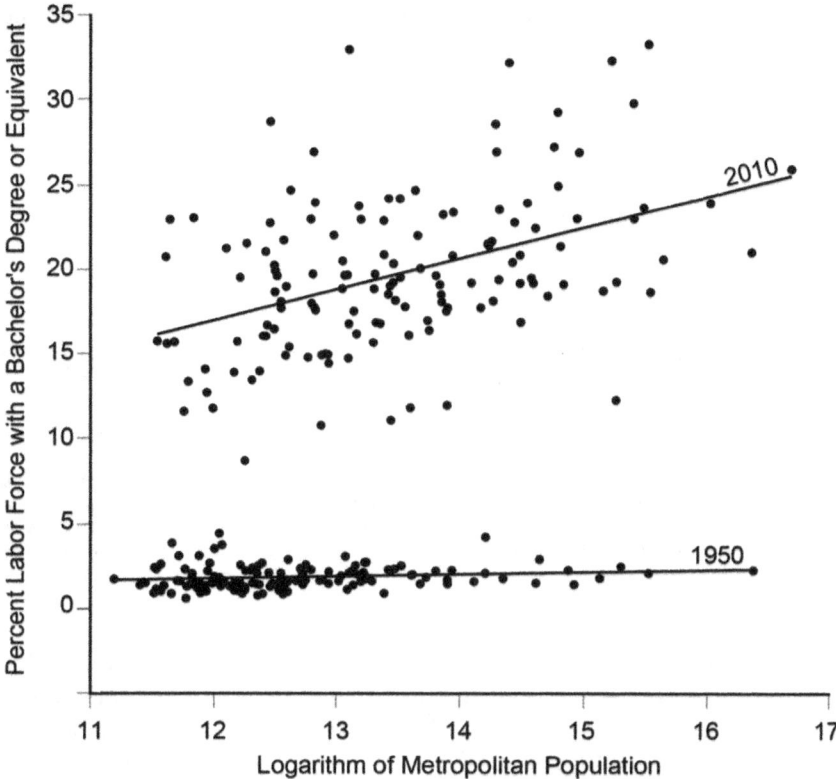

Fig. 8.2 Percent of the labor force with a bachelor's degree or equivalent versus the logarithm of population in US metropolitan areas, 1950 and 2010; regression lines are shown. Data presented in the figure represent the 139 metropolitan areas that appear in *both* of the years 1950 and 2010 in US Department of the Census sources. Source: Integrated Public Use Microdata Series (IPUMS-USA)

remarkably modest. Differences between the ten largest and all other metropolitan areas in regard to advanced educational qualifications were also notably small in 1950. By 2010, the percentage of workers with a bachelor's degree or better had increased in all occupational categories—in some cases radically—even those characterized by blue-collar work, and, symptomatically, the overall lead held by the ten largest metropolitan areas compared to the others had increased. The main concentrations of individuals with advanced educational qualifications in 2010 were in occupations that involve significant levels of cognitively and culturally inflected forms of work, with

Table 8.3 Percentage of labor force with a bachelor's degree or equivalent in different occupational categories in US metropolitan areas, 1950–2010[a]

Occupational category	Top ten metropolitan areas		All other metropolitan areas	
	1950	2010	1950	2010
Managerial and professional occupations	14.2	75.8	12.5	69.5
Sales occupations	2.9	33.5	2.9	26.3
Administrative support occupations	2.7	22.8	2.5	18.1
Service occupations	0.8	10.3	0.7	8.1
Precision production, craft and repair occupations	0.9	8.8	0.6	6.8
Operators, fabricators, and laborers, except transport occupations	0.4	5.6	0.3	4.5
Transport occupations	0.5	7.7	0.3	5.9

[a]Data presented in the table are based on the 139 metropolitan areas that appear in *both* of the years 1950 and 2010 in US Department of the Census sources. The top ten metropolitan areas (in 1950) are Boston, Chicago, Detroit, Los Angeles-Long Beach, New York, NY-Northeastern NJ, Philadelphia, Pittsburgh, St. Louis, San Francisco-Oakland-Vallejo, and Washington. Nb.: Any given metropolitan area may vary in geographic extent from one year to the next. Source: Integrated Public Use Microdata Series (IPUMS-USA)

managerial and professional occupations again clearly in the forefront. Sales and administrative support occupations, which in 1950 were almost entirely lacking in personnel with advanced educational credentials, show evidence of very significant upgrading by 2010.

An additional light on these matters is cast by Fig. 8.3, which plots values of 26 different human capital and work performance indexes in relation to three different size classes of metropolitan areas in the United States. These size classes are defined in terms of population, as follows: (a) small: less than 250,000, (b) medium: between 250,000 and one million, (c) large: more than one million. The indexes themselves were constructed by combining measures of human capital and work performance (published by the US Department of Labor) with employment data per

Fig. 8.3 (continued) values are normalized relative to this base. Metropolitan size classes are defined in terms of population as follows: (a) small: less than 250,000, (b) medium: between 250,000 and one million, and (c) large: more than one million. Population data are for the year 2000. Source: A. J. Scott and A. Mantegna, "Human capital assets and structures of work in the US metropolitan hierarchy (an analysis based on the O*NET information system)," *International Regional Science Review*, 32, 2009, 173–194

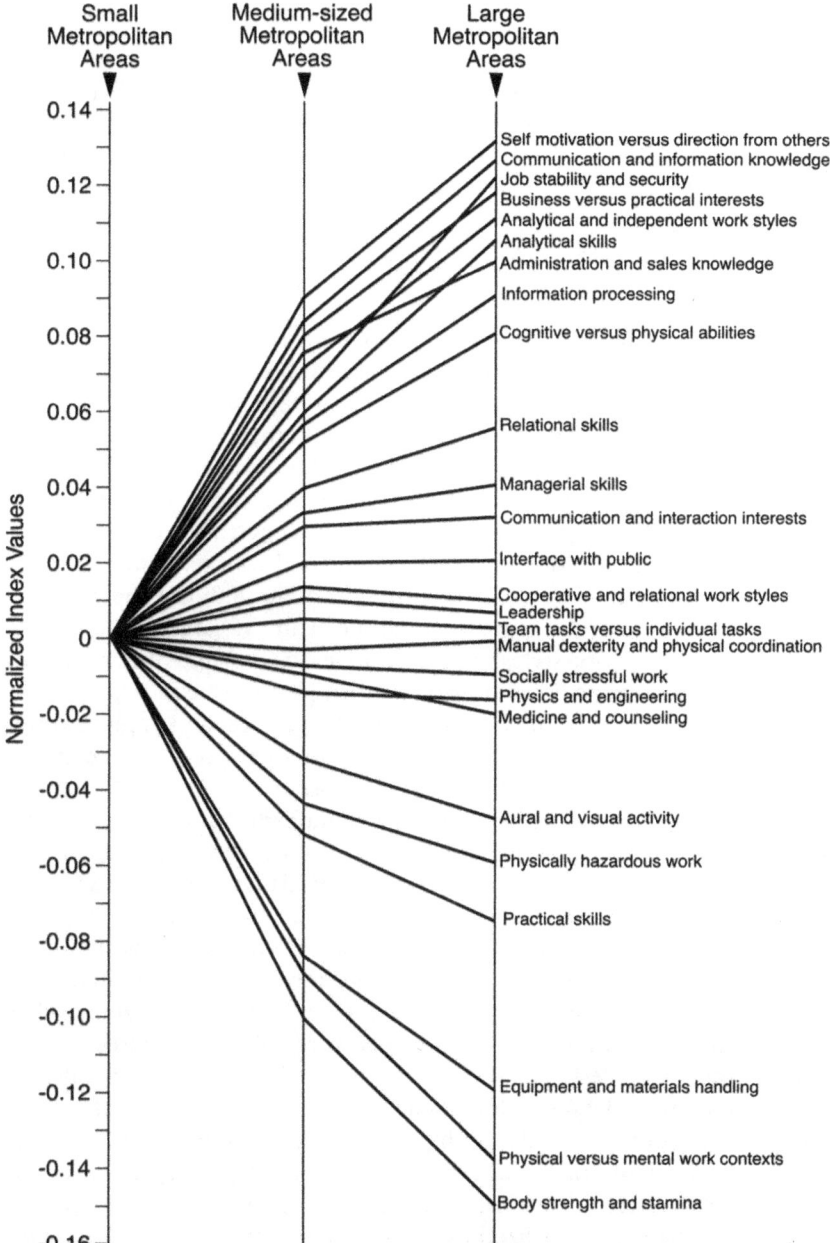

Fig. 8.3 Human capital and work indexes by metropolitan size class in the United States. For comparative purposes, the index for each type of human capital and work is set equal to zero for the smallest metropolitan size category, and all other

detailed occupation (as defined by IPUMS-USA for the year 2000).[12] The numerical scores of all indexes are normalized by setting the values for small metropolitan areas equal to zero and adjusting all other values relative to this base. The results set out in Fig. 8.3 reveal a remarkably systematic set of data patterns, and these rather clearly betoken the differential play of the social changes currently proceeding in American metropolitan areas as the cognitive-cultural economy penetrates ever more deeply into their functional fabric.

Thus, types of human capital and work performance that are primarily cognitive and interactive in nature (e.g. self-motivation, analytical skills, relational skills) increase notably in their representation within the labor force as we progress from small, through medium, to large metropolitan areas.[13] Conversely, the incidence of types of human capital and work performance that involve physical labor and applied know-how (e.g. body strength and stamina, physical versus mental work contexts, and equipment and materials handling) is inversely related to size of metropolitan area. Many additional intricacies are evident in Fig. 8.3. On the cognitive and interactive side of the human capital spectrum, variables like analytical and independent work styles, administrative and business interests, and information-processing activities play a much greater role in larger metropolitan areas than in the smaller ones. On the physical and applied know-how side, practical skills, hazardous work, and aural and visual acuity are relatively important in smaller metropolitan areas.

Between these two polarities lies a set of indexes that are more equally distributed across metropolitan size classes. Among these, the manual dexterity and physical coordination index is of special interest. The values of this index are quite evenly distributed across all three metropolitan size classes, and, moreover, this is the only index related to physical/applied labor that has a positive standardized score for large metropolitan areas. The explanation for this state of affairs can be found in all likelihood by noting that much of the practical physical work still concentrated in large cities is concerned less with repetitious manual operations or muscular exertion than with detailed motor skills and aptitudes in sectors that often have a strong contingent relationship to the wider cognitive-cultural economy. Two segments of the urban economy, in particular, illustrate this point, namely, craft industries, such as clothing, furniture, and jewelry (commonly forming specialized districts in core areas of major cities), and low-wage service operations focused on physical tasks such as making deliveries, taxi driving, repair trades, kitchen work, housekeeping, and so on.

Demographic Divisions

The Immigrant Connection

One of the familiar aspects of the growth of cities in capitalism, both in the United States and elsewhere, is their tendency to function as magnets for successive waves of immigrants (from both near and far), who are drawn into the orbit of the city by prospective opportunities for improved incomes and livelihoods and sometimes for physical security.[14] Moreover, the expansionary dynamic of the city continually calls for replenishment and expansion of the labor force, and immigrants play an important role in filling the concomitant gaps in the labor market, both in regard to the skilled labor demands and even more insistently in regard to the low-wage, unskilled labor needs of the large metropolis.[15] In these ways, decade after decade, changing streams of migrant populations have moved into, and continue to move, not only into the cities of wealthy countries, but also into the cities of low- and medium-income countries. In the latter case, numerical overloads of in-migrants frequently result in the formation of disproportionately large pools of unemployed individuals. In the United States, in the era of classical fordism, a major component of these streams of urban-bound migrants consisted of diverse racial, ethnic, and national groups such as African Americans from the southern states as well as Irish, Italians, Poles, and Eastern European Jews from various parts of Europe.[16] Since the 1970s and 1980s, low-wage immigrants moving into American cities have been increasingly originating in Asian and Latin American countries.

Race, Ethnicity, Gender

The information given in Table 8.4 partially illustrates these remarks by indicating the changing racial, ethnic, and national-origins composition of the labor force in the 139 American metropolitan areas for the years 1950, 1980, and 2010.

In 1950, when fordism was in full swing, African Americans constituted the largest minority group in American cities, with 9.3% of the labor force, while people born in Europe came second, with 8.4%. At this time, Asians and Hispanics constituted quite negligible minorities. In 1980, fordism was drawing rapidly to a close and the cognitive-cultural economy was

Table 8.4 Percentage of the labor force composed of African Americans, Asians, Hispanics, and European-born in US metropolitan areas, 1950, 1980, 2010[a]

Selected population groups	1950		1980		2010	
	Population	Percent	Population	Percent	Population	Percent
African American	7,811,247	9.3	18,994,626	14.29	28,828,824	14.74
Asian	260,375	0.31	2,645,158	1.99	12,502,197	6.44
Hispanic	1,990,608	2.37	10,700,261	8.05	36,730,057	18.84
European birthplace	7,013,324	8.35	4,240,228	3.19	4,620,377	2.38
Total population	83,991,903	–	132,922,502	–	194,133,492	–

[a]Data presented in the table are based on the 139 metropolitan areas that appear in *both* of the years 1950 and 2010 in US Department of the Census sources. Nb.: The designated population groups are not necessarily mutually exclusive. Source: Integrated Public Use Microdata Series (IPUMS-USA)

beginning its ascent; equally, 1980 represents a transitional year in terms of demographic change in the labor force in American cities. In 1980, the African-American population began to stabilize as a percentage of the total labor force though it was still the largest minority at this time. A slight increase in Asians is also evident in 1980 together with a significant and accelerating rise of Hispanics. And a sharp decline of individuals born in Europe has clearly set in by this time. By 2010, Hispanics have become by far the largest minority in the 139 metropolitan areas, followed by African Americans, who have much the same percentage representation in the metropolitan population in 2010 as they had in 1980, and whose numbers were actually falling in the largest metropolitan areas. In 2010, too, a significant increase in Asians as a percentage of the metropolitan population is evident, while the percentage made up by the European-born is even lower than in 1980.

Table 8.5 indicates how the four population groups in question here are distributed in percentage terms over the seven occupational categories previously examined and how these distributions have changed from 1950 to 2010 in step with the evolution of the American economy from a dominant fordist regime to a dominant cognitive-cultural regime. These data are again drawn from our standard 139 metropolitan areas. A plus sign attached to any number in Table 8.5 indicates that the corresponding index of representation is greater than 1.2; a negative sign indicates an index of less

Table 8.5 Percentage occurrence of selected population groups in selected occupational categories in US metropolitan areas, 1950 and 2010[a]

Occupational category	1950					2010				
	African American	Asian	Hispanic	European birthplace		African American	Asian	Hispanic	European birthplace
Managerial and professional occupations	2.9⁻	0.3	1.1⁻	10.3⁺		9.0⁻	8.3⁺	7.9⁻	3.3⁺	
Sales occupations	2.0⁻	0.2⁻	1.4⁻	7.1		12.2	6.5	15.1	2.2	
Administrative support occupations	3.4⁻	0.2⁻	1.3⁻	3.7⁻		14.5	5.2	14.0⁻	2.2	
Service occupations	31.7⁺	0.9⁺	2.4	12.9⁺		21.0⁺	6.8	24.8⁺	2.6	
Precision production, craft and repair occupations	4.1⁻	0.2⁻	1.6⁻	12.1⁺		9.5⁻	3.5⁻	26.6⁺	3.1⁺	
Operators, fabricators, and laborers, except transport occupations	15.1⁺	0.2⁻	3.4⁺	12.5⁺		18.7⁺	4.8⁻	27.2⁺	1.9⁻	
Transport occupations	10.2	0.1⁻	2.0	6.0⁻		21.5⁺	3.5⁻	20.5	2.5	
Percent of employed labor force	9.3	0.31	2.4	8.4		14.7	6.4	18.8	2.4	

[a]The numbers in the main body of the table represent the percentage of employment in the corresponding occupational category that is accounted for by the specified population group in the specified year. Numbers with a plus sign are associated with an index of representation greater than 1.2; numbers with a negative sign are associated with an index of representation less than 0.8. Data presented in the table are based on the 139 metropolitan areas that appear in both of the years 1950 and 2010 in US Department of the Census sources. Nb.: The designated population groups are not necessarily mutually exclusive.
Source: Integrated Public Use Microdata Series (IPUMS-USA)

than 0.8. The index of representation is defined as the percentage incidence of any given population group in any given occupation divided by the same group's percentage share of the total labor force. A high value of the index thus informs us that this population group is over-represented in the designated occupation, and a low value indicates under-representation. The information laid out in Table 8.5 is much too copious to warrant a full verbal description, but we can simplify matters by considering a few highlights that reveal some of the subtle and not-so-subtle ways in which the production system and the stock of available human resources embodied in the racial and ethnic character of the labor force combine with one another via the social logic of labor markets in US cities.

In 1950, the labor force across the board in major US cities was clearly dominated by native-born Americans divided into a broad range of white-collar and blue-collar occupations. Of the total labor force, 9.3% were African Americans, most of whom were concentrated in the lower half of the employment system in manufacturing and service occupations. The immigrant population in 1950 was dominated by individuals born in Europe who comprised 8.5% of the labor force and who were distributed fairly widely over different occupational groupings. At this time, Asians and Hispanics constituted only a negligible fraction of the total labor force.

This relatively simple pattern of racial and ethnic differentiation in American urban labor markets in the period of fordism gave way to a much more varied configuration as the new economy moved into high gear after the turn of the century and as immigration from Asia and Latin America accelerated rapidly thus widening the pool of available human resources. By 2010, Asians (of whom 66.8% were foreign-born) and Hispanics (of whom 40.0% were foreign-born) had now become both absolutely and proportionally much more present in the labor market, though in very different ways. With their generally higher levels education, Asians by this stage had made significant inroads into high-level cognitive and cultural forms of employment in management and the professions, including engineering, whereas Hispanics were concentrated in low-wage service and blue-collar occupations. In effect, Hispanics, and especially non-native-born Hispanics, make up a large segment of the new servile class in American metropolitan areas, a circumstance that reflects the relatively low average levels of formal education of Hispanic immigrants together with the fact that they are in numerous cases undocumented and thus often inhibited from asserting their civil rights such as their entitlement to at least a minimum wage.[17]

African Americans marginally increased their presence in the labor force of US metropolitan areas over the period from 1950 to 2010, and also made small advances in occupational status, but have undoubtedly progressed less rapidly than they might have done had the playing field in regard to life chances for this group been more evenly laid out. In addition, there has been some erosion in recent years of the African-American labor force in larger metropolitan areas, probably due in part to declines in manufacturing activity, but no doubt too as a consequence of competition in the labor market from low-wage immigrants. If we examine detailed low-wage occupational categories like waiters and waitresses, sewing machine operators, or electronics assembly operations, we find an anomalously low representation of African Americans within them as compared with immigrant Asians and Hispanics, despite unusually high unemployment rates among the former group. It is highly likely that many employers of workers in occupations like these have a conscious or unconscious preference for politically marginalized immigrant workers over those, like African Americans, who can more aggressively assert their rights in regard to minimum wages and working conditions. Tangible evidence in favor of this claim is provided by the frequently noted discouraged-worker effect among African Americans in regard to certain kinds of jobs for which they are otherwise entirely eligible.[18] By 2010, European immigrants had come to form a very minor fraction of the US labor force.

Of course, gender is also differentially and markedly articulated with the occupational division of labor in American cities (see Table 8.6). In both 1950 and 2010, women workers were most obviously concentrated in administrative support and service occupations, both of which involve many stereotypically feminized tasks especially in instances where a human interface or emotional transfer is involved, as in the case of personnel officers, hotel receptionists, restaurant servers, manicurists, health support, and childcare.[19] Women were also well represented in sales occupations in both 1950 and 2010, but their rate of relative concentration in this category declined somewhat over the intervening six decades. Whereas women in 1950 were significantly underrepresented in managerial and professional occupations, they have begun in recent years to enter these labor market niches in increasing numbers. The relative incidence of women in managerial and professional occupations is now approximately equal to their rate of participation in the labor force as a whole, though according to recent information from the American Community Survey,

Table 8.6 Percentage occurrence of female workers in selected occupational categories in US metropolitan areas, 1950 and 2010[a]

Occupational category	Female workers	
	1950	2010
Managerial and professional occupations	24.9	50.4
Sales occupations	36.2+	50.9
Administrative support occupations	60.2+	77.6+
Service occupations	56.0+	61.4+
Precision production, craft and repair occupations	4.7	8.2
Operators, fabricators, and laborers, except transport occupations	27.8	22.0−
Transport occupations	1.0−	12.0−
Percent of employed labor force	29.9	48.4

[a]Each number in the table represents the percentage of employment in the corresponding occupational category that is accounted for by female workers in the specified year. Numbers with a plus sign are associated with an index of representation greater than 1.2; numbers with a negative sign are associated with an index of representation less than 0.8. Data presented in the table are based on the 139 metropolitan areas that appear in *both* of the years 1950 and 2010 in US Department of the Census sources. Source: Integrated Public Use Microdata Series (IPUMS-USA)

their median income in these occupations is just 71.8% of the median income of their male colleagues.

These findings on demographic trends in the deployment of labor in cities are obviously highly specific to the United States and cannot be directly transferred to the case of other countries. What they do suggest in general is that in every specific social formation in the capitalist world, we are likely to find peculiar and opportunistic arrangements of labor processes, wage structures, stocks of human capital, and demographic differentials that come into operational relationship with one another via the competitive, efficiency-seeking dynamics of the urban production system. The stability of these arrangements, however, is always subject to erosion not only as an outcome of the path-dependent course of economic evolution, but also as a result of challenges by the least advantaged workers in the political arena.

Identity Versus the Melting Pot

Cities consistently exhibit highly variegated patterns of social life derived from the interactions of the division of labor, forms of human capital, and demographic differences (among other variables), though in widely differing qualitative expressions in different historical and geographical circumstances. The towns of early industrial Britain, the fordist cities of twentieth-century North America and Western Europe, and the global centers of cognitive-cultural capitalism today are all strongly marked by internal social differentiation of various kinds. Indeed, exemplary cases can be found virtually everywhere, from the cities of modern China with their cohorts of rural migrants, through the case of Brazilian cities and their communities of Japanese and Korean settlers, to large urban areas in francophone West Africa where Lebanese communities have deep roots.

Still, group identities in capitalist cities are rarely, if ever, fixed in stone. Distinctive identities are continually being negotiated and renegotiated, as it were, by the experience of life in the temporal and spatial swirl of the urban land nexus, and especially by the ways in which work activities and community life interact with one another in the wider context of the city. These constructed identities may be relatively stable over a few generations and yet are also highly mutable as the assimilation of subsequent generations sets in. In American cities, groups with subdominant cultural identities have usually been integrated over the course of three or four generations into mainstream society, though a large segment of the African-American population—which has experienced significant discriminatory barriers to upward social mobility—remains a stubborn exception to this statement.[20] Furthermore, the socialization and upward-mobility processes traditionally characteristic of American urban society have regularly eroded the conditions under which cheap exploitable labor at the bottom of the employment ladder can be internally reproduced. The concomitant vacuum has then invariably been filled by new rounds of immigration and new rounds of social fragmentation to be followed eventually by new rounds of social assimilation.

This, at least seemed to be the way things worked in the American metropolis throughout much of its history until the demise of fordism. In the new cognitive-cultural order, the deep social and economic bifurcation of urban existence has become so strongly ingrained that upward mobility appears to have slowed considerably over these last few decades.[21] Concomitantly, the traditional melting-pot dynamics of American society may well turn out to operate less effectively in the future than they have done hitherto, at least until significant political reform of current social and economic relationships has been achieved.

Precariousness, Poverty, and Informality

The Urban Slum

Wherever capitalism has ushered in processes of urbanization, poverty and slums have almost always followed in their wake. This predicament stems from a diversity of circumstances, depending on local conditions, including factors like the vagaries of competitive labor markets, the existence of population surpluses due to high rates of net migration to the city, ingrained prejudices that disadvantage particular social groups, and any combination of these factors. The neoliberal retreat from public spending on welfare in many different societies in recent decades has had particularly injurious effects by allowing poverty and social marginalization to fester in cities far and wide. Moreover, when numbers of persistently impoverished and marginalized individuals accumulate in cities, they typically gather together in the urban land nexus to form communities of the dispossessed, where they can find a degree of mutual support and material aid to counter the hardships of social marginalization. These communities vary greatly from one city to another and assume many different designations in different countries, but no matter whether they are referred to as slums, skid row areas, shantytowns, shack settlements, *bidonvilles*, *barrios*, or *favelas*, among many other terms (all of them with more or less derogatory implications), they represent the deep underbelly of the city and the extreme antithesis of the prosperous business and residential quarters where the successful frontrunners of capitalism stake out their privileged urban existence.

In nineteenth-century North America and Western Europe, the slum was a commonplace element of large cities, and it acquired a notorious reputation in popular lore as a place where the out-of-work, the destitute, the homeless, the physically and mentally incapacitated, and other lost souls congregated together, and where socially deviant behaviors such as crime, prostitution, and alcoholism ran rife. Lurid accounts of slum conditions are common currency in nineteenth-century enquiries into urban existence. An excerpt from a report by the superintendent of police in Glasgow provides a glimpse of life in some of the more deprived residential districts in the city in 1842[22]:

> The houses ... are unfit even for sties, and every apartment is filled with a promiscuous crowd of men, women and children, all in the most revolting

state of filth and squalor. In many houses, there is scarcely any ventilation; dunghills lie in the vicinity of the dwellings; and from the extremely defective sewerage, filth of every kind constantly accumulates. In these horrid dens the most abandoned characters of the city are collected, and from thence they nightly issue to disseminate disease, and to pour upon the town every species of crime and abomination.

The parallels between this description and Engels' contemporaneous account of slum housing in Manchester are striking. It is not surprising in the light of these comments to note that the urban slum in nineteenth-century North America and Western Europe constituted one of the principal "social problems" of the day, and, as outlined by Gareth Stedman Jones in his classic study *Outcast London*, was the object of numerous schemes of putative reform.[23]

Urban areas that have descended to the level of social degradation observable in the slums of Glasgow in 1842 are no longer a significant feature of cities in the advanced capitalist countries of the twenty-first century, especially given the vigorous implementation of programs of urban renewal and social housing construction over the post-War decades. However, neighborhoods marked by penury and deprivation are still frequently in evidence in these countries, often in association with racially or ethnically ghettoized populations. Vivid examples are offered by impoverished African-American neighborhoods in parts of New York, Los Angeles, and Chicago, or by refugee and Roma encampments in a number of European urban areas, or by pockets of homeless individuals virtually everywhere in the world. Moreover, while urban renewal and social housing have unquestionably ameliorated the conditions of life for large numbers of underprivileged individuals, they have also in many cases only succeeded in displacing the problems they were intended to resolve to other parts of the city.[24] The alienating tower blocks, or *habitations à loyer modéré*, with their racially and ethnically segregated populations and frequent high levels of social breakdown, criminality, and violence that form a discontinuous ring of suburban communities around the core of Paris, offer a rather startling object lesson in this kind of failure.[25]

Informality and Marginalization in Developing Countries

In numerous parts of Africa, Asia, and Latin America, where standards of living are considerably lower than those in North America and Western

Europe, and where cities are often inundated by immigrants from poor rural areas, problems of deprivation and casualization in urban areas are liable to take on massive proportions. In some countries, war and violence have also created streams of impecunious migrants to the city, as exemplified by chronic unrest in the eastern regions of the Congo Democratic Republic, causing large numbers of refugees to flee to the slums of Kinshasa. Davis describes several situations like this where large cohorts of "surplus humanity" are drawn to the city and yet are systematically excluded from more normatively sanctioned structures of employment and urban life.[26]

The persistent migration from rural to urban areas in less-developed countries appears at first glance to be something of a paradox given that population influxes to the city in these contexts so often results in prolonged unemployment and deprivation rather than in immediately improved material circumstances for the individual migrant, and *a fortiori*, for any accompanying family members. Certainly, urban wages in these countries are usually higher than rural wages for any given level of skill. It has been shown that in several African countries, for example, the urban wage, even in the informal sector, is often double and sometimes more than double the rural wage, for in spite of the massive cityward drift of population, appropriately skilled and socialized workers can evidently command a significant wage premium.[27] But why does migration to the city persist given that exceptionally high rates of unemployment are endemic? Harris and Todaro have provided a suggestive answer to this question by proposing that rural-urban movement in low-wage countries is regulated by the *expected* urban wage relative to the rural wage, and where, to simplify, the expected wage is defined as the actual urban wage adjusted in relation to the probability of finding a job.[28] Migration will then continue until the expected urban wage and the rural wage are equal. To put the matter in somewhat analogous terms, rural residents know that the prospects of attaining higher income levels are negligible so long as they remain where they are, but if they migrate to the city, there is always the possibility that they will eventually—at some indefinite time in the future—find adequately remunerative work.

A pervasive calculus of this sort probably helps to account for much of the hyperurbanization that is so characteristic of low- and middle-income countries, and this is almost always accompanied by a syndrome of slum development, where the chronically poor crowd together in dense and frequently insalubrious settlements. Some of these slum dwellers are able to find jobs in the formal sector, but most are marginalized in what we might call *para-capitalist* conditions of life that comprise for the most part a subservient relationship to the formal social and economic order of the city. This relationship assumes many different guises, including informal small-scale service provision and sweated labor in run-down workshops and factories that locate in slum areas in order to tap into the local pool of cheaply available workers while simultaneously engaging in noxious activities, such as leather tanning or foundry operations, that are barred from areas of the city subject to more rigorous environmental regulation. In many parts of the world, the slum economy is also based on the recycling of assorted waste products from rags to electronic scrap cast off from businesses and residents in more affluent quarters of the city. In its most degraded aspect this labor of recycling includes the retrieval of items salvaged from the city's garbage dumps, just as slum dwellers of London in Dickens' day supplemented their livelihoods by rummaging through the city's "dust heaps" (see Chap. 3).

According to the 2013 UN-Habitat report on the state of the world's cities, as many as 828 million urban dwellers worldwide reside in slum or informal settlements, an increase of 20.2% since 1990.[29] In sub-Saharan Africa, some 62.0% of the urban population lives in such settlements, a figure that rises to a remarkable 95.9% in the Central African Republic where the capital city of Bangui accounts for most of the country's slum population. According to Davis "the five great metropolises of South Asia (Karachi, Mumbai, Delhi, Kolkata, and Dhaka) alone contain 15,000 distinct slum communities whose total population exceeds 20 million."[30] Wherever they may occur in the world, these slum communities typically develop on land that is unattractive to other denizens of the city. Sometimes they emerge on steep hill slopes; sometimes they are located in areas subject to flooding; sometimes they form on top of old waste disposal sites; sometimes they are pushed out to the far periphery of the city; indeed, they can be found wherever the possibility of extra-legal land appropriation and squatting exists.[31] McGee has identified a form of slum development in Indonesia and other parts of Southeast Asia where interpenetrating bands of informal settlements and rural land, or what he calls *desakota* patterns of urbanization, occur in sprawling extensions of large cities.[32]

Poverty and irregular employment are central features of life in the majority of slums, and so also are such predicaments as the dearth of infrastructure, the poor quality of housing (often built by the occupier), overcrowding, the absence of social services, health hazards, and relatively high crime rates.³³ Slum areas are also usually marked by complex patterns of land occupancy and housing tenure, often of doubtful formal legality depending on the specific jurisdiction in which they are located. In any case, security of tenure is very generally fragile, which means that these kinds of settlements are highly susceptible to removal or redevelopment when they begin to impose social costs (crime, drug dealing, prostitution, health hazards, etc.) on the rest of the city or when changes in the structure of the urban land nexus make it worthwhile for powerful private or public interests to attempt to appropriate the land. One of the most notorious cases of this type of intervention was the forced movement of black families in 1955 from Sophiatown, an informal settlement on the edge of Johannesburg, South Africa, and its redesignation as a residential area for whites. But this is just one out of a large and continuing number of such instances of dispossession across the Global South.

The Peruvian economist Hernando de Soto, in his book *The Mystery of Capital*, has proposed that the quality of life of slum dwellers in developing countries might be significantly ameliorated by giving them formal legal title to the land and the housing that they occupy, enabling them thereby to acquire a stock of capital to be used at their discretion.[34] This proposal has received a mixed reception from scholars and policy-makers, however, perhaps most pointedly from those who argue that in the absence of parallel reforms in matters of market regulation, banking and financial systems, and judicial arrangements, any such scheme is likely to flounder for want of effective institutional safeguards protecting slum dwellers from the predatory practices of professional land developers and others who are in a position to take advantage of the less well informed. In many ways, some of the most imaginative and effective responses to the multiple problems of slums have been constructed by social and political movements originating in the slums themselves, and grass-roots experiments in this vein now proliferate across cities in all parts of the developing world. The Slum Dwellers International, started in 1999 as a global social movement of the urban poor, has been especially effective in building a far-flung network of local agencies and associations that diffuse advice about community development and other relevant goals.

The cities of the developing world are face-to-face with a deepening anomaly. On the one hand, large numbers of them are increasingly and successfully contesting global markets for sophisticated products and services that reflect their deepening command of the essential technologies and skills of the cognitive-cultural economy. On the other hand, they invariably harbor masses of impoverished individuals who are trapped in the vortex of informality and social marginalization. The explosive nature of this situation is well illustrated by the riots in São Paulo in early 2016, which were initially triggered by increases in public transport costs but which then led on to much wider political contestation over economic and social inequalities generally.[35] Tensions like this are legion throughout cities in low- and middle-income countries, and they have undoubtedly been aggravated by worldwide macroeconomic shifts in recent decades. In particular, they have specifically been fueled by the rigors of international financial policy, starting with the Washington Consensus at the end of the twentieth century when the World Bank and the International Monetary Fund succeeded in imposing structural adjustment programs on their clients in developing countries, and culminating in the global neoliberalism of the early twenty-first century.

Theoretical Coda

In view of these remarks on urbanization in low- and middle-income countries, it seems useful to pause briefly at this point to reconsider some of the main concepts of this book in relation to certain alternative voices.

In a few words, my own main claim is that wherever cities are found, a minimal common set of propositions can be adduced to describe their genesis and internal organization by reference to the division of labor, agglomeration, and the urban land nexus. These propositions provide a language of spatio-temporal analysis that encapsulates the essential variables of polarization, density, proximity, differentiation, and path dependency that characterize all cities. It is not a language that captures every detailed nuance much less the full complexity of actual cities, but it is a language that is at once fundamental in terms of the central processes of urbanization, and that makes it possible for particular discursive systems such as urban economics, urban political analysis, urban ethnography, urban design studies, and so on, to maintain a disciplined anchor in the *urban* as such. To many contemporary scholars, claims such as these raise the red flag of "universalization," which they see as a blind alley on the grounds that cities or particular groups of cities are inherently and necessarily incommensurable with one another. As I have already indicated in Chap. 5, post-colonial scholars add the further specific complaint that cities in the Global South are *innately* dissimilar to cities in the Global North and therefore that theories developed to account for urbanization processes in the North are irrelevant to cities in the South.[36] These scholars are hence prone to call for a repudiation of any overarching concept of urbanization that purports to apply equally to the North and the South, and, as a corollary, to suggest that urban theory must be "provincialized."[37]

By contrast, and in the light of the arguments presented here, it is far from evident as to why we should not treat cities in general as an object of theoretical enquiry, despite the high risks involved in this maneuver. The point, after all, is not whether generalization, or the construction of ideal types, or "universalization" are legitimate or illegitimate in principle, but whether or not the theoretical propositions that are made with respect to a specific circle of empirical *relata* have the explanatory power that they claim for themselves. In this book I offer a particular theoretical synthesis, one of whose basic claims is that it enables us to distinguish between the essential and the contingent in the urbanization process. I make these points, moreover, while insisting that my proposed synthesis remains fully open to the possibilities of hybridization with any number of other theoretical issues that intersect with the logic of the city and that it in no manner entails suppression of the very real empirical diversity, difference, and complexity that are inherent in the urban arena. *A propos*, post-colonial theorists do advance a very viable contention when they point to the relative paucity of the literature on the cities of low- and middle-income countries, though this gap is already rapidly diminishing as researchers domiciled outside North America and Western Europe publish more and more investigative studies of urban geography, sociology, and economics in their own native territories.

Appendix

Composition of Main Occupational Categories Used in the Analysis

The designated occupational titles are derived from the OCC1990 variable as given by the Integrated Public Use Microdata Series (IPUMS-USA). Only occupations whose definition remains unchanged from 1950 to 2010 are represented. Occupations that are considered to be irrelevant to the purpose at hand (such as agricultural and mining occupations) are excluded from this list.

APPENDIX

Managerial and professional occupations (core cognitive-cultural workers)
4 Chief executives and public administrators
14 Managers in education and related fields
18 Managers of properties and real estate
19 Funeral directors
22 Managers and administrators, n.e.c.
23 Accountants and auditors
25 Other financial specialists
28 Purchasing agents and buyers, of farm products
29 Buyers, wholesale and retail trade
33 Purchasing managers, agents and buyers, n.e.c.
36 Inspectors and compliance officers, outside construction
43 Architects
44 Aerospace engineer
45 Metallurgical and materials engineers, variously phrased
47 Petroleum, mining, and geological engineers
48 Chemical engineers
53 Civil engineers
55 Electrical engineer
56 Industrial engineers
57 Mechanical engineers
59 Not-elsewhere-classified engineers
68 Mathematicians and mathematical scientists
69 Physicists and astronomers
73 Chemists
75 Geologists
76 Physical scientists, n.e.c.
77 Agricultural and food scientists
78 Biological scientists
79 Foresters and conservation scientists
84 Physicians
85 Dentists
86 Veterinarians
87 Optometrists
89 Other health and therapy
95 Registered nurses
96 Pharmacists
97 Dietitians and nutritionists
105 Therapists, n.e.c.
154 Subject instructors (HS/college)
156 Primary school teachers
164 Librarians
166 Economists, market researchers, and survey researchers
167 Psychologists
169 Social scientists, n.e.c.
174 Social workers
175 Recreation workers
176 Clergy and religious workers
178 Lawyers
183 Writers and authors
185 Designers
186 Musician or composer
187 Actors, directors, producers
188 Art makers: painters, sculptors, craft-artists, and print-makers
189 Photographers
193 Dancers
194 Art/entertainment performers and related
195 Editors and reporters

Sales occupations
243 Supervisors and proprietors of sales jobs
254 Real estate sales occupations
255 Financial services sales occupations
256 Advertising and related sales jobs
274 Salespersons, n.e.c.
276 Cashiers
277 Door-to-door sales, street sales, and news vendors
283 Sales demonstrators/promoters/models

Administrative support occupations
313 Secretaries
318 Transportation ticket and reservation agents
328 Human resources clerks, except payroll and timekeeping
329 Library assistants

337 Bookkeepers and accounting and auditing clerks
347 Office machine operators, n.e.c.
348 Telephone operators
349 Other telecom operators
355 Mail carriers for postal service
356 Mail clerks, outside of post office
357 Messengers
359 Dispatchers
364 Shipping and receiving clerks
375 Insurance adjusters, examiners, and investigators
378 Bill and account collectors
379 General office clerks
383 Bank tellers

Service occupations
405 Housekeepers, maids, butlers, stewards, and lodgings cleaners
426 Guards, watchmen, doorkeepers
434 Bartenders
435 Waiter/waitress
436 Cooks, variously defined
439 Kitchen workers
446 Health aides, except nursing
447 Nursing aides, orderlies, and attendants
453 Janitors
454 Elevator operators
458 Hairdressers and cosmetologists
459 Recreation facility attendants
462 Ushers
464 Baggage porters
469 Personal service occupations, n.e.c.

Precision production, craft and repair occupations
505 Automobile mechanics
508 Aircraft mechanics
519 Machinery maintenance occupations
523 Repairers of industrial electrical equipment
527 Telecom and line installers and repairers
535 Precision makers, repairers, and smiths
544 Millwrights
549 Mechanics and repairers, n.e.c.
563 Masons, tilers, and carpet installers
567 Carpenters
575 Electricians
579 Painters, construction and maintenance
583 Paperhangers
584 Plasterers
585 Plumbers, pipe fitters, and steamfitters
588 Concrete and cement workers
589 Glaziers
593 Insulation workers
595 Roofers and slaters
597 Structural metal workers
599 Construction trades, n.e.c.
615 Explosives workers
616 Miners
628 Production supervisors or foremen
634 Tool and die makers and die setters
637 Machinists
643 Boilermakers
645 Patternmakers and model makers
649 Engravers
657 Cabinetmakers and bench carpenters
666 Dressmakers and seamstresses
668 Upholsterers
677 Optical goods workers
679 Bookbinders
686 Butchers and meat cutters
687 Bakers
695 Power plant operators
696 Plant and system operators, stationary engineers

Operators, fabricators, and laborers, except transport occupations
703 Lathe, milling, and turning machine operatives
707 Rollers, roll hands, and finishers of metal
709 Grinding, abrading, buffing, and polishing workers
713 Forge and hammer operators
719 Molders, and casting machine operators

724 Heat treating equipment operators
727 Sawing machine operators and sawyers
736 Typesetters and compositors
739 Knitters, loopers, and toppers textile operatives
745 Shoemaking machine operators
748 Laundry workers
749 Misc. textile machine operators
756 Mixing and blending machine operatives
759 Painting machine operators
766 Furnace, kiln, and oven operators, apart from food
773 Motion picture projectionists
774 Photographic process workers
779 Machine operators, n.e.c.
783 Welders and metal cutters
887 Vehicle washers and equipment cleaners
889 Laborers outside construction

Transport occupations
804 Truck, delivery, and tractor drivers
808 Bus drivers
809 Taxi cab drivers and chauffeurs
823 Railroad conductors and yardmasters
824 Locomotive operators (engineers and firemen)
825 Railroad brake, coupler, and switch operators
829 Ship crews and marine engineers
848 Crane, derrick, winch, and hoist operators
853 Excavating and loading machine operators
859 Misc. material moving occupations
885 Garage and service station related occupations

Notes

1. L. Wirth, "Urbanism as a way of life," *American Journal of Sociology*, 44, 1938, 1–24.
2. T. Piketty, *Capital in the Twenty-First Century*, Cambridge, MA: Harvard University Press, 2014.
3. No attempt is made to correct for changes in the geographic boundaries of individual metropolitan areas between reference years. This way of proceeding undoubtedly introduces distortions into the analysis, but it also comprises an element of implicit self-correction since boundary changes typically follow changes in the built-up area (though admittedly with a time lag), and hence in part reflect the growth of social and economic activity at the edges of the metropolitan area.
4. C. Guilluy, *Le Crépuscule de la France d'en Haut*, Paris: Flammarion, 2016.
5. M. Reich, D. M. Gordon and R. C. Edwards, "A theory of labor market segmentation," *American Economic Review*, 63, 1973, 359–365.
6. All relevant data are available at https://usa.ipums.org/usa/
7. T. Berger and C. B. Frey, "Did the computer revolution shift the fortunes of US cities? Technology shocks and the geography of new jobs," *Regional Science and Urban Economics*, 57, 2016, 38–45.
8. For parallel developments in London, see C. Hamnett, "Gentrification and the middle-class remaking of inner London, 1961–2001," *Urban Studies*, 40, 2003, 2401–2426. The issue of gentrification will be dealt with in Chap. 9.

9. An extended account of the statistical problems in constructing city-specific measures of human capital is provided by A. J. Scott and A. Mantegna, "Human capital assets and structures of work in the US metropolitan hierarchy (an analysis based on the O+NET information system)," *International Regional Science Review*, 32, 2009, 173–194.
10. See, for example, P. McHenry, "The geographic distribution of human capital: measurement of contributing mechanisms," *Journal of Regional Science*, 54, 2014, 215–248; E. Glaeser, G. A. M. Ponzetto and K. Tobio, "Cities, skills and regional change," *Regional Studies*, 48, 2014, 7–43.
11. Cf. M. Bacolod, B. S. Blum and W. C. Strange, "Skills in the city," *Journal of Urban Economics*, 65, 2009, 136–153.
12. For details on how these indexes are constructed see: A. J. Scott and A. Mantegna, *op. cit.*, 2009.
13. Cf. C. H. Wheeler, "Do localization economies derive from human capital externalities?" *Annals of Regional Science*, 41, 2007, 31–50.
14. D. Ward, *Cities and Immigrants*, New York: Oxford University Press, 1971.
15. A. Portes and J. Walton, *Labor, Class, and the International System*, New York: Academic Press, 1981.
16. D. Ley, *A Social Geography of the City*, New York: Harper and Row, 1983; D. Ward, *op. cit.*, 1971.
17. A. J. Scott, "The manufacturing economy: ethnic and gender divisions of labor," pp. 215–255 in R. Waldinger and M. Bozorgmehr (eds.) *Ethnic Los Angeles*, New York: Russell Sage Foundation, 1996.
18. Cf. J. P. Blair and R. H. Fichtenbaum, "Changing black employment patterns," pp. 72–92 in G. C. Galster and E. W. Hill (eds.) *Metropolis in Black and White: Place, Power, and Polarization*, New Brunswick: Transaction Publishers, 2012.
19. M. Gatta, H. Boushey and E. Appelbaum, "High-touch and here-to-stay: future skills demands in US low wage service occupations," *Sociology*, 43, 2009, 968–989; A. Hochschild, *The Second Shift: Working Parents and the Revolution at Home*, New York: Penguin, 1989; M. Kang, "The managed hand: the commercialization of bodies and emotions in Korean immigrant-owned nail salons," *Gender and Society*, 17, 2003, 820–839; L. McDowell, *Working Bodies: Interactive Service Employment and Workplace Identities*, Chichester: Wiley-Blackwell, 2009.
20. D. S. Massey and B. P. Mulligan, "Processes of Hispanic and black spatial assimilation," *American Journal of Sociology*, 89, 1984, 836–873; D. T. Rodgers, "Tradition, modernity, and the American industrial worker," pp. 217–243 in T. K. Rabb and R. I. Rotberg (eds.) *Industrialization and Urbanization: Studies in Interdisciplinary History*, Princeton: Princeton

University Press, 1981; O. Zunz, *The Changing Face of Inequality: Urbanization, Industrial Development, and Immigrants in Detroit, 1880–1920*, Chicago: University of Chicago Press, 1981.
21. Cf. M. Corak, *Income Inequality, Equality of Opportunity, and Intergenerational Mobility*, Discussion Paper No. 7520, Bonn, Germany: Institute for the Study of Labor, 2013.
22. As quoted in W. Ashworth, *The Genesis of Modern British Town Planning*, London: Routledge and Kegan Paul, 1954, p. 49.
23. G. Stedman Jones, *Outcast London: A Study in the Relationship between Classes in Victorian Society*, Harmondsworth: Penguin, 1976.
24. Cf. D. Harvey, *Seventeen Contradictions and the End of Capitalism*, Oxford: Oxford University Press, 2014.
25. L. Wacquant, *Urban Outcasts: A Comparative Sociology of Advanced Marginality*, Cambridge: Polity, 2008. See also: M. Dikeç, *Badlands of the Republic: Space, Politics and Urban Policy*, Malden, MA: Wiley-Blackwell, 2007.
26. M. Davis, *Planet of Slums*, London: Verso, 2006.
27. A. de Brauw, V. Mueller and H. L. Lee, "The role of rural-urban migration in the structural transformation of sub-Saharan Africa," *World Development*, 63, 2013, 33–42.
28. J. R. Harris and M. P. Todaro, "Migration, unemployment and development: a two-sector analysis," *American Economic Review*, 60, 1970, 126–142.
29. UN-Habitat, *State of the World's Cities 2012/2013*, New York: Routledge, 2013.
30. M. Davis, *op. cit.*, p. 26.
31. J. E. Perlman, *The Myth of Marginality: Urban Poverty and Politics in Rio de Janeiro*, Berkeley: University of California Press.
32. T. G. McGee, "The emergence of desakota regions in Asia: expanding a hypothesis," pp. 299–325 in N. Ginsburg, B. Koppel and T. G. McGee (eds.) *The Extended Metropolis: Settlement Transition in Asia*, Honolulu: University of Hawaii Press, 1991.
33. UN-Habitat, *The Challenge of the Slums*, London: Earthscan, 2003.
34. H. de Soto, *The Mystery of Capital: Why Capitalism Triumphs in the West and Fails Everywhere Else*, New York: Basic Books, 2000. For an insightful critique, see: C. Woodruff, "Review of de Soto's *The Mystery of Capital*," *Journal of Economic Literature*, 39, 2001, 1215–1223.
35. Cf. T. P. R. Caldeira, "Social movements, cultural production and protests: São Paulo's shifting political landscape," *Current Anthropology*, 56, 2015, S126–S136.
36. See, for example, A. Roy, "Slumdog cities: rethinking subaltern urbanism," *International Journal of Urban and Regional Research*, 35, 2011,

223–236; J. Robinson, *Ordinary Cities: Between Modernity and Development*, London: Routledge, 2006.
37. E. Sheppard, H. Leitner and B. Maringanti, "Provincializing global urbanism: a manifesto," *Urban Geography*, 34, 2013, 892–900; M. Lawhon, J. Silver, H. Ernstson and J. Pierce, "Unlearning (un)located ideas in the provincialization of urban theory," *Regional Studies*, 40, 2016, 1611–1622.

CHAPTER 9

Through the Kaleidoscope

Introduction

The urban land nexus is in the first instance an expression of powerful forces of spatial convergence, but it is also in the second instance a site of divergence and fragmentation. These contradictory tendencies are played out through the quest on the part of individual firms and households for locations that offer overall accessibility to the rest of urban space while also conferring positive externalities and as much insulation as possible from negative externalities. The quest is in its turn mediated by land rent and the rent-paying abilities of different land users. Given these circumstances, cities are always characterized by kaleidoscopic patterns of land use as represented by the irregular but demonstrable partitioning of the urban land nexus into functionally differentiated districts, neighborhoods, and channels of communication.

At one level, this pattern disaggregates into production space, social space, and circulation space; at a more refined level, each of these spaces splits into yet more diverse subspaces. The detailed spatial discontinuities brought into being in this manner are especially evident in the cities of contemporary capitalism. Thus, the production space of the city breaks down into multiple subunits composed of elements like inner-city industrial quarters, business districts, suburban technopoles, commercial parks, office clusters, and retail ribbons. Social space is divided along the lines of class and ethnicity together with a host of other social and cultural criteria ranging from religion to lifestyle. These divisions are nowhere more detectable in the

United States at the present time than in Los Angeles, vividly described by Charles Jencks as an archetypical *Heteropolis*, where the internal space of the city decomposes into a multiplicity of finely grained micro-territories.[1] Circulation space, too, and more generally the assortment of networks representing the infrastructural nervous system of the city are, in the words of Graham and Marvin, becoming more and more "splintered" as a function of the diversification of their material forms and the increasing shift in ownership of these networks away from old public monopolies in favor of privatization.[2] All of these different spaces and subspaces form a changing patchwork that reflects the operational imperatives of urban existence, but that is also replete with social predicaments and political conflicts.

THE URBAN COMMUNITY

Over the last century and more, much scholarly writing on the city has emphasized the qualities of urban areas as dense congeries of social encounters where large numbers of individuals carve out simultaneously intermingled but also contrasting ways of life rooted in disparate communities. Simmel's paper, "The Metropolis and Mental Life," published in 1903, was a seminal contribution to this manner of seeing the city and was also an important source of inspiration for Wirth's celebrated 1938 statement.[3] But it was the Chicago School's theory of urban dynamics based on biologistic notions of ecological dominance and succession that constituted the most ambitious and influential attempt in the first half of the twentieth century to understand the variegated social space of the city. This theory is nowadays more or less thoroughly discredited in favor of economic and sociological approaches that variously invoke issues of spatial organization on the one side, and logics of social reproduction on the other as entry points to urban analysis. I now attempt to provide a synthetic overview of how these factors structure the internal organizational patchwork of the city (with special reference to residential space). I shall then go on sketch out some of the more important features of the changing contours of this patchwork over the last century and more.

Crosscurrents: Accessibility and Neighborhood

There can be little doubt that the daily journey to work plays an important role in most individuals' or households' choice of residential location. This choice can be analyzed in a first round of reasoning as reflecting trade-offs between land rent, commuting costs, and the amount of residential space consumed relative to the location of workplaces. In order to initiate the exposition, we will assume that we are dealing with a city in the manner of Alonso, Mills, and Muth where workplaces are taken to be concentrated at the geometric center of the urban land nexus (though we will relax this assumption later).[4] In this imaginary world, residential locations with high levels of accessibility to the city center (and hence with low commuting costs) will command elevated land rents per unit area; conversely, locations with low levels of accessibility will be associated with correspondingly reduced land rents. If all residential lots were fixed in size and every household confined to a single standard lot, then in theory the sum of commuting costs and land rent would be equal to a constant value over the whole of residential space, and housing density would also be invariant everywhere. This is manifestly not the case in reality for endemic land development processes in the city will tend to induce higher densities of housing at more accessible central locations and lower densities at less accessible peripheral locations. Such an outcome is in fact observable in actual cities and can typically be expressed in terms of a negative exponential curve of population density as a function of increasing distance from the city center.[5]

These population density variations will also be modulated in various ways as a function of intraurban social structure. Henri Lefebvre captures what is centrally at stake in this matter in the following formulation:

> [Urban] space contains more or less appropriately located *social relations of reproduction*, that is, bio-physiological relations between the sexes and different age groups in the specific context of the family—and *relations of production*, that is, the division of labor and its organization, and hence hierarchized social functions. These two sets of relationships, production and reproduction, cannot be separated: the division of labor is reflected and sustained in the family; conversely, family organization influences the division of labor.[6]

This quotation is partly translatable into the further idea that patterns of social life in the city are marked by the division of labor and occupational status while socio-cultural processes reflecting the dynamics of family and communal interrelationships have significant impacts on the qualities and capabilities of the labor force, and, we might add, on the structure of residential space.

I have already indicated in earlier chapters that the structure of residential space in the classical fordist city can be broadly identified in terms of a bipartite division of households into white-collar and blue-collar categories. In the presence of latent intragroup neighborhood externalities with positive effects on social reproduction, each of these categories will have a tendency to crystallize out in the urban milieu into a more or less socially homogeneous community. This is even more likely to happen if latent negative externalities are present under conditions of spatial mingling of the two categories. In the simplest case of a monocentric city, this crystallization will evidently assume the shape of two concentric zones around the center, as in Burgess' schematic map of Chicago, though we must still pose the question as to which social group will occupy which zone and why. The immediate answer in principle to this question is that the inner zone will be occupied by the group from which superior land rents can be extracted.[7] In classical fordist cities, this group in practice comprised blue-collar workers. These workers were willing to settle at high density at the core of the city in exchange for reduced transport costs, for even though central locations command high land rents per unit area, elevated density levels mean that per capita rents are correspondingly reduced. By contrast, the white-collar workers were willing to accept higher transport costs in exchange for low population densities in the urban fringe, where they could pursue their preferred suburban lifestyle. However, in order to complete the argument about the socio-spatial segregation of these two groups, we must also elaborate further on certain mechanisms of social reproduction that kept them much more apart from one another in the intraurban space than would in all likelihood have been the case if density differentials and transport costs were the only factors contributing to their separation.

In the first place, then, low-income blue-collar neighborhoods in central-city areas, despite their relatively disfavored housing conditions, possessed noteworthy positive qualities that flowed from their status as socially specialized residential enclaves enabling them to function as viable repositories of working-class life. Sampson has proposed the term "collective efficacy" as a way of capturing these qualities, which, in detail, break down into forms of social capital like mutual aid in regard to childminding, information sharing about employment opportunities, informal restraints on disruptive behavior, and communal responses to negative externalities generally.[8] Collective efficacy assumes even greater value in neighborhoods occupied by minority groups that are excluded from the rest of residential space by reason of their distinctive racial or ethnic identities, and where, in addition, their members can find support in familiar cultural and linguistic environments.[9] Similarly, collective efficacy is notably relevant to inhabitants of slum areas in cities in low- and middle-income countries.[10]

In the second place, white-collar workers, aided and abetted by municipal action ranging from infrastructural investments in peripheral land to advantageous urban planning regulations, successfully constructed a set of outcomes involving spacious suburban communities and styles of domestic life based on stable nuclear households. Increasing rates of car ownership after the First World War made suburbanization a yet more attractive option for this social group. Over much of the fordist era, the "suburban solution," as Walker called it,[11] accorded well with social prejudices that placed individual home ownership and the traditional family high on the list of priorities for achieving successful domesticity and a positive image in the workplace and in the society at large. More to the point, suburbs offered a framework for the social construction of powerful ideological currents about exemplary forms of life and functioned as instruments by which white-collar workers could secure for themselves symbolic legitimization of their position in society and transmit it successfully to the next generation by raising and schooling their children in supportive social and environmental conditions. The social integrity of white-collar neighborhoods, and above all, their resistance to invasion by low-income individuals were in many cases safeguarded by restrictive zoning ordinances and building codes ensuring that housing density, lot size, and the number of families allowed per building accorded with the overall domestic ethos of the suburbs.

All the same, this simple bipartite pattern of blue-collar and white-collar residential zones was constantly subject to social adjustments. For one thing, some fractions of the white-collar labor force, even in the fordist era, have always preferred to live in inner-city areas, where they form exclusive enclaves close to the central business district. For another, and right from the start, many blue-collar workers followed decentralizing industrial jobs to suburban areas, leading, after the Second World War, to notable declines in the population of numerous inner-city areas. Since the 1980s, the pace of change in the social structure of intraurban residential spaces has become especially intense.

Beyond the Monocentric City

While the overarching principles that underlie the argument thus far have wide application, we must also take into account, as just suggested, the fact that neither employment locations in the city nor lifestyles with their attendant reflections in residential behavior are invariant across time and space.[12] In nineteenth-century Paris, for example, the urban renovation projects initiated by Haussmann, pushed much industrial development out to peripheral communes such as Ivry-sur-Seine and St. Denis to the southeast and north of the city, respectively. At the same time, large numbers of low-income households were displaced from the center by Haussmann's projects, and many of them resettled in and around these peripheral communes, which rapidly became dense centers of working-class life. Many small-scale artisanal and labor-intensive varieties of production remained within the limits of the city of Paris together with dependent workers' communities (as in the case of the northeastern *arrondissements*[13]), but the *bourgeois* and *rentier* classes retained a durable hold over the old historical fabric of the core areas with their patrimonial assets and their grand Haussmannized boulevards.

Even in US cities in the early decades of the twentieth century, as we have seen, some manufacturing plants located preferentially in the suburbs, sometimes giving rise to peripheral industrial clusters. In many instances, this trend also encouraged the development of blue-collar communities in the urban fringe, as exemplified by Dearborn in the suburbs of Detroit where Henry Ford built his River Rouge plant in the years following 1917.[14] After the Second World War, these trends intensified greatly in US cities, and with the steady abandonment of core areas by manufacturing plants, the foundations of the traditional working-class neighborhoods that had developed nearby were gradually undercut. These neighborhoods continued to dominate most of the residential space of the inner city, but over the 1950s and 1960s, they were subject to considerable physical and social deterioration along with the retail and service functions that they had supported. The official answer to this progressive decay at the core of American cities was the Federal Housing Act of 1949 (reinforced by the 1954 Housing Act), enabling municipalities, under the euphemism of "urban renewal," to acquire and clear properties in blighted areas of the core. Typically, the land was then sold at a discount to private developers, who, in the place of long-standing and vibrant working-class communities, built sterile new blocks of public housing and sometimes luxury apartments, as in the notorious cases of Boston's West End and Philadelphia's Society Hill, or sought to hoard the land by transforming it into parking lots with a view to future speculative gain.[15] Urban freeway construction, subsidized under the Federal-Aid Highway Act of 1956, greatly intensified this process of central land clearance and redevelopment while concurrently fostering further outward sprawl of low-density suburban and peri-urban tracts.

By the 1970s, the waning fortunes of the fordist economy as a whole were compounding the already bleak outlook for inner-city areas and their urban working-class residents. These years ushered in a seemingly permanent urban crisis not only in the formerly thriving Manufacturing Belt of North America but also in many of the old industrial urban centers of Western Europe. In the mid-1970s, even New York City came to the verge of bankruptcy as its economy deteriorated and its tax base plummeted downwards.

Toward a New Urbanism

The foundations of capitalist urbanization began to shift into new configurations after the early 1980s as the machine age of fordism steadily gave way before a more knowledge-intensive and culturally inflected socio-economic system based partly on emerging digital technologies and a significantly widening range of human capital. This shift has been accompanied by a great global expansion of capitalism and the resurgence of ever more intricate and extended networks of international trade and human migration. The geographic mainstay of these developments is constituted by a web of city-regions that function as powerful gravitational hubs in the new global order. Wherever these city-regions may be found, from the San Francisco Bay Area, to London, to Singapore and Beijing, large numbers of immigrants flow in from far and wide to take up jobs in various segments of the economy. Many of these immigrants are highly qualified individuals seeking work in the upper reaches of the cognitive-cultural economy. Equally, many immigrants flow in from less prosperous areas and are in large degree assimilated into low-wage service occupations in the same city-regions. Some analysts have suggested that these low-wage immigrant populations are less segregated than they once were in host cities, though they still tend to settle at the outset in distinctive communities in the social space of the city.[16] All of these different waves of immigration, together with ever rising incursions of exotic influences, bring new cultural vernaculars into the city and inject significantly mounting levels of cosmopolitanism into urban life. In some instances, however, notably in cities of Western Europe that have recently absorbed large influxes of refugees from the Middle East, latent cosmopolitanism has often given way to distrust and xenophobia, accentuated no doubt by the increasing insecurities of existence in centers of cognitive-cultural capitalism where rapid change, labor-market instabilities, and competitiveness are an intrinsic part of the everyday order of things.

There is undoubtedly a growing perception in urban areas today that overall social order and security may be deteriorating in the context of the deeply divided heteropolitan city. The great expansion of gated communities in recent years, not only in American metropolitan areas, but in cities virtually everywhere from Brazil to China bears testimony to this affirmation.[17] In the United States, gated communities actually date from the nineteenth century, but they have become more and more pervasive of late, to the extent that by 1997, according to Blakely and Snyder, there were 20,000 of them in the United States alone.[18] These communities are typically organized as self-governing homeowner associations designed to offer, in varying combinations, a prestigious address, customized lifestyle opportunities, security measures, and, to an increasing degree, retirement facilities for their occupants. Above all, perhaps, they offer a degree of refuge from the stresses of the wider urban milieu, where social polarization is endemic and where fears about threats and risks often run rife. Some gated communities are reserved for working-class residents, but by far the majority are occupied by middle- and upper-class households.[19] In Southern California, for example, they proliferate in upscale areas like Malibu, Newport Beach, and Palm Springs where they offer seclusion combined with high levels of environmental quality to a wealthy clientele.[20] In the city of São Paulo in Brazil, where, as Caldeira writes, the "population is obsessed by security and social discrimination," gated communities with high walls and armed guards have become middle-class sanctuaries in what is often seen as a surrounding sea of social disorder.[21]

At the same time, the outward expansion of cities is proceeding apace everywhere, and is increasingly swallowing up peripheral municipalities as urban boundaries are pushed deeper and deeper into the hinterland. In consequence, city-regions increasingly resemble polynucleated spaces marked by fractal patterns of agglomeration and sub-agglomeration, as illustrated by the cases of the Northeastern Megalopolis of the United States, Southeast England, the Paris Basin, the Tokyo metropolitan region, and the Shanghai conurbation.[22] In some instances, these polynucleated spaces have become so distended that they actually comprise multiple metropolitan areas. Most large metropolitan areas of the Global South are affected by similar processes of aggressive, indeed hyperaggressive, lateral extension.

A number of urban scholars have recently begun to write about the phenomenon of "post-suburbia" as a way of referring to these kinds of developments in the urban periphery.[23] The classic concept of suburban space in fordist cities amounted essentially to a picture of a homogeneous expanse of white-collar, single-family residences forming a ring of low-density dormitory settlements around the outer edge of the monocentric city (even if the suburbs never existed in reality with this stark degree of descriptive simplicity). The post-suburban syndrome, by contrast, is much like a replication of the complex interweaving of land uses and functionally specialized districts characteristic of the core areas of the large metropolis. Post-suburbia is socially heterogeneous, not only in the sense that it comprises neighborhoods of varying densities and income levels but also because it is increasingly interspersed with communities in which racial and ethnic minorities predominate, a state of affairs that used to be thought of as an exclusive peculiarity of central cities. Post-suburbia is also a locus of sometimes architecturally ambitious industrial and business parks many of which are given over to firms that blend smoothly into the new cognitive-cultural economy, ranging from high-technology equipment and software producers to financial and commercial service providers and their back offices. The landscape of post-suburbia is further distinguished by proliferating shopping and commercial centers, many of them, like the South Coast Shopping Plaza in Costa Mesa in Orange County, California, offering branded luxury items of the sort that were formerly confined to exclusive downtown shopping havens.

Firman, drawing on the original work of McGee, has alluded to a roughly analogous though perhaps rather less alluring sort of post-suburban condition in the hyperextended *desakota* fringes of the Jakarta metropolitan region.[24] An even more remarkable example in Southeast Asia is offered by the Multimedia Supercorridor in Malaysia, initiated in 1996, and which, in spite of continuing obstacles to its full realization, represents a massive infrastructure and urbanization project stretching some 30 miles from Kuala Lumpur southward to the new international airport.[25] The Supercorridor comprises two main functional centers, namely, Putrajaya, where many governmental administrative offices are housed, and Cyberjaya, which is projected to become a major cluster of software, information, and new media producers. Similar developments are starting to emerge in the fringes of cities in other parts of the Global South, one noteworthy instance being the planned Konza Technology City to the south of Nairobi, Kenya. We might say, as Garreau already suggested in 1988 in his "edge city" concept, that while the traditional dichotomy between the core and the suburbs is far from being entirely eliminated, it is now considerably blurred in terms of the physical development of these two urban zones.[26] This sense of spatial continuity and interpenetration has been greatly strengthened by the deepening physical integration of the central city and the suburbs as a consequence of their mutual accessibility via ever more efficient multimodal transport infrastructures.

Just as post-suburban dynamics are changing the face of the peripheral territories of large metropolitan areas, so, too, are central cities currently experiencing remarkable shifts in their economic structure and residential fabric. Resurgent central business districts are thriving on the basis of expanding office functions, revivified tertiary economic activities, and burgeoning cultural infrastructures. Perhaps even more remarkable are the changes taking place in many old neighborhoods within the central city where diverse forms of gentrification are transforming large swaths of formerly working-class housing and other land uses into upscale residential communities. Gentrification in its modern form can be traced back to the immediate post-War years in Britain and the United States. Already in the 1950s, fashionable real estate agents in London were extolling the merits of former working-class houses converted into "bijou" residences in parts of the city like Chelsea and Hampstead. The term *gentrification* itself was first coined by Ruth Glass in 1964 in reference to the upgrading and colonization of working-class housing and old Victorian properties that had seen better days by the "upper-middle classes" in areas like Islington, North Kensington, and Paddington in central London.[27] Glass related the changes she observed to the urge among the growing cohorts of professional workers and their like in the greater London region to avoid the need to commute from the ever-extending suburbs to the center of the city. She also pointed to the fact that gentrification was starting to "push away" low-income individuals from their long-established communities, as land values increased and as landlords boosted property rental rates in response to rising demand for inner-city housing. In this manner, Glass also helped to initiate the long tradition of political critique that has typified much of the literature on gentrification and that has consistently pointed out both its disruptive effects on otherwise socially cohesive low-income neighborhoods in central-city areas and its adverse personal impacts on the original residents as properties are taken over—sometimes under duress—and repurposed for more affluent newcomers.[28]

The particular instances of gentrification identified by Glass predate by a number of decades the advent of the new capitalism as such, but they are almost certainly related to the expansion of white-collar foci of employment in London in the immediate post-War decades, especially in banking and finance, and they can undoubtedly be seen as harbingers of the massive shifts that were to occur after the crisis years of the 1970s in response to changes wrought by the advent of the cognitive-cultural economy. Indeed, as I shall argue more fully below, the deepening incidence of gentrification in cities all over the world in the twenty-first century can be very plausibly correlated with the growth of the new capitalism and the role of central business districts as privileged spatial concentrations (among others) of a significant portion of the jobs that it generates. As these trends have gathered momentum, the literature on gentrification, together with debates about its essential etiology and political resonances, has expanded exponentially.[29] Along with this efflorescence has come a corresponding tendency in some parts of this literature to interpret virtually any and all types of redevelopment—urban and rural, downtown and suburban, residential and commercial—as symptoms of gentrification. This broad notion of gentrification has unquestionably served well heretofore as a forensic tool of urban analysis, and it certainly continues to offer useful ways forward, but it has now become so overloaded with disparate substantive and conceptual cargo that some serious reconsideration of its import is urgently required.

LAND REDEVELOPMENT

The argument that I propose to make here is that gentrification is an important but essentially special case of the much more pervasive phenomenon of land redevelopment in general. I shall indicate in analytical terms how a broad concept of land redevelopment can be established and how the basic dynamics of gentrification can be accommodated within this concept.

Conceptual Preliminaries

Along with Ruth Glass, the late Neil Smith can be counted as one of the most influential early theorists of gentrification, if not *the* most influential. In a series of papers dating from 1979, he single-handedly charted the intellectual and political course followed by a significant segment of the literature on this topic down to the present day.[30]

Smith's analysis starts from the premise that middle-class individuals can earn sizable monetary and psychic benefits by taking over and rehabilitating (i.e. gentrifying) properties in deteriorated districts of the central city where low-income neighborhoods or run-down commercial buildings dominate the pattern of land use. These districts, being adjacent to the core of the city, are characterized by relatively high land values (or equivalently, land rents). Even so, according to Smith, these values are typically at a lower level than they would be if the land were converted from working-class residences to "higher and better" uses, namely, middle-class housing. Smith states that the difference between the potential and actual land values in these districts can be identified as an anomalous depression in the otherwise-smooth gradient of the urban rent curve, and he labels the corresponding deficit as "the rent gap." There is unquestionably a high probability that the value of land occupied by swaths of low-income households or failing businesses would tend to be depressed, and in his monumental 1933 study of land values in Chicago, Hoyt claims to recognize something like rent gaps or "deep valleys" coinciding with blighted areas around the central Loop.[31] To this extent, Smith's notion of the rent gap possesses a degree of verisimilitude, though as we shall see, his particular formulation of the land conversion process in urban areas represents a very special case. Smith goes on to aver that middle-class gentrifiers, motivated by speculative interests, stand to gain financially from land-use conversion at sites where the rent gap is high. Still, recent empirical attempts to measure the rent gap by analysts such as Clark in Sweden and Ley in Canada have not been especially convincing, possibly because the rent gap as Smith defined it had long ago disappeared in the cases investigated, for once relevant land-use changes start to get under way, there is a strong likelihood that forward-looking market forces will eliminate any anomalous land rent pattern of the type that Smith took to be the mainspring of gentrification.[32] In any event, there is absolutely no reason why gentrification or, more generally, property conversion processes should not occur even when a rent gap *à la* Smith is absent.[33] This contention stems from a consideration of land redevelopment dynamics in general, and it can be defended in two essentially equivalent ways depending on whether we are referring to conversion for housing or for commercial purposes. The discussion that follows presumes for simplicity of exposition that redevelopment does not entail any change in type of land use, but extension to this case is entirely straightforward.

We may take it that the total capital outlay required for the conversion of any given property for *housing* purposes is equal to the purchase price of the original property (including land) plus the expense of rehabilitation (or demolition and reconstruction). A preliminary definition of the opportunity cost of conversion is then given as the expected resale price of the property on completion of the conversion minus the capital outlay. The expected resale price will reflect not just the initial capital outlay but also other relevant economic or psychic factors such as the accumulated present-value of savings on commuting costs and time or externality effects that impinge on the property. There is clearly an inducement to proceed with conversion if the opportunity cost is positive. In a competitive land market, the realized opportunity cost will technically be transformed into an increment to land rent, and this will be appropriated by the owner of the land should there be a division of proprietorship between the house and the land on which it stands.

In the case of land-use conversion for the purposes of *commercial* exploitation, the overall opportunity cost can be defined in an analogous manner, but it will now be most convenient if we proceed on the basis of annualized monetary quantities. The critical quantity to be identified here is the expected annual revenue to be obtained from production activities at the rehabilitated property. The opportunity cost is now, therefore, this same annual revenue less the annually discounted capital outlay less whatever additional annual production costs (including normal profit) are incurred when the property is fully operational. Again, conversion will proceed when the opportunity cost is positive. In the early stages of land-use conversion, this quantity will take the form of excess profit, but its location-contingent elements will once more be absorbed into total land rent as other properties in the vicinity are redeveloped and as the land market responds to rising demand by developers.[34]

Given these considerations, land-use conversion or intensification for housing or commercial purposes will tend to be most active where actual or anticipated rents are already at an elevated level, that is, where the payoff to any given type of land use is high. It is tempting to identify the opportunity cost defined above as a sort of *enhanced rent gap* because it includes any element of a Smith-style rent gap, should it exist, and because it can also in principle rise well above this hypothesized level. Furthermore, even if there is no Smith-style rent gap, the general calculus of land-use intensification (i.e. augmented investment per unit of land) remains unaltered from its formulation above. Unfortunately, this analysis still does not complete the story in so far as the specific case of housing gentrification is concerned, for we also need to know why blue-collar neighborhoods were a durable element of central cities at one period in time, and why they became objects of concerted middle-class conversion at another. I will deal with this issue in the following section.

Meanwhile, these two forms of property conversion, that is, for housing and commercial purposes, are equivalent in that they represent types of land-use intensification leading to augmented personal benefits or revenues, and ultimately to increased land rent. For the sake of clarity, I advocate that we refer to these processes under the general heading of *land redevelopment*, while confining the term *gentrification*, as such, to the special case of the redevelopment of housing units originally occupied by low-income individuals (usually, but not necessarily, in the central city) by individuals of higher income and social status. Merrifield has used the phrase "neo-Haussmannization" to refer to gentrification and its associated pathology of exacerbated socio-economic bifurcation in the city.[35] However, Haussmann's dramatic replanning of Paris in the middle of the nineteenth century went very far indeed beyond any of the specific sorts of land-use redevelopment considered here, for besides its concern with replacing slums by bourgeois housing, it had numerous other cultural, strategic, public health, transport, economic, and imperial ambitions that make "Haussmannization" much too grandiose a term to substitute for "gentrification" in its usually accepted meaning.

The Social Dimensions of Gentrification

The basic feature of gentrification (in the narrow sense as defined above) as it first emerged in the cities of the United States and Western Europe over the 1950s and 1960s is that it took the specific form of middle-class residential colonization of working-class neighborhoods in areas. These neighborhoods had sprung up in the inner city in response to the employment offered by the factories, workshops, and warehouses that since the nineteenth century had flourished nearby. Despite the relatively low income levels of the original residents, not to mention the social problems often associated with poor neighborhoods, community life was by and large well developed and usually evinced a high degree of collective efficacy. Many residents of these neighborhoods engaged in "reverse commuting" to jobs in the urban fringe in the 1950s and 1960s, but deterioration of the local social fabric tended frequently to set in as reverse commuting was succeeded by active relocation of blue-collar families to intermediate and suburban tracts of the city.[36] The simultaneous expansion of white-collar jobs in corporate offices and allied service functions in the central business districts of large metropolitan areas (such as London) in the 1950s and 1960s was also now starting to make the inner city an attractive residential location for adventurous middle- and upper-middle-class individuals who preferred to economize on housing by means of gentrification rather than to seek residences in already established but expensive middle-class enclaves in the central city. We may characterize this stage of the process as first-generation gentrification.

By the late 1970s and 1980s, downtown areas were expanding rapidly as the cognitive-cultural economy started its expansionary thrust, leading to the accelerated growth of managerial, professional, and vocational employment in downtown areas, hence greatly increasing the attractiveness of adjacent parts of the city for middle-class residents, and stimulating a second and a much more aggressive generation of gentrification. This second surge is in part typified by the conversion of houses that have been independently and willingly sold by their occupants. However, a powerful element of involuntary displacement if not outright coercion among other residents can also be detected in contemporary gentrification processes. Displacement is actively promoted by locally rising land values, rents, and taxes, especially in the case of tenants who can be easily evicted on the termination of their lease, just as other tenants can be cheaply bought out if their lease has not yet expired. The use of physical threats on the part of unscrupulous landlords eager to reap the benefits of higher property values and by overzealous city councils anxious to enhance the image of the city has also been documented.[37] Developments like these and the general crisis of affordable housing in large metropolitan areas frequently result in political mobilization and street protests on the part of negatively affected residents. One out of the many ways of illustrating this remark can be found in the protests in Vancouver's Downtown Eastside in 1995, where a large-scale land conversion project raised fears that it would lead to soaring land values and trigger further displacement of the poor in the surrounding areas.[38] Another is represented by the strong local opposition that was organized in the face of the eviction of residents from the Mission District in San Francisco in the late 1990s as the dot-com boom gathered steam, and the district became a target for both residential gentrification and commercial redevelopment.[39]

In some instances, a transitional or pregentrification phase can be observed in disadvantaged areas in the inner city (including areas of run-down commercial property) when intrusions of artists, bohemians, and diverse individuals on the fringes of mainstream society start to occur. Lloyd has shown for the case of Chicago[40] and Zukin for New York[41] that this sort of neo-bohemian development is often accompanied by the establishment of bars, music venues, and other services reflecting the lifestyle of these trailblazers. Then, as middle-class individuals move in, further transformation occurs and eventually full-scale gentrification is apt to take hold. This process of upgrading may actually go so far as to result in the emergence of an expensive and highly fashionable neighborhood complete with high-end boutiques, restaurants, and art galleries, as happened in the case of SoHo in New York after the 1970s. Long before the arrival of this ultimate stage of development on the urban landscape, the former neo-bohemian pioneers will have moved on to other waning neighborhoods in the inner-city, where the developmental cycle leading to advanced gentrification is apt to reappear.

Gentrification has become an insistent feature in the twenty-first century not only in the cities of advanced capitalism but also in cities as far-flung as Abu Dhabi, Buenos Aires, Cairo, Cape Town, Istanbul, Karachi, Lagos, Santiago, and Taipei, among many others.[42] Each individual instance of gentrification is, of course, marked by local specificities, especially regarding occupancy rights and the political power relations between different social classes. Ghertner has charged that these specificities undermine any claims to generality on the part of gentrification theory,[43] but since the central mechanism typically revolves around residential displacement of relatively poor and politically marginalized groups by relatively wealthy and powerful groups or their political agents, predominantly in the core areas of large cities, it seems reasonably defensible to treat these specificities as local variations on a distinctly common theme. This call to conceptual generality is bolstered by consideration of the striking growth of employment opportunities in advanced cognitive-cultural sectors such as finance, business services, media, advertising, and fashion and design from the early 1980s onward in central cities, first in the advanced capitalist countries and later in many parts of the Global South. As this growth has occurred, adjacent residential neighborhoods have become increasingly attractive to college graduates and others employed in these sectors, an assessment that has been offered not only by Glass herself but also by analysts such as Hamnett and Ley.[44]

The social character of central-city areas has thus been subject to dramatic change over these last few decades. This point is well illustrated by data for the Unites States showing the changing incidence of college-educated workers living in the cores of major metropolitan areas. Official census sources allow us to compile a consistent data set of this sort for the central cities of 45 metropolitan areas for both of the years 2000 and 2014. In 2000, college-educated individuals comprised 18.3% of the total population of these 45 central cities taken in aggregate. In 2014, college-educated individuals comprised 25.4%. Concomitantly, the number of college-educated individuals in the 45 central-city areas grew by 36.8% while that part of the population lacking this qualification fell by 10.0%. Not all of this change will have been associated with gentrification in the strict sense (i.e. when individuals of relatively high social rank renovate and settle in properties formerly inhabited by individuals of lower social rank), but it does provide a strong sense of the changing residential character of the inner zones of American metropolitan areas, and a large literature suggests that the overall rate of actual displacement of one social group by another is quite high. A further illustration of recent inner-city gentrification is offered by the case of central Manchester, whose population had fallen to only a few hundred in the 1980s, whereas today, after extensive housing rehabilitation and rebuilding, the population is over 20,000.[45] The literature also indicates that gentrification is proceeding rapidly not only in central-city areas but is now extending to parts of the inner suburbs as well.[46]

A nuance that must be added to these comments is that the middle-class individuals living in central cities today are often distinguishable from other upper-tier workers—certainly in Britain and the United States—by their special demographic and social characteristics, marked as they are by an unusually high representation by young professionals, childless families, people in same sex unions, apartment sharers, condominium dwellers, metrosexual singles, cohabiting couples, and the like.[47] To an increasing extent, moreover, many of these individuals are not first-generation gentrifiers, but are occupants of property that has been converted by some previous owner.

Commercial Land Redevelopment and Aestheticization

Investment in commercial properties represents the second main dimension of land redevelopment in urban areas. But whereas the former entails an element of consumer psychology in regard to housing choice, the latter is bound up with calculations about the revenues from goods and services, including residential units for rent or sale, that can be produced on a given unit area of land. It follows immediately that property redevelopment for commercial purposes will be most intense (in terms of dollars invested per square meter) in parts of the city where the land is most productive per unit of investment. Since land rents reflect excess profits from production (i.e. above and beyond normal profits) that have been bid away in competitive land markets, this means in practice that land-use intensification will tend to occur most aggressively at locations where rents are already high. In line with this argument, construction and renovation projects for commercial purposes in the city will tend to be the thickest on the ground in central business district areas and other highly accessible nodes in the urban land nexus where local peaks of land rent occur. Homer Hoyt's commentary on this redevelopment process in Chicago in the inter-War years points to the apparent paradox that "thirteen storey skyscrapers with a structural life of a century or more have been torn down to give room to twenty-two or forty-four storey tower buildings."[48] An ancillary point that ensues from this logic is that commercial property booms when land redevelopment proceeds at an unusually rapid pace derive intrinsically from rising expectations about the opportunities for excess profits from productive activity in the city.

Major projects of commercial land-use intensification represent in one sense narrow exercises in economic rationality, but also frequently include major architectural gestures as part of an overall program of redevelopment. These gestures quite possibly result in long-run economic payoffs but they also generate valuable symbolic capital for building owners and users, particularly in the case of large-scale office buildings in downtown areas where avant-garde architectural idioms are commonly on display. We might refer to gestures like these as entailing processes of what I have called elsewhere *aestheticized land-use intensification*, an admittedly unwieldy term, but one that captures the essence of much of the lavish building activity that is a familiar feature of the landscape of central business districts in large cities everywhere.[49] Indeed, the association between land-use intensification and creative building design has always been a feature of the core areas of large cities in advanced capitalism, and a very plausible argument might be advanced to the effect that the generalized architectural agendas promulgated by leading practitioners of this sort of building did not come solely out of abstract aesthetic impulses, but also out of the practical and technical problems that needed to be solved in pursuit of land-use intensification, and more specifically in the effort to construct higher and higher buildings in order to maximize the productivity of each unit of land.

Chicago at the end of the nineteenth century, for example, was a major focus of iconic and innovative architectural projects whose driving principle was summarized in Louis Sullivan's slogan "form follows function." Most of these projects were concentrated in the Loop where Burnham, Richardson, Sullivan, and others were active in designing visionary, thickset buildings decorated with Romanesque motifs for banks and other commercial enterprises. These were multi-storey buildings but their reliance on load-bearing outer walls restricted the maximum height that they could attain. Eventually, the protomodernism initiated by these Chicago architects gave way to the full-blown modernist architecture stripped of superfluous decoration launched by Gropius, Mies van der Rohe, and others under the banner that "less is more." This architecture came to dominate the central business districts of large American metropolitan areas over a significant part of the twentieth century as load-bearing central columns and outer curtain walls allowed buildings to attain to hitherto unheard of heights.[50] The notion of aestheticized land-use intensification is especially appropriate today when cognitive-cultural capitalism is driving major transformations of the functional attributes of central business districts and bringing in its wake dramatic new kinds of architecture more given to bombast, playfulness, and idiosyncrasy than the chaste geometries of classical modernism.[51] Moreover, the complex volumetrics of so much of this architecture is achievable only by means of the digital technologies and software applications that have been developed within the new capitalism. This new architecture is all of a piece with the diverse cerebral, creative, and cultural activities that now take place in the core areas of city-regions across the entire globe. In the same way, as Sklair has pointed out, the new architecture accords well with the cosmopolitan worldview espoused by the privileged transnational capitalist class that sustains the global business connections linking these city-regions into a closely knit mesh of competitive and cooperative relationships.[52]

Bold iconic architectural themes also increasingly serve as branding and marketing devices for cities with global ambitions. The point is well exemplified by megaprojects (often signed by celebrity architects and subsidized by governmental agencies) such as London's Docklands, Kuala Lumpur's Petronas Towers, Shanghai's World Financial Center, Dubai's

Burj Khalifa, and a host of comparable schemes designed to attract the attention of the world's elite and to signal a special kind of urban panache. Large-scale cultural ventures like Bilbao's Guggenheim Museum and Los Angeles' Disney Hall (both designed by Frank Gehry) further enhance the verve of the cities in which they are located and function as beacons for the international tourist trade. In these ways, the visual form and cultural resources of selected cities are being mobilized to ever greater degree by private investors and entrepreneurial municipalities as strategic weapons in the global intercity competitive race to attract inward investment, human capital, megaevents (such as the Olympic Games), and tourist's expenditures.[53] In addition, the downtown areas and other important nerve centers of major cities are increasingly interlaced by consumer-oriented amenities such as gallerias, department stores, upscale restaurants, boutique art galleries, and other facilities serving a well-heeled clientele and adding to the glamour of metropolitan life for a favored minority. As the core areas of numerous large cities undergo these different forms of aestheticized land-use intensification, they experience waves of regeneration distinguished by spectacular visual displays and assertive urban symbols.[54] In the emerging social and economic milieus of these areas, the real or perceived incompatibilities between production space and residential space that once seemed to be an indelible aspect of life in the preceding versions of capitalist urbanization—at least insofar as more privileged members of the workforce were concerned—now appear to be receding. Instead, a new sort of balance is evidently making its appearance as these spaces become more spatially interwoven and more functionally compatible with one another. Parts of post-suburbia, too, display similar kinds of ecologies, where verdant industrial parks with high-technology firms and other commercial ventures housed in glossy modern buildings are often to be found alongside sweeping residential estates and gated communities dominated by the new cognitariat.

Notwithstanding this apparent new-found harmonization of social and economic functions in certain quarters of the metropolis, one of the more prominent ironies of urban life in cognitive-cultural capitalism is the contrast between the allure and glitter of its immediate outward form in upscale precincts of the city and the squalor of its murkier underside where the burgeoning new servile class, sweatshop workers, and diverse left-behinds attempt to keep body and soul together.[55] Nowhere is this contrast more apparent than in the world's major financial centers like London, New York, and Tokyo, where in the daytime, one brigade of highly paid workers occupies the sleek office towers that serve as cathedrals of international finance while at night-time another brigade made up of minimum-wage and often undocumented workers takes over in order to prepare the premises for the next day's onslaught of frenetic trading activity.

The Political Logic of the Kaleidoscope

As David Harvey has pointed out on numerous occasions, cities are intrinsically susceptible to periodic outbreaks of political conflict.[56] The density and mutual proximity of large numbers of people in cities facilitate the rise of political movements and the organization of mass demonstrations of political discontent. Cities represent favorable environments for this kind of activity, not only because their physical arrangement lends itself to rapid popular mobilization but also because the urban land nexus itself is deeply conflictual in any number of different dimensions.[57]

Cities have always been cauldrons of political ferment where, from time to time, those who make up the lower reaches of society rise up against authority to demand redress of their grievances and to seek social justice. Multitudinous cases of this propensity in the modern era may be cited, ranging from the revolutionary movements in Paris, Prague, Budapest, Vienna, and other European centers in 1848 to the aborted Arab Spring that started in Tunisia in late 2010 and then spread across the cities of North Africa and the Middle East. Yet other examples are provided by the anti-apartheid marches in South African cities in the 1950s and 1960s, the "water war" of Cochambamba, Bolivia, in response to the privatization of municipal water supply in the late 1990s, and the international Occupy movement that sprang up in New York in 2011 as a protest against social inequality and that subsequently diffused rapidly to cities elsewhere in the world. Nowadays, possibilities for the mobilization of protest movements in cities are enormously enhanced by widespread access to social media. In the same way, political ideas and demands diffuse from city to city across the entire globe with increasing rapidity and effectiveness. The city is without question a major fulcrum of emancipatory potentials, though its capacities for political expression are also sometimes exploited by reactionary currents, as in the case of the Pegida anti-immigration demonstrations in Dresden and other German cities in 2014.

The proclivity of dense aggregates of individuals to promote political solidarity and to provide a ready-made setting for social protest and spontaneous demonstrations has been confirmed over and over again in practice. But what is it that constitutes the specifically *urban* in these matters? Formal and informal mechanisms of diffusing information and fomenting public assemblies like spontaneous crowds or prearranged mass gatherings and marches are certainly one way in which the urban, and more specifically, the urban land nexus, lends itself to the initiation and maintenance of political movements in cities. Yet what can we say about the substantive content of these movements and their relationship to the urban as such? It is almost certainly not fruitful to insist too strongly on a rigorous distinction between the essentially urban and the contingently urban content of political issues, especially as some of these issues are hybrid in nature, as in the case of class conflicts (e.g. over employment or housing issues) that have their roots in society-wide mechanisms of social organization but that have numerous urban manifestations. Still, what we *can* say in substantive terms about the urban political arena in the strict sense is that it revolves centrally around conflicts and collisions that are endemic to the urban land nexus, particularly given its status as a dense kaleidoscopic amalgam of widely varying human interests.

In this book, I have persistently alluded to this condition in terms of the multiple externalities, the shared resources, the communal solidarities and differences, and the wayward evolutionary tendencies that materialize in the urban land nexus in the context of specific social formations and the ways in which they inject concrete meaning into these matters. All these aspects of the urban land nexus represent points of tension in that they generate outcomes whose costs and benefits are almost always distributed unequally across the citizenry at large. Specific kinds of institutions of governance typically seek to manage the urban dysfunctionalities and social perplexities generated by this turbulent scene and to chart out strategic plans of action, though political restraints and blowback mean that these institutions are subject to considerable pressure from many different interest groups. A democratic urbanism capable of facing up to this complex field of predicaments must not only be able to mobilize technical problem-solving know-how but must also ensure that these institutions are capable of comprehending and grappling with the peculiar political conflicts of the urban land nexus, as such. In the same way, Manuel Castells' work on urban politics and protest movements points urgently to the inherently problematical nature of urban existence and the need for transparency in governance.[58] In line with the general argument presented here, Castells emphasizes three generic imperatives that are consistently intertwined with political tensions and requirements in cities, both in rich and in poor countries, namely, investment in collective consumption and the allocation of public goods; the search for cultural identity, conviviality, and community in relationship to a definite territorial base; and the importance of flexibility and expertise in the policy-making capacities of urban governance as it responds to local needs and demands.

Notes

1. C. Jencks, *Heteropolis: Los Angeles, the Riots, and the Strange Beauty of Hetero-Architecture*, London: Academy Editions, 1993.
2. S. Graham and S. Marvin, *Splintering Urbanism: Networked Infrastructures, Technological Mobilities and the Urban Condition*, London: Routledge, 2001.
3. G. Simmel, "The metropolis and mental life," pp. 409–424 in K. H. Wolff (ed.) *The Sociology of Georg Simmel*, New York: Free Press, 1950.
4. W. Alonso, *Location and Land Use*, Cambridge, MA: Harvard University Press, 1965; E. S. Mills, *Studies in the Structure of the Urban Economy*, Baltimore: Johns Hopkins University Press, 1972; R. F. Muth, *Cities and Housing*, Chicago: Chicago University Press, 1969; see also M. Straszheim, "The theory of urban residential location," pp. 717–757 in E. S. Mills (ed.) *The Handbook of Regional and Urban Economics*, Vol. 2: *Urban Economics*, Amsterdam: Elsevier-North Holland, 1987.
5. Such a model was first empirically calibrated by Clark in the early 1950s; see C. Clark, "Urban population densities," *Journal of the Royal Statistical Society*, Series A, 114, 1951, 490–496.
6. H. Lefebvre, *La Production de l'Espace*, Paris: Editions Anthropos, 1974, p. 41.
7. Glaeser, Kahn and Rappaport suggest that low-income individuals are concentrated at the center of the city because this part of the city offers an abundance of public transport opportunities. This suggestion is no doubt partially correct, but the relationship is surely reflexive, for the high density of population also encourages relatively high rates of investment in public transport facilities at the center of the city. See E. L. Glaeser, M. E. Kahn and J. Rappaport, "Why do the poor live in cities? The role of public transportation," *Journal of Urban Economics*, 63, 2008, 1–24.
8. R. J. Sampson, *Great American City: Chicago and the Enduring Neighborhood Effect*, Chicago: University of Chicago Press, 2012. See also J. Bodnar, *Workers' World: Kinship, Community, and Protest in an Industrial Society, 1900–1940*, Baltimore: Johns Hopkins University Press, 1982.
9. I. Katznelson, *City Trenches: Urban Politics and the Patterning of Class in the United States*, New York: Pantheon, 1981.

10. See, for example, K. Boo, *Behind the Beautiful Forevers: Life, Death and Hope in a Mumbai Undercity*, New York: Random House, 2012; T. P. R. Caldeira, *City of Walls: Crime, Segregation, and Citizenship in São Paulo*, Berkeley: University of California Press, 2000.
11. R. A. Walker, "A theory of suburbanization: capitalism and the construction of urban space in the United States," pp. 383–429 in M. Dear and A. J. Scott (eds.) *Urbanization and Urban Planning in Capitalist Society*, New York: Methuen, 1981.
12. See, for example, M. Ellis, R. Wright and V. Parks, "Geography and the immigrant division of labor," *Economic Geography*, 83, 2007, 255–281; S. Gera and P. Kuhn, *Occupation, Locational Pattern, and the Journey to Work*, Ottawa: Economic Council of Canada, 1978; A. J. Scott, "Patterns of employment in Southern California's multimedia and digital visual effects industry: the form and logic of an emerging local labor market," pp. 30–48 in H-J. Braczyk, G. Fuchs and H-G. Wolf, *Multimedia and Regional Economic Restructuring*, London: Routledge, 1999.
13. See, for example, J. Gaillard, *Paris, La Ville, 1852–1870*, Paris: Honoré Champion, 1977.
14. H. B. Barrow, "The American disease of growth: Henry Ford and the metropolitanization of Detroit, 1920–1940," pp. 200–220 in R. Lewis (ed.) *Manufacturing Suburbs: Building Work and Home on the Metropolitan Fringe*, Philadelphia: Temple University Press, 2004.
15. C. W. Hartman, "The housing of relocated families," *Journal of the American Institute of Planners*, 30, 1964, 266–286; N. Smith, "Toward a theory of gentrification: a back to the city movement by capital not people," *Journal of the American Planning Association*, 45, 1979, 538–548.
16. D. S. Massey and N. A. Denton, *American Apartheid: Segregation and the Making of the Underclass*, Cambridge, MA: Harvard University Press; W. A. V. Clark, E. Anderson, J. Östh and B. Malmberg, "A multiscalar analysis of neighborhood composition in Los Angeles, 2000–2010: a location-based approach to segregation and diversity," *Annals of the Association of American Geographers*, 105, 2015, 1260–1284.
17. T. P. R. Caldeira, *op. cit.*, 2000; N. M. Yip, "Walled communities without gates: gated communities in Shanghai," *Urban Geography*, 33, 2012, 221–236.
18. E. J. Blakely and M. G. Snyder, *Fortress America: Gated Communities in the United States*, Washington, DC: Brookings Institution, 1997.
19. E. Vesselinov, M. Cazessus and W. Falk, "Gated communities and spatial inequality," *Journal of Urban Affairs*, 29, 2007, 109–127.
20. R. Le Goix, "Gated communities: sprawl and social segregation in Southern California," pp. 131–151 in R. Atkinson and S. Blandy (eds.) *Gated Communities*, London: Routledge, 2006.

21. T. P. R. Caldeira, *op. cit.*, 2000, p. 232. See also P. Pérez, "Buenos Aires: fragmentation and privatization of the metropolitan city," *Environment and Urbanization*, 14, 2002, 145–158; M. L. de Souza, "Metropolitan decentralization, socio-political fragmentation and extended suburbanization: Brazilian urbanization in the 1980s and 1990," *Geoforum*, 32, 2001, 437–447.
22. P. Hall and K. Pain, *The Polycentric Metropolis: Learning from Mega-City Regions in Europe*, Abingdon: Earthscan, 2006; J. Gottmann, *Megalopolis: The Urbanized Northeastern Seaboard of the United States*, Cambridge: MIT Press, 1964.
23. J. C. Teaford, "Suburbia and post-suburbia: a brief history," pp. 15–34 in N. A. Phelps and F. Wu (eds.) *International Perspectives on Suburbanization: A Post-Suburban World?* London: Palgrave Macmillan, 2011.
24. T. Firman, "Post-suburban elements in an Asian extended metropolitan region: the case of Jabodetabek (Jakarta Metropolitan Area)," pp. 195–209 in N. A. Phelps and F. Wu (eds.) *International Perspectives on Suburbanization: A Post-Suburban World?* London: Palgrave Macmillan, 2011; J. C. Teaford, *op. cit.*, 2011.
25. T. Bunnell, "Multimedia utopia? A geographical critique of high-tech development in Malaysia's Multimedia Supercorridor," *Antipode*, 34, 2002, 265–295; M. Indergaard, "The webs they weave: Malaysia's Multimedia Supercorridor and New York's Silicon Alley," *Urban Studies*, 40, 2003, 379–402.
26. J. Garreau, *Edge City: Life on the New Frontier*, New York: Doubleday, 1988. See also R. Keil and J-P. D. Addie, "It's not going to be suburban, it's going to be all urban: assembling post-suburbia in the Toronto and Chicago regions," *International Journal of Urban and Regional Research*, 2015, DOI: 10.1111/1468-2427.12303
27. R. Glass, "Aspects of change," pp. xiii–xlii in *London: Aspects of Change*, Centre for Urban Studies Report No. 3, London: MacGibbon and Kee, 1964.
28. T. Slater, "The gentrification of the city," pp. 571–585 in G. Bridge and S. Watson (eds.) *The New Blackwell Companion to the City*, London: Wiley-Blackwell, 2011; T. Slater, "The eviction of critical perspectives from gentrification research," *International Journal of Urban and Regional Research*, 30, 2006, 737–757.
29. As many as 8,570 references to gentrification were recorded in Google Scholar in the year 2016 alone.
30. N. Smith, "Gentrification and capital: theory, practice and ideology in Society Hill," *Antipode*, 11, 1979, 24–35; N. Smith, "Toward a theory of gentrification: a back to the city movement by capital, not people," *Journal of the American Planning Association*, 45, 1979, 538–548.

31. H. Hoyt, *One Hundred Years of Land Values in Chicago: The Relationship of the Growth of Chicago to the Rise of its Land Values, 1830–1833*, Chicago: Chicago University Press, 1933.
32. E. Clark, "The rent gap and transformation of the built environment: case studies in Malmö, 1860–1985," *Geografiska Annaler*, 70, 1988, 241–254; D. Ley, "Alternative explanations for inner-city gentrification: a Canadian assessment," *Annals of the Association of American Geographers*, 767, 1986, 521–535.
33. A point that is also made by S. C. Bourassa, "The rent gap debunked," *Urban Studies*, 30, 1993, 1731–1744.
34. It is an easy matter to transform this analysis to the case of agricultural land, and to incorporate it into a dynamic von Thünen framework generally. The analysis can also be readily extended to include the issue of the *timing* of land-use conversion decisions, see D. M. Nowlan, "The land market: how it works," pp. 3–37 in L. B. Smith and M. Walker (eds.) *Public Property?* Vancouver: Fraser Institute, 1977.
35. A. Merrifield, *The New Urban Question*, New York: Pluto Press, 2014.
36. R. Vernon, "The economics and finances of the large metropolis," *Daedalus*, 90, 1961, 31–47; J. O. Wheeler, "Occupational status and work-trips: a minimum distance approach," *Social Forces*, 45, 1967, 508–515; Q. Gillard, "Reverse commuting and the inner-city low-income problem," *Growth and Change*, 3, 1979, 12–18.
37. T. Slater, "The eviction of critical perspectives from gentrification research," *International Journal of Urban and Regional Research*, 30, 2006, 737–757; L. Wacquant, "Relocating gentrification: the working class, science and the state in recent urban research," *International Journal of Urban and Regional Research*, 32, 2008, 198–205.
38. N. Blomley, *Unsettling the City: Urban Land and the Politics of Poverty*, London: Routledge, 2004; R. Enright (ed.) *Body Heat: The Story of the Woodward's Redevelopment*, Vancouver: Blueimage, 2010.
39. L. Lees, T. Slater and E. Wyly, *Gentrification*, London: Routledge, 2007.
40. R. Lloyd, "Neo-Bohemia: art and neighborhood development in Chicago," *Journal of Urban Affairs*, 24, 2002, 517–532.
41. S. Zukin, *Loft Living: Culture and Capital in Urban Change*, Baltimore: Johns Hopkins University Press, 1982.
42. See, for example, L. Lees, H. B. Shin and E. López-Morales (eds.) *Global Gentrifications: Uneven Development and Displacement*, Bristol: Policy Press, 2015.
43. D. A. Ghertner, "Why gentrification theory fails in much of the world," *City*, 19, 2015, 552–563.
44. C. Hamnett, "Gentrification and the middle-class remaking of inner London, 1961–2001," *Urban Studies*, 40, 2003, 2401–2426; D. Ley, *The*

New Middle Class and the Remaking of the Central City, Oxford: Oxford University Press, 1996.
45. K. Ward, C. Fagan, L. McDowell, D. Perrons and K. Ray, "Class transformation and work-life balance in urban Britain: the case of Manchester," *Urban Studies*, 47, 2010, 2259–2278.
46. B. Badcock, "Thirty years on: gentrification and class changeover in Adelaide's inner suburbs, 1966–96," *Urban Studies*, 38, 2001, 1559–1572; M. Wulff and M. Lobo, "The new gentrifiers: the role of households and migration in reshaping Melbourne's core and inner suburbs," *Urban Policy and Research*, 27, 2009, 315–331.
47. A. Haase, S. Kabisch, A. Steinführer, S. Bouzarovski, R. Hall and P. Ogden, "Emergent spaces of reurbanisation: exploring the demographic dimension of inner-city residential change in a European setting," *Population Space and Place*, 16, 2010, 443–463; C. Hamnett and D. Whitelegg, "Loft conversion and gentrification in London: from industrial to postindustrial land use," *Environment and Planning A*, 39, 2007, 106–124.
48. H. Hoyt, *op. cit.*, 1933, p. 335.
49. A. J. Scott, "Emerging cities of the third wave," *City*, 15, 2011, 289–381.
50. A. R. Cuthbert, *The Form of Cities: Political Economy and Urban Design*, Oxford: Blackwell, 2006.
51. H. Schmid, W-D. Sahr and J. Urry (eds.) *Cities and Fascination: Beyond the Surplus of Meaning*, Farnham: Ashgate, 2011.
52. L. Sklair, *The Transnational Capitalist Class*, Oxford: Blackwell, 2000; L. Sklair, "Iconic architecture and the culture-ideology of consumerism," *Theory, Culture and Society*, 27, 2010, 135–159.
53. M. Kaika, "Architecture and crisis: re-inventing the icon, re-imag(in)ing London and rebranding the City," *Transactions of the Institute of British Geographers*, 35, 2010, 453–474.
54. J. Hannigan, *Fantasy City: Pleasure and Profit in the Postmodern Metropolis*, London: Routledge, 1998.
55. E. Currid-Halkett and A. J. Scott, "The geography of celebrity and glamour: reflections on economy, culture, and desire in the city," *Cities, Culture and Society*, 4, 2013, 2–11.
56. See, for example, D. Harvey, *Rebel Cities*, London: Verso, 2012. See also: E. Swyngedouw and M. Dikeç, "Theorizing the politicizing city," *International Journal of Urban and Regional Research*, 2017, DOI: 10.1111/1468-2427.12388
57. G. Rabrenovic, "Urban social movements," pp. 239–254 in J. S. Davies and D. L. Imbroscio (eds.) *Theories of Urban Politics*, London: Sage, 2009.
58. M. Castells, *The City and the Grassroots: A Cross-Cultural Theory of Urban Social Movements*, Berkeley and Los Angeles: University of California Press, 2003.

CHAPTER 10

The Urban Commonwealth

THE CITY AND THE COMMONS

Background and Definitions

I have made much in previous chapters of the distinction between the individual and the collectivity and the different ways in which these two domains of ownership and action play out in the context of the urban land nexus. In the present chapter, I seek to modify this line of discussion by adding a complementary and partially hybrid domain involving communal assets. Some of these assets are gifts of nature, others are the unintended result of purely private action, and yet others have their roots in collective enterprise, both governmental and civil. All of them entail forms of property that are in varying degree accessible outside of competitive market arrangements to a wider public, whether it be the citizenry at large or only selected groups of individuals. Examples of assets like these are the atmosphere or the visual landscape of the city, or property held in public trust such as a park or a monument, or goods and services supplied by government such as a road network or street lighting. These assets, or *commons*,[1] represent important if underacknowledged elements of contemporary urban life, and, if anything, are becoming ever more diverse in a world marked by increasing levels of technological and social complexity.

The term "commons" refers originally to the organization of the village economy of pre-Enclosure England where an area of waste or common land was typically open to all members of the community for pasturing livestock. In his celebrated paper *The Tragedy of the Commons*, published in 1968, Garrett Hardin pointed to a potential liability in this communal arrangement.[2] There is, he suggested, a strict upper limit on the number of cattle that can be efficiently grazed on any given common, and any infringement of this limit will entail diminished aggregate income for the village as a whole. However, every individual villager has an incentive, on the basis of a purely personal calculation, to put more and more cattle on the common. The net result, in the absence of formal or informal restraints on overgrazing, is that diminishing returns will set in, leading in the long run to the exhaustion of the productive capacity of the common and reduced income for everyone. This type of dilemma, or free-rider problem, is inherent in situations where assets of any kind are held in common, and as Hardin indicates, there are two principal ways of dealing with it. One is represented by privatization (i.e. enclosure of the common into individual holdings); the other is collective governance. The latter solution was actually widely practiced in much of rural England before the Industrial Revolution in the form of customary understandings or joint agreements between users as to rights of access to the common together with relevant policing operations so as to enforce local rules and regulations. It might be noted, as an aside, that the benefits of this apparently exemplary republicanism in pre-Enclosure England were to a significant extent skimmed off by the lord of the manor.

Hardin's paper was intended to draw attention to modern-day environmental predicaments, but as it happens, the metaphor of the commons is equally pertinent to the case of the modern city. There have always been many different kinds of commons in cities and in capitalism more broadly, and in the twenty-first century, the metaphor has taken on insistent new meaning to the point that some analysts have suggested that capitalism itself may be eroding away in the face of current extensions of the commons. Before we come to this contentious question, however, much further clarification about the urban commons and their many different expressions in terms of their physical forms and modes of governance is in order.

Commons Versus Markets

In their purest expression, commons such as national defense or the ideas that circulate through society are not only freely at the disposal of all, but are also immune from depletion or congestion with increases in the number of individuals who benefit from them. These types of commons are akin to Samuelson's notion of a public good or a "collective consumption good."[3] In many instances, however, resources held in common are indeed subject to deterioration as usage increases, which means that they are liable to take on severely suboptimal configurations unless regulatory restraints, such as fee structures, or legislative control, or exclusion of certain categories of users, are imposed to ensure orderly use. Regulation of this sort is frequently, but by no means always, provided by governmental agencies, as in the case of air pollution controls and road pricing schemes in large metropolitan areas. In other instances, the pure form of the commons gives way to what we might call quasi-commons, or what Elinor Ostrom has identified as *common-pool resources*, which are held jointly and exclusively in diverse sorts of self-managing joint ownership or joint control agreements, such as cooperative housing projects or community gardens (as well as the commons of pre-Enclosure English villages).[4] These arrangements assume many different guises including hierarchical, nested, and polycentric forms of association, which in turn may be profit-oriented or not.[5]

In the urban context, the commons in the widest sense, from pure public goods through unplanned spillover effects, to common-pool resources, emerge in the first instance as overlapping mixes of externalities, community property, and collectively supplied goods or services that occur in the city by reason of its densely packed structures of human activity and interaction. In the words of Hardt and Negri, the urban commons represent a concentration of "people living together, sharing resources, communicating."[6] In more specific terms that directly reflect the logic and dynamics of the urban land nexus—itself an extensive multiplex of different private and communal property regimes[7]—the city is the site of numerous and many-sided commons stemming from its status as a jointly created space marked by profuse interlocational overflows and synergies together with accumulated reserves of tradition and social memory. The urban commons thus constitute a conspicuously heterogeneous collection of artifacts, spaces, and institutions that interlock with one another across the urban land nexus.[8]

From the perspective of mainstream economic theory, the commons are an incongruity, a domain of market failure that has not yet been brought within the scope of private property and competitive market discipline and hence, in this view, a source of inefficiency and resource misallocation. This conventional insistence on the notion of market failure, however, grants far too much, by implication, to the market as a taken-for-granted normative ideal of social organization. In opposition to this notion, the commons do not stand simply as a collection of aberrant or irrational secondary outcomes relative to the market. Even when privatization of the commons might work well in market terms, they are often imbued with value-laden substance that is hostile to purely market-oriented criteria of evaluation, whether for reasons of aesthetics, amenity, culture, tradition, ethics, communal sentiment, public order, or social justice. It is certainly the case that inefficiency and resource misallocation can and do occur in numerous spheres where market forces are absent, and good reasons can be offered in favor of competitive price signals as a means of coordinating many aspects of life.[9] That said, two arguments that extend the points already stated above must also immediately be taken into account as to why markets cannot in any case provide an all-encompassing framework of urban organization.

First, market rationality is myopic in its terms of reference, so that quite apart from any technicalities of market failure, the wider demands of social rationality mean that much broader standards of judgment inevitably apply to the evaluation of many urban outcomes. This reasoning pertains with special force when the city is seen for what it is, that is, a *commonwealth* that exceeds by far the sum of the private holdings, individual interactions, and market relationships that constitute an important but far from complete inventory of the substantive contents of the city. Second, and as already indicated, not only are wide swaths of the urban commons immune from intrusions of market order, but effective governance of their functions can often be achieved by quite varied formal and informal institutional agencies. What is especially important here is that these agencies are usually subject to political forces reflecting normative visions of urban life, and they are thus much better able than markets to express the complex compromises and pressures that come into play in any attempt to balance prosperity and growth with economic and social evenhandedness for all. Of course, the compromises that are realized in practice always reflect the political balance of power in society. In this respect it is important to mention that despite the evident extension of the commons in contemporary society, anticipations of "life beyond capitalism"[10] remain a distinctly distant prospect. Although the commons offer crucial enhancements of democratic citizenship, they are in practice highly congruent elements of extant social arrangements, and it would certainly be premature to think of them as harbingers of a post-capitalist order.

Varieties of Urban Commons

I have already offered a few examples of commons as a way of pushing the analysis forward, but a much more systematic account of the many diverse types of commons embedded in the urban land nexus is now needed in order to fill out the discussion. Figure 10.1 provides a schematic overview of some basic varieties of urban commons and their relationships to one another. I should stress that the figure is entirely provisional; it is not exhaustive and nor are the designated categories or boxes representing specific types of commons completely watertight. The figure is constructed as a tentative hierarchical taxonomy branching out from the root category of the urban commons as a whole and arranged in terms of the formal and functional attributes of different categories of commons.

A first branching point emerging out of the root of the diagram distinguishes between a category representing commons that can be defined as including all the elements of the public domain versus a category identified in terms of common-pool resources. The public domain in turn gives way to three major categories that I have designated as externalities, government-controlled facilities, and public-private hybrids, where the latter are defined as commons that allow for public access to and gatherings on property that is nevertheless privately held. I now deal with each of these categories and their declensions in turn.

The box labeled "externalities" subsumes an unusually large number of more detailed cases. This broad category actually overlaps significantly with other types of commons in other branches of the hierarchy. However, I designate it here as a hierarchical element in its own right to signify that it comprises assets (and liabilities) that originate as spontaneous unplanned excrescences of the urban land nexus and hence can be distinguished from planned externalities resulting from different types of public goods and private-public hybrids. The diversity and scope of the externalities referred to explicitly in Fig. 10.1, range from intraurban economies of scale and scope, through socialization processes, to the positive and negative overspill effects that emanate from urban environmental resources. Since these externalities are produced in a largely unplanned and spontaneous manner, their impacts are typically distributed across the urban land nexus with a significant degree of arbitrariness in regard to who benefits and who bears the ill effects. Moreover, and importantly, even where these externalities are equally accessible to all, it does not necessarily follow that the (positive or negative) payoffs are always equal.

220 10 THE URBAN COMMONWEALTH

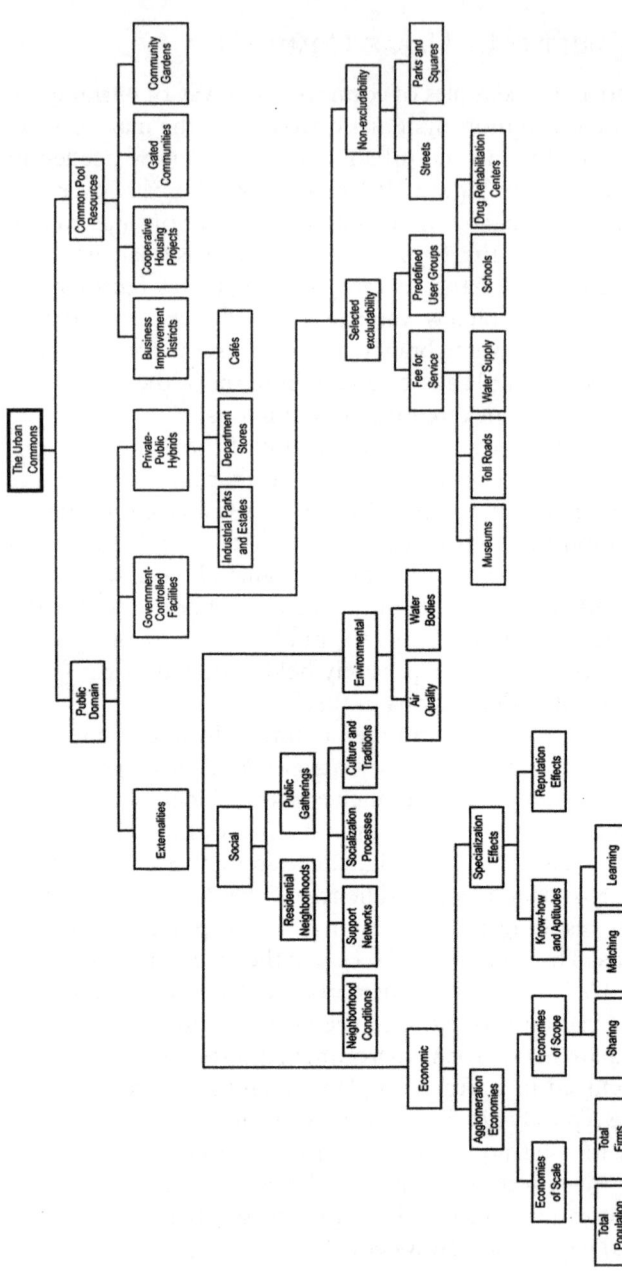

Fig. 10.1 Hierarchical classification of the urban commons; the diagram is suggestive only and is not intended to be exhaustive. The designated categories are purely exemplary and are not necessarily mutually exclusive

Externalities can in turn be systematically codified in terms of economic, social, and environmental subtypes, and these then divide into yet more finely defined categories. At these levels of the taxonomy, we can also readily identify specific types of institutional responses that come into being in the effort to augment the positive effects and to curtail the negative impacts of these different elements of the commons. For example, public authorities may seek to boost agglomeration economies by means of new infrastructural investments or by establishing forums that stimulate interfirm learning processes; land use zoning ordinances and informal local associations can often be designed in ways that bring significant improvement to neighborhood conditions; and air pollution issues can be addressed by means of emissions controls and other restrictions on the activities of source points. These modes of corrective intervention may be more or less effective in shoring up the positive values and curtailing the negative effects of intraurban externalities, but they rarely accomplish as much as they might in principle, partly because of the complexity of the tasks involved and partly because in capitalist society there are always irresolvable tensions between the logic of the commons and the claims of private interests. A notable instance of this sort of tension is represented by disruptive incursions of private developers and gentrifiers into established urban neighborhoods and communities endowed with subtle but powerful logics of mutual support, security, and socialization that have been built up over many decades. Blomley has alluded to such a case in regard to property redevelopment in a poor neighborhood of Downtown Eastside in Vancouver, where contending forces with radically opposing ideological positions in regard to the nature of property confront one another. In the face of demands by private investors to redevelop this area, Blomley writes that it is also necessary "to acknowledge the existence of counterposed claims that are collective in scope. The developer's right to exclude is countered by the claim that the poor have a right not to be excluded."[11]

If we now return to the box labeled "public domain" in Fig. 10.1, a further branching point leading to the category of government-controlled facilities becomes apparent, and a new set of commons with their own peculiar characteristics come into view. These particular commons can be differentiated into those that offer only selective access and those that are free public goods. In the first category are types of commons where consumers are excluded either by means of fee schedules (e.g. toll roads) or where exclusion is secured by predefining user groups (e.g. schools).

In the second category are types of commons (e.g. streets and public parks) that are accessible to all without charge. Much of the infrastructural and public service apparatus of the city is contained within these two special instances of commons. Government supply and regulation of these commons can be seen in part as being necessitated by technical market failures because in many instances these represent assets that resist effective enclosure and metering in ways that would make it possible for private firms to collect individual user fees. This is only part of the story, however. Facilities like road networks, sewage systems, schools, and drug rehabilitation centers, for example, can indeed be supplied by private enterprise, but rarely in adequate quantities or in sufficiently well-calibrated qualities relative to social needs, so that if these kinds of facilities were to be privatized, we might well expect dysfunctional deficits in urban welfare to occur. At the same time, the supply of urban public goods is by its nature subject to insistent politicization, and all the more so given the familiar discrepancies across urban space and across the vertical spectrum of urban society between the taxes and levies raised for public investment purposes on the one hand, and the benefits received relative to social needs on the other hand. Indeed, conflicts over the cost and spatial allocation of public goods are a major source of political ferment in the urban land nexus.

There is a further element of the public domain that I have labeled in Fig. 10.1 as private-public hybrids (or, as they are sometimes labeled, privately owned public spaces).[12] These consist of sites within the city that are privately owned, such as department stores, cafés, theaters, or malls but that nonetheless function as places of public encounter.[13] It is possible no doubt to quibble as to whether this category really represents a commons at all, but clearly it does constitute an important component of the public life of the city just as it also helps to sustain the communal and convivial attributes of urban existence. Also, in many cities today different kinds of business and commercial activities congregate together in privately held industrial parks and estates to share services in common and to engage in beneficial forms of mutual interaction.

Finally, the idea of the urban commons can also be extended to incorporate the special category of common-pool resources. This category comprises jointly held or jointly administered resources whose benefits are accessible only to accredited individuals, and, as Fig. 10.1 indicates, it can be separated into detailed subcategories such as business improvement districts, cooperative housing projects, gated communities, and communally managed gardens. In many instances, the formation of common-pool resource organizations is facilitated by local or national legislation specifying the responsibilities and privileges of the different participants. The homeownership associations that manage gated communities, for example, are typically incorporated under local government legal codes. Similarly, business improvement districts are usually set up as officially designated non-profit entities formed by groups of property owners to promote local commercial development, as in the case of Times Square in New York and the Fashion District of Los Angeles.

It is evident from this brief commentary that large portions of the urban land nexus remain free from the constraints of private property and are socially produced as commons that touch in many different ways on the lives of the entire citizenry. Even the monetary value of urban land is generated out of the collective forces that reside within the urban land nexus as a whole. A striking paradox of contemporary urbanization, then, is the glaring contrast thrown into relief by the status of so much of the urban land nexus as a public resource while so many of the benefits that it generates are unequally appropriated for purely private purposes. In the same way, a continual struggle exists between the integrity of the commons and the urge to privatize many of the more lucrative opportunities that they offer. An open question at this stage is how this tense and chronically antagonistic balance between the commons and the private realm will shift as the cognitive-cultural order of the twenty-first century comes yet more forcefully to the forefront. That said, the increasing entrepreneurialism of numerous municipalities and their often-aggressive inclination to externalize many of the ownership obligations and service responsibilities that were formerly taken more or less for granted as the legitimate domain of local government suggests that we are likely to see continued erosion of at least some parts of the commons.[14] Where this has already occurred, it has typically compromised the welfare of the less fortunate social strata of the city.

The Urban Commons in Cognitive-Cultural Capitalism

I have tried to describe in this chapter so far the multidimensional character of the urban commons and the different and not infrequently ambiguous ways in which they are intertwined with both the state and civil society. A similar kind of ambiguity hangs over the role of the commons as resources for capital and labor. As Amin and Howell have written, we cannot simply presume that the commons are invariably "the antithesis of commodification."[15] In fact, large segments of the urban commons function as essential inputs to commodity production, and, by the same token, are important components of the competitive advantage of cities. This aspect of the commons has assumed a special significance in view of the role of place, propinquity, and agglomeration in the new economy, even as globalization continues to move erratically but continually forward.

Competitive Advantage and the Commons

At the outset, and to pick up on a by-now-familiar refrain, the urban land nexus functions as a fertile terrain of agglomeration economies and specialization effects that help to underpin the competitive dynamics of the new economy. The specific benefits of this terrain derive from its role as a site of sharing, matching, and learning, and as a pool of know-how, aptitudes, and reputational evaluation. Among these benefits, the powers of the urban land nexus to stimulate creative and innovative processes must be counted as being among the most sensitive and significant. These powers derive from many different facets of the urban commons. For one thing, the urban milieu is partly constituted as a web of interactions between production units in ways that shape patterns of innovation and entrepreneurship. For another, it is also interpenetrated by extensive residential spaces where labor is reproduced, and where many traditions, customs, and cultural values affecting workers' aptitudes for resourcefulness and ingenuity are kept alive. Neighborhoods play a special role in this regard since they are sites where communal patterns of socialization and habituation within the labor force are bolstered via local interrelationships and family life. Equally important as stimuli of innovation impulses are many kinds of educational and business-service institutions (such as technology and business advice centers) inserted into the urban land nexus and supplied as public goods. I have referred elsewhere to these broad aspects of the urban commons as a "creative field," that is, a multifaceted spatial system of interactions, cues, influences, and resources providing materials for imaginative appropriation by individuals as they pursue the business of work and social existence.[16] In the cognitive-cultural economy, with its typically dispersed and bottom-up forms of innovation and the frequently shifting product and process configurations of individual producers, the contribution of the creative field to localized competitive advantage is almost always of crucial importance. Wherever this field comes into existence, its potentialities are further enhanced by the mutual entanglement of firms and workers in transactional exchanges with one another so that they receive and emit signals charged with information that is susceptible to combination with other pieces of freely floating information in a manner that recurrently generates new insights. The application of these multifarious creative energies in specific forms of technological, commercial, and cultural innovation helps to unleash an urban dynamic of intensifying competitive advantage. Partly on these bases, large cities in many different countries function as communal springboards facilitating the capacity of producers in the cognitive-cultural economy to contest national and global markets by means of uniquely configured products.

A recent twist on the latter observation is that firms in the new economy are strongly disposed—as already demonstrated in Chap. 7—to adopt Chamberlinian competitive strategies that exploit unique kinds of local resources rooted in the urban commons. The exploitation of these resources enables firms to stamp the quality and design of their products with virtually inimitable characteristics thus enabling them to command definite market niches. Conspicuous examples of this phenomenon can be found in high-technology production regions like Silicon Valley where advanced informational assets and communal intellectual property make it possible for local firms to maintain positions close to the frontier of innovation and technical design. Similarly, financial centers such as London, New York, and Tokyo are typically endowed with interlocking local networks of idiosyncratic skills and commercial know-how giving them an overall competitive edge that is far greater than the simple sum of each individual producer's capacity to contest markets. A further illustration is provided by major centers of the cultural economy like Los Angeles, London, Paris, and, increasingly, former Third World cities like Bangkok, Beijing, Mumbai, Seoul, Buenos Aires, and Mexico City where deep pools of place-specific aptitudes, traditions, and creative talent are deployed in the production of diverse products, from film to fashion. These place-specific assets are then expressed in the look, sound, and feel of local outputs, providing them with an aura of authenticity that may perhaps be imitated by firms in other places but that can never be truly captured by reproductions. Even many small urban centers around the world tap increasingly into local cultural resources in order to promote goods and services like handicrafts, music, cuisine, dance, and tourist attractions for international consumption.

It is quite conceivable that in the absence of localized commons with place-specific cultural and creative resources of these kinds, the economic geography of contemporary capitalism might have been even more concentrated and uneven than it actually is. By the same token, many smaller centers that have in practice managed to carve out market niches for themselves in the world division of labor, would in all likelihood have been unable to initiate a durable dynamic of prosperity and growth. These remarks stem from the observation that Chamberlinian advantages give many initially small or laggard production centers the capacity to face up to competition from larger and more established centers with well-developed agglomeration economies, and even to contest global markets. Hollywood was once widely predicted to emerge victorious as the sole viable global center of film and television entertainment on the basis of its acquired stock of common assets. Yet Hollywood has seen its market share eroded by the resurgence of alternative film production locales whose competitive advantages are drawn precisely from the unique patrimony of locally inflected idioms, cultural values, and skills that they are able to harness. These alternative locales comprise not only the widely cited cases of Bollywood (Mumbai), Hong Kong, Beijing, Seoul, and Tokyo but also dozens of other centers with burgeoning regional markets from Bogotá through Lagos and Istanbul to Manila.

Social Reproduction

The effects of the commons on the economic fortunes of the city are complemented and reinforced by their related impacts on general processes of socialization, notably via the influence of work-based and community-based routines on habits of thought and behavior. Child-rearing and schooling practices, with their roots going deeply into neighborhood life, are also shaped in various respects by a broad ethos deriving from the commons. With increasing global integration, however, and especially with the development of cyberspace, the scalar dimensions of many segments of the commons now extend far beyond any single urban area. A matter of particular note in this respect is that purely localized socialization processes are becoming steadily entangled with and partially submerged by effects that spring from a wider mediasphere embedded in the global commons. Accordingly, the mediatic environment, the workplace, and the city tend to act as mutually interpenetrating forces shaping forms of culture and consciousness that in essence emerge as hybridized outcomes of local and global influences. In the light of this statement, Hardt and Negri's idea that the "metropolis is to the multitude what the factory was to the industrial working class," is partially correct but clearly overblown.[17]

Hardt and Negri have nevertheless argued persuasively that the intensification of these socialization processes over the twentieth century and into the twenty-first has proceeded to the point where the commons have now steadily become implicated in biopower relations across the whole of advanced capitalist society.[18] The term "biopower" here refers to the social construction of the lifeworld of individual subjects and the concomitant alignment of human subjectivity with the driving purposive directions (like capital accumulation and competitive markets) built into the overall structure of capitalist society. This development is consistent with what Rossi, drawing from Foucault, calls the "entrepreneurialization of the self," a phrase with special resonance at the present moment in history, where implicit subjective consent to participation in the free-for-all of individualistic neoliberalism is being actively manufactured in the cognitive-cultural commodity system.[19] The widening impacts of cognitive-cultural capitalism on prevailing forms of consumerism surely have a great deal to do with this state of affairs. Or, to put the matter more directly, much if not most of the cultural commons at the present time is fundamentally molded by capitalist firms engaged in the production and distribution of commodified beliefs, information, and attitudes. As it happens, these same firms are themselves important engines of twenty-first-century urban development through their production and employment activities.

In contradistinction to the state of things in the nineteenth century when subsumption of the individual was to a large degree formal (i.e. imposed from without), and in the twentieth century when subsumption started to become "real" (i.e. assented to without coercion), subsumption today is taking over large swaths of social and mental existence in ways that make it difficult for radically alternative conceptions of life's possibilities to secure a hearing. This condition is manifest in the mutually supportive realignments of work, social being, and consciousness that are proceeding in cognitive-cultural capitalism. This contention is not intended to echo in any literal sense the old nightmare scenario of the Frankfurt School with its claims about the wholesale stupefaction of the rank and file by means of the knowing manipulation of popular culture by capitalist enterprise. However, as argued by Peters and Bulut, the interplay of the media, commodified entertainment, and consumption generally in contemporary capitalism most certainly operates as a systematic inducement to tacit acquiescence in the broad architecture of society as currently constituted.[20]

In any case, we can probably expect the urban dimensions of these realignments to widen as the cognitive-cultural economy, in its role as a focus of employment and as a source of cerebral and emotional distraction, extends its hold over urban life. Newly emerging city-centric ideologies and technologies, as manifest in current creative city and smart city proposals are closely bound up with these trends. The net effect of such proposals is likely to be significant enlargement of segments of the urban commons, though not necessarily always in a positive direction. Thus, in the one case, much of the literature on creative cities at the present time favors investments in amenities and cultural resources that to all intents and purposes represent disproportionately large public subsidies for the already privileged upper stratum of urban society.[21] In the other case, and granted that embedded sensors and information-gathering agencies in the digital city help to boost the efficiency of urban public services and intraurban flows,[22] these devices also immediately raise the specter of greatly heightened mass surveillance and social control. Smart technologies also offer intimations of a post-political city where supposedly unerring algorithms may well increasingly be promoted as superior alternatives to public debate and collective decision-making in regard to social needs.

From all that has been said above, it is clear that the commons comprise many features that contribute significantly to the social, cultural, and economic lifeblood of the city. There is accordingly a pressing need for more responsive municipal institutions not only to manage these resources in the public interest, but also to protect their positive contributions to urban existence from the privatizing impetus of neoliberal urbanism. It is equally evident, however, that the actually existing urban commons represent economically and politically equivocal phenomena, quite far removed from the *communard* dream of a collective utopia.

Capitalism and the City Revisited

Durability and Resilience

The issues raised in this chapter point directly to a series of major questions about capitalism and the city in the era of the so-called sharing economy. Several influential commentators have recently offered predictions about the prospect of imminent shifts in capitalist society driven by digital technologies and a widening cybernetic commons. These shifts are notably symptomatized by the rise of social media and the Internet of Things. Some of these commentators then claim that these trends are actually undermining capitalism itself, and that a radical expansion of the commons is bringing in its train a prospective collapse of purely capitalistic property, price, and wage relationships.

There are assuredly important opportunities for extending the commons in benign ways and for enlarging the scope of democratic participation and social interaction in cognitive-cultural capitalism. Peer-to-peer networks, for example, make it possible for huge numbers of far-flung virtual communities to coalesce in cyberspace. Benkler speculates on the basis of developments like these that the Internet will eventually liberate the production of culture and information from commercial interests and will largely overturn received conceptions of intellectual property.[23] Rifkin conjectures that digital technologies and the Internet of Things (including three-dimensional printing) are leading to the emergence of a society in which positive prices will eventually disappear because the possibility of reproducing unlimited quantities of outputs at close to zero marginal cost is becoming an ever more concrete possibility.[24] Rifkin goes on to suggest that a collaborative commons based on an extensive sharing economy will rapidly start to supplant competitive capitalism. In an even more radical vein, Vercellone and Negri, among other post-*operaismo* theorists, argue on the basis of Marx's brief discussion of "general intellect" in the *Grundrisse* that the sphere of ideas and information generally is coming to occupy a central role in modern society, and that this turn of events signals the advent of new modalities of production and value formation and the imminent onset of widespread practices of social cooperation.[25] Like-minded theorists have begun to argue that the prospect of the comprehensive socialization of knowledge as a result of new technological possibilities now makes it necessary and urgent to legislate in favor of a universal social wage.[26]

Some of these arguments no doubt point in interesting and alluring directions, but for the most part they are almost certainly unduly exaggerated. They correctly draw attention to the unstable and ambiguous boundary between the digital commons on the one hand and the rights of private property owners on the other, and they also laudably pay attention to the democratic possibilities—as well as the dangers—opened up by the new technologies. Still, some tempering of these speculations about the radical retreat of capitalism in the twenty-first century is surely in order.

Thus, whereas cooperation, sharing, and open-source inputs to economic and social life are unquestionably pushing the boundaries of some kinds of commons outwards, the equally dramatic upsurge of product differentiation (i.e. Chamberlinian competition) together with the swiftly widening practice of distinguishing outputs by means of firm- and place-specific branding, copyright, patenting, and AOC devices, suggests that individual producers will be able to exercise increasing degrees monopolistic or oligopolistic control in many different markets. Hence, even given the highly improbable case where marginal costs fall across the board to zero, producers who are protected by these devices can always extract positive prices or rents from consumers. Much of the digital realm, besides, can only be accessed by means of websites and applications created and held by private profit-making firms that, again, are more often than not protected by the ownership of intellectual property rights. Increasing numbers of these firms, like Facebook, Twitter, Uber, and Airbnb are able to assert their capacities as profit-making entities by reason of the unique services that they offer in cyberspace. The sharing element of these producers does not represent an anti-capitalist undercurrent, but a means of creating new enclosable resources, new needs, and new opportunities for profit and rent.

For these reasons, speculations about the deliquescence of the individual capitalist firm under pressure from an expanding commons must remain extremely theoretical to say the least, especially given the fact that cyberspace itself is daily opening up enormous numbers of new entrepreneurial prospects within the cognitive-cultural economy. We must also be cautious about widespread claims that cyberspace and the global commons are now threatening the very existence of the city as an agglomeration of interacting firms and individuals.[27] The continued rapid growth of urban clusters in countries at all levels of economic development suggests that, at least for the present, cyberspace is far from undermining the spatial integrity of the city, for as stressed in these pages, the core elements of the urbanization process, from productive work to domestic life, are still based to a significant degree on grounded analog communities and interactions that in turn generate important place-centered synergies. As cyberspace expands, urban clusters certainly become caught up within globalized networks, but despite the claims made by theorists of planetary urbanism, the continued vibrancy of the relationships entrenched within the urban land nexus ensures that they remain as powerful localized articulations of social life and collective order.

Tasks Ahead

The urban land nexus is not a talisman for the final resolution of all debates on matters of urban theory, though it is a means of clarifying the persistent enigma as to what the city *is*. With all due acknowledgment to Perec's warning, as quoted in Chap. 2, that any attempt to define the city is more than likely to result in error,[28] I propose that a stable concept of the city can indeed be established by reference to the urban land nexus as the material expression of urbanization processes. I make this claim not because the concept reduces everything about the city to a single descriptive figure, far from it, but because it provides us with a preliminary language for dealing with the genetics of urban clustering and for revealing how specific kinds of space-sorting processes lead on to determinate forms of intraurban space that are in turn imbued with unique historical and geographical substance generated in interaction with wider social frameworks and dynamics. Similarly, while the triumphs and tribulations of the city that I referred to in my opening chapter take on very different aspects in different conjunctures, they are always jointly expressed in the form and functions of the urban land nexus.

The manifestly short period of historical time over which the cities of cognitive-cultural capitalism have made their appearance means that anticipations in regard to future urban developments are liable to be especially untrustworthy, and this in its turn makes political advocacies doubly hazardous. In spite of this difficulty, several critical articulations of the urban land nexus are clearly at the core of a number of indurated social predicaments. In the light of the foregoing analysis three of these predicaments call urgently for concerted public debate and corrective action.

First, as capitalism in general and cognitive-cultural capitalism in particular have tightened their hold over major world cities, a significantly deepening bifurcation of labor markets, incomes, and life chances has also occurred, leading to widespread deprivation among lower-income families and to growing social disaffection of a large fraction of the working population. This bifurcation leaves deep traces on the urban land nexus, as manifest above all, in the radically contrasting qualities of employment, housing, and neighborhood life in major cities, where the disparities between the cognitariat and the new servile class is most apparent. In cities in low- and middle-income countries, these disparities are even more marked so that the festering problems of slum areas in these cities are of an altogether more intense order of magnitude from those of poor neighborhoods in cities of the advanced capitalist societies of the twenty-first century. To be sure, effective correction of many of these problems requires political action and reform at levels well above the scale of the urban land nexus, yet there is still much that municipal authorities can do to alleviate the worst forms of social and economic distress in contemporary cities.

Second, the competitive and mercenary temper of work and life in these cognitive-cultural times is an ideal breeding ground for the possessive individualism and narcissism that appear to be rampant in cities today, and most strikingly of all among members of the upper tier of the cognitive-cultural labor force. This syndrome is quickened by the instrumentalization of human relationships brought on by the increasingly potent but ambiguous ideology of self-fulfillment through career advancement together with potentially massive monetary rewards to individual success in the context of atomized competitive labor markets. Castells has made a related remark to the effect that interrelationships even between people in the same city are tending to depersonalization as web-based forms of exchange intensify.[29] Hence, despite the widely circulated claim advanced by Florida that the so-called creative class thrives in urban milieus where tolerance, openness, and social diversity are prominent,[30] it is probably more accurate to say that to the degree that these proclivities exist, they are more apt to be a reflection of indifference and cynicism rather than meaningful engagement with the fulsomeness of urban life. The recovery of more immediate forms of social cohesion together with the consolations and pleasures of community are therefore important desiderata in any political reconstruction of the city in the interests of more meaningful and rewarding modalities of urban existence.

Third, as demonstrated in the present book, the expanding cognitive-cultural economy has induced a great resurgence of agglomeration effects in the form of localized economies of scale and scope. These effects are a fundamental component of the urban commons, and they have major impacts on the productive capacities and competitive advantages of many cities. Since they are almost entirely spontaneous and unplanned, however, neither their quantity nor their qualitative attributes are likely to attain to anything that comes close to overall social optimality. The evident deduction is that very much more effective collective coordination of agglomeration processes in the city is required in order to calibrate the local economy, not just with regard to profitability but also with a clear view to social welfare generally. Storper *et al.* have recently shown that well-informed non-governmental institutions can play a crucial role in guiding strategies for harvesting these benefits and for steering development into productive channels.[31]

In all of these matters, the urban land nexus functions as both an object of remedial action and a field of latent possibilities within the framework of the wider constraints and potentials presented by society as a whole. As the technological foundations and social relations of cognitive-cultural capitalism evolve further forward, we can expect many dramatic changes to occur in the urban land nexus. Even so, the transcendence of capitalism and the advent of a future collaborative society alleged by Rifkin and others to be imminently in the offing—at whatever geographic scale we care to imagine—remains far from assured. The current situation is one where decisive shifts in the quality of work and life in cities are under way, but these are far removed from anything resembling the putative atrophy of capitalist social and property relations. In spite of this declaration, the long, slow efforts of progressive political movements around the world to push social and economic reform forward will certainly continue despite inevitable setbacks and disappointments. Even in an era of globalization and digitized communication, urban areas, with their dense populations and public spaces, continue to function as robust forums for the articulation of enlightened political demands, as they have done since the time of the Greek polis.

Notes

1. I use the singular when referring to a specific communal asset; otherwise, I use the plural.
2. G. Hardin, "The tragedy of the commons," *Science*, 162, 1968, 1243–1248.
3. P. A. Samuelson, "The pure theory of public expenditure," *Review of Economics and Statistics*, 36, 1954, 387–389.
4. E. Ostrom, *Governing the Commons: The Evolution of Institutions for Collective Action*, Cambridge: Cambridge University Press, 1990; E. Ostrom, "Beyond markets and states: polycentric governance of complex economic systems," *American Economic Review*, 100, 2010, 641–672.
5. E. Ostrom, J. Burger, C. B. Field, R. B. Norgaard and D. Policansky, "Revisiting the commons: local lessons, global challenges," *Science*, 284, 1999, 278–282.
6. M. Hardt and A. Negri, *Commonwealth*, Cambridge, MA: Belknap Press, 2009, p. 251.

7. D. W. Bromley, "The commons, property, and common-property regimes," pp. 3–16 in D. W. Bromley (ed.) *Making the Commons Work*, San Francisco: Institute for Contemporary Studies, 1992.
8. For detailed overviews of the diversity of the urban commons and the management problems that they pose see: S. R. Foster, "Collective action and the urban commons," *Notre Dame Law Review*, 87, 2011, 57–134; and N. S. Garnett, "Managing the urban commons," *University of Pennsylvania Law Review*, 160, 2012, 1995–2027.
9. A robust and balanced defense of the usefulness of price signals in urban policymaking is presented in P. C. Cheshire, M. Nathan and H. G. Overman, *Urban Economics and Urban Policy: Challenging Conventional Policy*, Cheltenham: Elgar, 2015.
10. P. Chatterton, "Building transitions to post-capitalist urban commons," *Transactions of the Institute of British Geographers*, 41, 2016, 400–415.
11. N. Blomley, "Enclosure, common right and the property of the poor," *Social and Legal Studies*, 17, 2008, p. 316.
12. Cf. J. S. Kayden, *Privately Owned Public Space: The New York Experience*, London: Wiley, 2000.
13. S. Boydell and G. Searle, "Understanding property rights in the contemporary urban commons," *Urban Policy and Research*, 32, 2014, 323–340. See also P. Bresnihan and M. Byrne, "Escape into the city: everyday practices of communing and the production of urban space in Dublin," *Antipode*, 47, 2015, 36–54.
14. D. Harvey, "From managerialism to entrepreneurialism: the transformation in urban governance in late capitalism," *Geografiska Annaler*, Series B, *Human Geography*, 7, 1989, 3–17.
15. A. Amin and P. Howell, "Thinking the commons," pp. 1–17 in A. Amin and P. Howell (eds.) *Releasing the Commons: Rethinking the Future of the Commons*, London: Routledge, 2016, p. 5.
16. A. J. Scott, "The cultural economy: geography and the creative field," *Media, Culture, and Society*, 21, 1999, 807–817; A. J. Scott, "Cultural economy and the creative field of the city," *Geografiska Annaler*, Series B, *Human Geography*, 92, 2010, 115–130.
17. M. Hardt and A. Negri, *op. cit.*, 2009, p. 250.
18. M. Hardt and A. Negri, *op. cit.*, 2009. See also: Y. Moulier Boutang, *Le Capitalisme Cognitif, Comprendre la Nouvelle Grande Transformation et ses Enjeux*, Paris: Editions Amsterdam, 2007.
19. U. Rossi, *Cities in Global Capitalism*, Cambridge: Polity, 2017.
20. M. A. Peters and E. Bulut, "Introduction: cognitive capitalism, education, and the question of immaterial labor," pp. xxv–xl in M. A. Peters and E. Bulut (eds.) *Cognitive Capitalism, Education and Digital Labor*, New York: Peter Lang, 2011.

21. A. J. Scott, "Beyond the creative city: cognitive–cultural capitalism and the new urbanism," *Regional Studies*, 48, 2014, 565–578.
22. C. Rabari and M. Storper, "The digital skin of cities: urban theory and research in the age of the sensored and metered city, ubiquitous computing and big data," *Cambridge Journal of Regions, Economy and Society*, 8, 2015, 27–42. See also: C. Landry, *The Digitized City: Influence and Impact*, London: Comedia, 2016.
23. Y. Benkler, "Freedom in the commons: towards a political economy of information," *Duke Law Journal*, 52, 2003, 1245–1276; Y. Benkler, *The Wealth of Networks: How Social Production Transforms Markets and Freedom*, New Haven: Yale University Press, 2006.
24. J. Rifkin, *The Zero Marginal-Cost Society*, New York: Palgrave Macmillan, 2014.
25. C. Vercellone and T. Negri, "Le rapport capital/travail dans le capitalisme cognitive," *Multitudes*, 32, 2008, 39–50.
26. Y. Moulier Boutang, *Le Capitalisme Cognitif: Comprendre la Nouvelle Grande Transformation et ses Enjeux*, Paris: Editions Amsterdam, 2007.
27. In the 1990s, in particular, as consciousness about the potentialities of new communications technologies gathered momentum, it was proclaimed in many quarters that distance was effectively dead and that a radically new era of geographically deconcentrated interaction was about to replace purely local relationships. See, for example, F. Cairncross, *The Death of Distance: How the Communications Revolution will Change our Lives*, Boston: Harvard Business School Press, 1997; and R. O'Brien, *Global Financial Integration: The End of Geography*, London: Royal Institute of International Affairs, 1992.
28. G. Perec, *Espèces d'Espaces*, Paris: Galilée, 1974.
29. M. Castells, "The impact of the internet on society: a global perspective," pp. 132–133 in F. González (ed.) *Ch@nge: 19 Key Essays on How Internet is Changing our Lives*, Bilbao: BBVA, 2013.
30. R. L. Florida, *The Rise of the Creative Class: And How it's Transforming Work, Leisure, Community and Everyday Life*, New York: Basic Books, 2002.
31. M. Storper, T. Kemeny, N. P. Makarem and T. Osman, *The Rise and Fall of Urban Economies: Lessons from San Francisco and Los Angeles*, Stanford, CA: Stanford Business Books, 2015.

Index

A
Abu Dhabi, 202
Accra, 97
accumulation of capital, 106. *See also* capitalism
Ackroyden, 53
administrative support occupations, 160, 172
Aegean world, 24
aerospace complex, 138
aesthetic idioms, 142
aestheticization, 204. *See also* land redevelopment
African Americans, 167, 171, 173, 175
African-American migrants, 66
agglomeration, 138, 179. *See also* urban land nexus
agglomeration economies, 20, 221. *See also* increasing returns effects
agglomeration-specific skills, 138
air pollution, 221
air pollution controls, 217
Airbnb, 230
Akron, 137

algorithmic routines, 114
Alonso, W., 189
amenities, 143, 144, 146, 147
American Community Survey, 119, 171
Amin, A., 12, 223
Ancient Rome, 39
anti-apartheid movement, 207
AOC, 230
Appalachians, 46
Apple Inc., 141
Arab Spring, 207
architectural agendas, 204
architectural experimentation, 145
Argentina, 74
art centers, 146
art galleries, 206
artificial intelligence, 120
artists, 144
Arts and Crafts Movement, 52
Asian immigrants, 167
Asian Tigers, 112
Asians, 167
assemblage theory, 14
assembly line, 61

238 INDEX

assimilation, 173
atmosphere, 28
automation, 114, 117
Autor, D. H., 116
avant-garde architectural idioms, 204
Aztec cities, 24

B
Babylon, 21
back offices, 123, 195
backwash, 71
Bagnasco, A., 111
Bairoch, P., 18, 21, 40
Baldwin, R. E., 125
Balzac, H., 1
Bangui, 177
Barcelona, 51
barrios, 174
Bautès, N., 136
Becattini, G., 112
Beck, U., 114
Beijing-Tianjin-Tangshan, 98
Bell, D., 110, 121
Bellamy, E., 52
Benevolo, L., 50
Benkler, Y., 229
Bentham, J., 54
Berry, B. J. L., 83
Beveridge Report, 63
bidonvilles, 74, 174
bijou residences, 196. *See also* gentrification
Bilbao, 145, 206
biopower, 227
Birmingham, 44
Birmingham Small Arms Company, 48
Black Belt, 67
Blakely, E. J., 194
blighted areas, 192
Blomley, N., 221
blue-collar neighborhoods, 65, 190, 200
blue-collar suburbs, 66, 192

blue-collar workers, 62, 117, 132, 133, 156, 158, 190, 191
Bluestone, B., 109
bohemians, 202
Bollywood, 138, 226
boot and shoe industry, 44
Boston, 44, 193
Boswell, J., 1
Bournville, 53
Bradford, 53
branch plants, 74, 111, 148
branding, 230
Brasilia, 33
Brazil, 74
Brazzaville, 144
Brenner, N., 15, 31, 72, 100
Bridgeton, 48
Brusco, S., 112
Brussels, 51
Buenos Aires, 202
building codes, 191
Bulut, E., 227
Bunnell, T., 100
bureaucracy, 110
Burgess, E. W., 13, 66, 190
Burj Khalifa, 145, 206
Burnham, D., 205
business advice centers, 224
business cycle, 133
business ecosystems, 135
business improvement districts, 222
business parks, 195

C
Cabet, E., 52
Cairo, 92, 202
Caldeira, T. P. R., 194
Canberra, 33
Cape Town, 202
capital accumulation, 227
capitalism, 2–8, 14, 21, 26–30, 32, 39–59, 61, 71, 73, 78, 88, 94,

97, 101, 105–20, 122, 123, 125, 131–5, 138, 140, 143, 145, 158, 159, 161, 167, 173, 174, 187, 193, 194, 197, 202, 204–6, 216, 223–33
  rise of, 39, 40 (*see also* industrialization; mercantilism)
capitalist era, 3
car ownership, 191
Castells, M., 12, 13, 77, 208, 232
Catalano, G., 141
Çatal Hüyük, 17, 21
Central African Republic, 177
Central Andes, 18
central business district, 196, 197, 204, 205
central city, 196, 200
Chadwick, E., 50
Chamberlin, E., 139
Chamberlinian competition, 138–40, 225, 226, 230
Chelsea, 196
Chicago School of Urban Sociology, 12, 66, 188
chicken-and-egg relationships, 149
Childe, V. G., 18
Child-rearing practices, 226
China, 92
cholera epidemics, 50
circulation space, 187
city-regions, 124, 193, 205. *See also* global city-regions
Clark, E., 198
clerical and allied occupations, 117
clustering processes. *See* agglomeration economies; industrial districts
clusters, 135, 137
coal resources, 46
Cobbett, W., 1
Cochambamba, 207
Cochrane, A., 31
cognitariat, 231. *See also* cognitive cultural workers

cognitive-cultural economy/capitalism, 120, 131, 134, 139, 143, 156, 158, 159, 206, 223–8. *See also* gentrification; post-fordism; third wave
cognitive cultural workers, 133, 155, 159
collaborative commons, 229
collective action, 55
collective consumption, 217. *See also* public goods
collective efficacy, 190, 200
collective governance, 216
collectivity, 29, 215. *See also* commons
colonial outposts, 4
Colorado Springs, 148
Coming of Post-Industrial Society, The, 110
command and control centers, 14
commercial land redevelopment, 203–7. *See also* land redevelopment
commodity chains, 97
common-pool resources, 217, 219, 222. *See also* public goods
commons, 27–9, 215–18
commonwealth (urban), 218
communal assets, 215
communal gardens, 222
communications networks, 46
Communist Manifesto, 52
communitarian principles, 52. *See also* utopian socialists
community gardens, 217
community property, 217
commuting costs, 189, 199. *See also* journey to work
comparativism, 99
competitive advantage, 89, 113, 141, 224, 225
concentric zone model, 67
Condition of the Working Class in England, 49

240   INDEX

Congo Democratic Republic, 176
Constantinople, 39
constitutive outside of the city, 83
consumer cities, 146
consumer sovereignty, 146
convergence, 71
cooperative housing, 217, 222
copyright, 139, 230
core-periphery relationships, 71, 95
corporate command and control, 94
cosmopolitanism, 194
Costa Mesa, 195
craft industry, 77, 111, 112, 138
craftsworkers, 17
creative cities, 143–6, 228
creative cities script, 144
Creative City Network, 144
creative class, 121, 143, 146, 232
creative destruction, 134
creative field, 134–7, 224
creative talent, 225
creative-class theory, 136
creativity, 143
crime, 178
Crimean War, 48
critical discourse, 110
crowding, 49
cultural economy, 225
cultural industries, 107, 143
cultural infrastructures, 196
curtain walls, 205
cybercapitalism, 120
Cyberjaya, 195
cybernetic commons, 229
cyberspace, 226, 229, 230

D
Dakar, 144
Dallas-Fort Worth, 148
Davis, M., 176, 177
Dearborn, 66, 192

Death and Life of Great American Cities, 24
death of distance, 139
debt crisis, 75
decentralization, 47, 70, 75, 148, 161, 191
defense spending, 148
de Geer, S., 63
deindustrialization, 75, 109
Delhi, 177
democratic participation, 229
Democratic Republic of Congo, 86
democratic urbanism, 208
desakota, 177, 195
design ideologies, 139
deskilling, of worker, 61. *See also* division of labor
de Soto, H., 178
Detroit, 5, 64, 137, 192
Deutschland, 65
Devaraj, S., 117
Dhaka, 137, 177
Dickens, C., 50
digital city, 12, 228. *See also* smart city
digital technologies, 6, 95, 114, 193, 229
digital workshops, 123
Disney Hall, Los Angeles, 206
disneyfication, 146
divergence, 71, 187. *See also* decentralization
division of labor, 19–21, 42, 61, 179
    horizontal, 42 (*see also* old international division of labor)
    social, 61
    technical, 61
    vertical, 42
Docklands, London, 205
dormitory settlements, 195
dot-com boom, 201
Downtown Eastside, Vancouver, 201, 221

Dreiser, T., 66
drinking water, 50
drug rehabilitation centers, 222
Dubai, 205
Ducie Bridge, 49
Dunning, J. H., 140
Duranton, G., 22, 85
Durkheim, E., 20
dust heaps, 50, 177

E
Eastern European Jews, 167
Economic Manuscripts of 1861-63, 50
economies of scale, 22, 31, 61, 64, 73, 219, 232. *See also* increasing returns effects
edge city, 196
Edmonton, 51
education, 162
Edwards, R. C., 158
Egypt, Ancient, 18
Electronic News, 111
electronics and aerospace agglomerations, 148
embedded sensors, 228
Emilia-Romagna, 78
employment relation, 133
enabling legislation, 30
enemies of the city, 53
Engels, F., 49, 52, 175
entrepôt centers, 4
entrepreneurialization of the self, 227
entrepreneurship, 136
environmental assets, 140
excess profits, 204
export-oriented industrialization, 112
export processing platforms, 109
expressways, 72
externalities, 26–9, 219. *See also* spillover effects

F
Facebook, 230
face-to-face contact, 22, 132, 135
factorial ecology, 70. *See also* social area analysis
Factory Zone, 67
Fashion District, Los Angeles, 223
favelas, 74, 174
Federal Housing Act, 192
Federal-Aid Highway Act, 193
female workers, 172. *See also* women workers
feminism, 14
festivals, 140
financial centers, 225
financial institutions, 123
financial policy, 179
financial services, 107
Finchley, 51
Firman, T., 195
first wave, 4, 56
First World, 73
first-generation gentrification, 201
flexible accumulation, 120
flexible city, the, 131–7
flexible specialization, 77, 112
Florida, R., 121, 143, 146, 232
Ford, H., 5, 62, 192
fordism, 5, 148, 156, 158, 161, 167, 193. *See also* mass-production system
foreign direct investment, 74
formal subsumption, 50, 54
form follows function, 205
Foucault, M., 227
Fourier, C., 52
Foxconn, 54
Frankfurt School, 227
freelancers, 133
free-rider problem, 29, 54, 216
freeway construction, 193
Friedmann, J., 14, 94
Fuà, G., 112

G

Gabaix, X., 85
galleries, 146
Garden City Movement, 52
Garofoli, G., 112
Garreau, J., 196
gated communities, 27, 194, 206, 222
Gehry, F., 206
gender, 171
general intellect, 229
gentrification, 196, 200
geographical indications, 139
Ghertner, D. A., 202
gifts of nature, 215
gig economy, 133
Glaeser, E., 1
glamour, 206
Glasgow, 48
Glass, R., 196, 202
global city-regions, 87, 95. *See also* city-regions; world cities
global commons, 28, 226, 230. *See also* commons
Global Power City Index, 98
Global South, 14, 91, 99, 123, 179, 195, 202
globalization, 14. *See also* new international division of labor
Goertz, G., 40
gold standard, 109
golden age of capitalism, 108
Golden Triangle, 71, 111
Gordon, D. M., 158
Gottmann, J., 72
Gouldner, A., 110, 121
Graham, S., 188
Gramsci, A., 5, 62
Grant, R., 97
Great Convergence, 125
Gropius, W., 205
growth center, 64
growth poles, 62, 64

Grundrisse, 229
Guangzhou, 98
Guggenheim Museum, Bilbao, 145, 206
Guilluy, C., 158
gun industry, 47

H

habitations à loyer modéré, 175
habituated labor, 149
habituation, 138, 224
Hall, P., 47, 87, 94, 134
Hamburg, 145
Hammond, N. G. L., 24
Hamnett, C., 202
Hampstead, 196
handicrafts, 225
Hangzhou, 39
Hardin, G., 216
Hardt, M., 28, 217, 227
Harris, C., 67
Harris, J. R., 176
Harrison, B., 109
Harrison, J., 97
Harris-Todaro model, 176
Harvey, D., 13, 77, 207
Haussmann, Baron, 48, 51, 192, 200
headquarter offices, 124
health hazards, 177, 178
heritage, 140
Hershey, 53
Heteropolis, 188
Hicks, M. J., 117
hierarchical taxonomy, 219
highest and best use of the land, 29
Highland Park, 5
high-performance car-manufacturing, 138
high-technology industry, 78, 107
Hirschman, A., 71
Hispanics, 167

Hoefler, D. C., 111
Hollywood, 132, 137, 141, 226
homeowner associations, 194, 223
Hong Kong, 98
Housing Act, 1954, 192
housing conditions, 49
housing tenure, 178
Howard, E., 52
Howell, P., 223
Hoyler, M., 97
Hoyt, H., 67, 198, 204
hukou system, 123
human capital, 119, 143, 161–6
hunters and gatherers, 17
Hurd, R. M., 29
hybridization, vii, 180
hyperurbanization, 176

I

immigrants, 167
import substitution, 6, 75, 112. *See also* core-periphery relationships
import-substitution policies, 109
income inequalities, 157
increasing returns effects, 42. *See also* agglomeration
indigenous settlements, 4
Indonesia, 74
industrial atmosphere, 138
industrial complex, 62. *See also* input-output system; mass-production system
industrial decentralization, 6
industrial development, 40
industrial districts, 112. *See also* agglomeration economies
industrial parks, 222
industrialization, 2, 4, 39–59, 74, 75, 92, 111, 112, 114. *See also* capitalism; urbanization
Industrial Revolution, 21, 45

Indus Valley, 18
informal sector, 108, 176
informal settlements, 177. *See also* slum communities
information spillovers, 135
information-gathering agencies, 228
inner city, 191, 200
innovation, 89, 134, 136, 143, 224
input-output system, 42
Institute for the Formation of Character, 53. *See also* New Lanark
institutions, 228
institutions of governance, 29–31
intellectual property, 225, 229, 230
intelligent highways, 120
international division of labor, 73, 112
International Monetary Fund, 179
international system, 5
Internet, 229
Internet of Things, 229
interpersonal networks, 135
intraurban linkages, 21
intraurban space, 231. *See also* urban land nexus
IPUMS-USA, 159
Irish, 167
Irish immigrants, 49
Iron Age, 18
Islington, 196
Istanbul, 202
Italians, 167
Ivry-sur-Seine, 192

J

Jacobs, J., 12, 17, 24
Jakarta, 195
Japan, 6
Jayet, H., 134
Jefferson, M., 11, 45, 65
Jencks, C., 188

Jericho, 21
job loss, 109
job security, 158
Johannesburg, 92, 125, 178
Johnson, Dr. S., 1
Jones, G. S., 175
journey to work, 188

K
Karachi, 177, 202
Katz, L. F., 133
Kennedy, President John F., 72
Keynes, J. M., 63
Keynesian welfare-statism, 72, 75, 108, 113
Kilbowie, 48
Kinshasa, 144, 176
Klepper, S., 137
know-how, 138, 224
knowledge economy, 120
knowledge-intensive economy, 193. *See also* cognitive-cultural capitalism
knowledge workers, 7
Kolkata, 177
Konza Technology City, 196
Krueger, A. B., 133
Kuala Lumpur, 145, 195

L
labor control, 54
labor force, 43
labor markets, 107, 133
labor-intensive industries, 47, 77, 112. *See also* craft industries
Lagos, 202
laisser-faire, 139
Lancashire, 4
land development bottlenecks, 73
land market, 199
land redevelopment, 200. *See also* gentrification

land rent, 26, 27, 187, 189
land use. *See* urban land nexus
land use zoning, 221
landlords, 201
land-use intensification, 204. *See also* land redevelopment
large-batch production runs, 132
large-scale materials-intensive processing, 47. *See also* mass production system
Larsen, J. K., 135
late capitalism, 108–14
Latin American immigrants, 167
lead plants, 5, 62, 70
learning, 22, 136. *See also* innovation
Le Creusot, 44
Lefebvre, H., 13, 25, 76, 189
left-behinds, 206
less is more, 205
Letchworth, 52
Levy, F., 114
Lewis, S., 66
Ley, D., 198, 202
linkage networks, 132
Little Italy, 65
Little Poland, 65
Little Sicily, 67
Lloyd, R., 202
load-bearing outer walls, 205
lock-in problems, 29
London, 1, 40
Longhua Industrial Park, 54
Long Post-War Boom, 5, 63, 70
Looking Backward, 52
Loop, The, 67, 198, 205
lord of the manor, 216
Los Angeles, 148, 188
lost decade, 75, 109
low-wage countries, 161
low-wage labor pools, 148
low-wage service occupations, 193
low-wage service workers, 122, 155. *See also* new servile class

INDEX 245

low-wage workers, 121
Lubumbashi, 144
luxury apartments, 192

M
machine age, 193
macrocephalic urban system, 86
Malaysia, 74, 195
Malibu, 194
managerial and professional occupations, 160, 172
managerial authority, 50
managers and professionals, 117
Manchester, 49, 175, 203
Mandel, E., 110
manual dexterity, 166
Manufacturing Belt, 5, 63, 75, 109, 148, 193
  Europe, 5, 64
  North America, 5, 63
Mao Tse-Tung, 92
maquiladoras, 109
Marchand, B., 53
Maringanti, A., 100
market competition, 107
market failure, 29, 217, 218, 222. *See also* externalities; free-rider problem
Marshall, A., 28
Marvin, S., 188
Marx, K., 50, 52, 229
Marxian political economy, 77
Marxian urban theory, 13
mass-production society, 71
mass-production system, 61–3
  assembly, 62 (*see also* fordism)
  process, 62
mass surveillance, 228
MasterCard, 124
matching, 22, 224
McGee, T., 177, 195
McKenzie, R. D., 13, 66

mediasphere, 226
medical diagnosis, 119
Megalopolis, 72, 194
megaprojects, 205
megaregion, 87
melting pot, 172–3
mercantilism, 39
Merrifield, A., 200
Mesopotamia, 18
metrocentricity, 98
Metropolis and Mental Life, 188
Mexico, 74
Mezzogiorno, 6, 71, 111
microelectronics, 78
micro-territories, 188
Middle America, 18
middle-class sanctuaries, 194
Middle East, 194, 207
Midlands, 4
Mies van der Rohe, L., 205
military funding, 114
million cities, 45
Mills, E. S., 189
Mission District, San Francisco, 201
model factory villages, 53
Modena, 138
mode of social regulation, 107, 108
modernist architecture, 205
Mohenjodaro, 21
monocentric city, 192–3
monopolistic competition, 139
monopsonistic employer, 55
Mori Memorial Foundation, 98
Morris, W., 52
Multimedia Supercorridor, 195
multiplant corporations, 113
multiple nuclei model, 68
Mumbai, 125, 138, 142, 177, 225, 226. *See also* Bollywood
Mumford, L., 11
Murnane, R. J., 114
music venues, 146
Muth, R. F., 147, 189

Myrdal, G., 71
Mystery of Capital, The, 178

N
Nairobi, 196
narcissism, 232
national-champion industries, 64
natural harbors, 46
Naypyidaw, 33
negative exponential curve, 189
negative externalities, 54, 56, 187, 190. *See also* externalities
Negri, A., 28, 217, 227, 229
neo-bohemianism, 202
neoclassical models, 71
neoconservatism, 113
neo-fordism, 75. *See also* fordism
neo-Haussmannization, 200
neoliberalism, 108, 113, 179
Neolithic Age, 2
new citadels, 158
new class, the, 121
New England, 44
New Harmony, 52, 53
new industrial spaces, 78, 111, 148
new international division of labor, 76. *See also* globalization
New Lanark, 44, 53
newly industrializing countries, 74
new particularism, vi
Newport Beach, 194
New Right, 76
new servile class, 122, 206, 231. *See also* low-wage service workers
News from Nowhere, 52
New York City, 193
Nicaragua, 86
NICs. *See* newly industrializing countries
Nijman, J., 97
non-routine work, 115

North Africa, 207
North China Plain, 18
North Kensington, 196
Noteboom, B., 135

O
occupational status, 189
Occupy Movement, 207
old international division of labor, 40
oligopolistic competition, 139
Olympic Games, 206
operators, fabricators, and laborers, 160, 172
oppida, 18
opportunity cost, 199
Orange County, 148, 195
ordinary cities, 99
organic solidarity, 20
organization men, 122
origins of urbanization, 17–22. *See also* urbanization
Ostrom, E., 217
Our Mutual Friend, 49
Outcast London, 175
overcrowding, 177
Owen, R., 44, 52, 53

P
Paddington, 196
Pain, K., 87
Palm Springs, 194
Panopticon, 54. *See also* labor control
para-capitalist conditions, 177
Paris Basin, 194
Park, R. E., 13, 66
parking lots, 193
part-time work, 133
patenting, 135, 230

paternalism, 53. *See also* philanthropic capitalists
path dependency, 43, 149
patriarchal family, 110
patrimonial assets, 192, 226
pauperization, 7
Pearl River Delta, 98
Peck, J, 144
peer-to-peer networks, 229
Pegida, 207
Perec, G., 11, 231
Perroux, F., 62
Peters, M. A., 227
Petronas Towers, 145, 205
Philadelphia, 193
philanthropic capitalists, 53
Philippines, 86
Phoenix, 148
physical coordination, 166
pin factory, 61
Piore, M., 77, 112
planetary urbanism, 2, 15, 31, 230
Planning. *See* Urban planning
plant closure, 109
plutocracy, 155
polarization, 71
Poles, 167
polycentric metropolis, 87
polynucleated spaces, 194. *See also* city-regions
popular culture, 227
port cities, 45
Port Sunlight, 53
possessive individualism, 232
post-capitalist order, 218
post-colonial theory, 14, 98, 179
post-fordism, 78, 108–14. *See also* third wave
post-industrial society, 110
post-operaismo theorists, 229
post-political city, 228
post-structuralism, 14
post-suburbia, 195, 206
post-War decades, 133
poverty, 174
Prebisch-Singer hypothesis, 73
precision production, craft and repair occupations, 160, 172
Pred, A., 45
pre-Enclosure England, 215
pregentrification phase, 202
primate cities, 65, 86
Prison Notebooks, 62
private developers, 192
privately owned public spaces, 222
private property, 26, 229
private-public hybrids, 222
privatization, 216
Procter and Gamble, 141
product differentiation, 230. *See also* Chamberlinian competition
production networks, 97. *See also* input-output system
production space, 187
profits, 106
project-oriented teams, 122
property booms, 204
property conversion, 198, 200. *See also* land redevelopment
protomodernism, 205
provincialization, 15
psychosocial motivation, 136
public city, 27–31. *See also* commons
public domain, 219
public goods, 217, 221. *See also* collective consumption
public health, 50
public housing, 72, 192
public monopolies, 188
public subsidies, 228
public-private hybrids, 219
Puga, D, 22

Pullman, 53
Putrajaya, 195

Q
quattrocento, 111

R
Rajasthan, 136
Randstad-Holland, 94
rank-size rule, 84
rational comprehensive planning, 73
Reagan, President R., 76, 113
real subsumption, 55. *See also* subsumption
regime of accumulation, 41, 107. *See also* mode of social regulation
Reich, M., 158
Reich, R., 121
rent gap, 198
rentiers, 192
Report on the Sanitary Condition of the Labouring Population, 50
residential space, 13, 49, 188, 190
resource misallocation, 218
resource sites, 46
restrictive zoning ordinances, 191
restructuring crisis, 109
reverse commuting, 70, 200
Rhine-Ruhr, 94
rhizomatic networks, 14
Richardson, H. H., 205
Rifkin, J., 229, 233
Right to the City, The, 76
rights of labor, 48
risk society, 114
River Rouge, 62, 192
road pricing, 217
Robinson, J., 99
robotization, 119
Rogers, E., 135
Roma encampments, 175
Romanesque motifs, 205
Rossi, U., 227
routinization, 131
Roweis, S., viii
Roy, A., 99
rural-urban migration, 123, 176
Ruskin, J., 24, 52
Russo, M., 135
Rustbelt, 75

S
Sabel, C., 77, 112
Saint-Simon, H. de, 52
sales occupations, 117, 172
sales, services, and transport occupations, 160
Salt, Sir T., 53
Saltaire, 53
Sampson, R. J., 190
Samuelson, P. A., 217
San Diego, 148
San Francisco, 201
Santa Clara County, 148. *See also* Silicon Valley
Santiago, 202
São Paulo, 74, 179
Sassen, S., 14, 94, 124
Sassuolo, 135
Saunders, P., 16
Saxenian, A., 111
Schmid, C., 31, 100
Schneider Iron Works, 44
schooling, 226
Schumpeter, J., 114, 136
science-based industries, 148
Scott, A. J., 25
Second Industrial Divide, The, 112
second wave, 5, 6, 56. *See also* fordism
Second World, 73
sectoral model, 67
self-driving cars, 120
seniority, 133

Seoul, 138
service occupations, 115, 117. *See also* low-wage service occupations
sewage systems, 222
sex and the city, 16
shack settlements, 174
Shanghai, 194
shantytowns, 74, 123, 174
sharing, 22, 224
sharing economy, 228, 229
Shenzen, 54
Silicon Valley, 78, 111, 137, 138, 225
Silicon Valley Fever, 135
Simmel, G., 13, 66, 188
Sinclair, U., 66
Singer Sewing Machine Company, 48
skid row, 174
Sklair, L., 143, 205
slum areas, 94, 231
slum clearances, 50, 72
slum communities, 123
slum development, 176, 177
Slum Dwellers International, 178
slum housing, 175
Small Heath, 48
small-scale labor-intensive industries, 47
small-scale service provision, 177
smart city, 120, 228
Smith, A., 61
Smith, M, 24
Smith, N., 197
Snyder, M. G., 194
social area analysis, 13, 70
social capital, 145, 190
social control, 228
Social Darwinism, 13
socialism, 52
socialization, 224. *See also* habituation; labor control
Social Justice and the City, 77
social marginalization, 174, 179
social media, 229

social polarization, 194
social reformers, 51
social space, 27, 54, 67, 71, 187, 188, 193. *See also* residential space
social stratification, 155–66
social surveillance, 120
social welfare, 232
Society Hill, 193
socio-spatial segregation, 190
SoHo, New York, 202
Sophiatown, 178
South Africa, 207
South Coast Shopping Plaza, 195
Southeast Asia, 177, 195
Southeast England, 194
Southern California, 97
South Korea, 74
space-economy, 71
space-sorting mechanisms, 26
special economic zones, 109
Species of Spaces, 11
spillover effects, 217. *See also* externalities
spin-off, 137
sprawl, 193
spread, 18, 32, 40, 65, 71, 72, 88, 94, 100, 112, 140, 141, 207. *See also* backwash
St. Denis, 192
stagflation, 75
standardized work, 114
star architects, 145, 205
Storper, M., viii, 25, 232
strategic alliances, 140
street sweeping, 50
subcontracting, 140
sub-Saharan Africa, 177
subsidiarity principle, 30
subsumption, 227
suburban communities, 191
suburban solution, 191
suburban sprawl, 72

suburbanization, 6, 48, 70, 72, 73, 191. See also decentralization; sprawl
suburbs, 6, 27, 51, 66, 67, 70, 71, 191, 192, 195, 196, 203. See also urban fringe
Sullivan, L. H., 205
Sunbelt, 71, 74, 111, 146, 147. See also Manufacturing Belt
supercluster, 87. See also global city-regions
surplus humanity, 176
sweated labor, 177
symbolic analysts, 121
symbolic capital, 204
symbolic legitimization, 191
systems houses, 132

T

tacit knowledge, 132, 135, 139
Taipei, 202
Taiwan, 74
talent, 142, 143, 145, 225. See also creative class
Taylor, P., 21, 141
temporary work, 133
temporary work agencies, 133
tenants, 201. See also gentrification
textile towns, 44
Thatcher, Mrs. M., 76, 113
Theory of Economic Development, The, 136
Third Italy, 78, 111
third wave, 6, 7, 105, 108. See also cognitive-cultural capitalism
Third World, 73, 74
three-dimensional printing, 119, 229
Thrift, N., 12
Times Square, 223
Todaro, M. P, 176
Tokyo, 194
Toronto, 145
Toulouse, 138
tourism, 140, 206
tourist attractions, 225
Toyota, 141
trademarks, 139
trade unions, 113
Tragedy of the Commons, The, 216
trans-Atlantic networks, 39
transnational capitalist class, 94, 143, 205
transport networks, 46
transport nodes, 46
transport occupations, 172
triangular trading system, 39
trickle down, 71
tripartite world order, 5
Turkey, 74
Tuscany, 78
Twitter, 230
two-income families, 157

U

Uber, 230
Ullman, E., 67
unequal exchange, 73
UNESCO, 144
UN-Habitat report, 2013, 177
unionization, 108, 148
uniquitous principle, 24
universalization, 179
universal social wage, 229
urban communities, 136
urban continuum, 87
urban crisis, 193
urban fringe, 192. See also suburbanization
urban land nexus, 23–7, 131, 143, 145, 161, 174, 178, 179, 187, 207, 208, 215, 231. See also urbanization
urban periphery, 47, 65, 195. See also suburbs

urban planning, 55, 191
urban question, 33
urban renewal, 72, 192
urban slums, 174–5
urban system, 87
urbanization
  Africa, 92
  China, 92
  Global South, 175
  Latin America, 92
  mass-production metropolis, 61–81
  nineteenth-century Britain, 39–59
  (*see also* urban land nexus)
US Department of Labor, 164
utopian socialists, 52
utopianism, 51

V
Valette, E., 136
Vancouver, 201
Veneto, 78
Vercellone, C., 229
Verizon, 141
vertical disintegration, 112, 132
vertical integration, 61, 131
Vietnam War, 109
virtual reality, 120
Vuitton handbags, 138

W
wages, 106
Walker, R. A., 12, 191
Wallerstein, I., 73
Walthamstow, 51
warm winters, 146
Washington Consensus, 76, 179
waste land, 215. *See also* commons
water supply, 207
water war, 207
wave of capitalist development, 4, 41, 56, 105, 120, 124. *See also* regime of accumulation

Weber, M., 11
Welwyn Garden City, 52
West End, Boston, 193
white-collar neighborhoods, 65, 191
white-collar workers, 62, 133, 156, 158, 191
Wirth, L., 11, 13, 67, 155, 188
Wolff, G., 14, 94
women workers, 171
work performance indexes, 166
working class, 49
working-class housing, 196
working-class neighborhoods, 192. *See also* blue-collar neighborhoods
workshop and factory system, 4
World Bank, 94, 179
world cities, 14, 98, 225, 231. *See also* global city-regions
world city hypothesis, 94
World Financial Center, Shanghai, 205
world periphery, 73, 74, 112
World War I, 191
World War II, 191, 192
Worldwide Centers of Commerce Index, 124

X
xenophobia, 194

Y
Yangtze River Delta, 98
Yorkshire, 4
Yorubaland, 18

Z
zero marginal cost, 229
Zipf, G., 84
Zukin, S., 202

GPSR Compliance
The European Union's (EU) General Product Safety Regulation (GPSR) is a set of rules that requires consumer products to be safe and our obligations to ensure this.

If you have any concerns about our products, you can contact us on

ProductSafety@springernature.com

In case Publisher is established outside the EU, the EU authorized representative is:

Springer Nature Customer Service Center GmbH
Europaplatz 3
69115 Heidelberg, Germany